THE YELLOWSTONE HIGHWAY

DENVER TO THE PARK, PAST AND PRESENT

"First Autos to Enter Yellowstone Park"

They entered the park August 1, 1915,
the first day automobiles were allowed in Yellowstone.
The pictured autos entered via the east entrance, also known as the "Cody Road."
Note the Wyoming license plate number 1
registered to J. M. Schwoob of Cody, Wyoming.

THE YELLOWSTONE HIGHWAY

DENVER TO THE PARK, PAST AND PRESENT

LEE WHITELEY

On the cover: Postcard showing "auto trails" and the Burlington Railroad converging on Cody, Wyoming, on the east entrance road to Yellowstone National Park. The card is signed by William Frederick "Buffalo Bill" Cody and was mailed from the town of Cody to Denver on October 18, 1916. This was only three months before his death in Denver. Cody, best known for his Wild West Show, was a founder of the town of Cody. He strongly supported tourism and the "good roads" movement, including the admission of automobiles into Yellowstone National Park.

Postcard courtesy of the Denver Public Library, Western History Collection.

ISBN: 0-9671351-2-5

To
my wife Jane,
for sharing many experiences
along life's highway.

Bad section of road, unknown location.

**The American Automobile Association (AAA) was one of the sponsors
of the 1920 National Park-to-Park Highway dedication tour.**
In Wyoming, this "auto trail" followed the route of the Yellowstone Highway.

A. G. Lucier photograph, courtesy of the Hinckley Library, Northwest College.

Introduction

"**Auto Trails**" **were early automobile roads mapped, maintained, and promoted by local businessmen and "Good Roads Clubs.**" These colorfully named "highways" appeared in the early 1910s, years before state or federal money was available for road maintenance. The auto trails evolved from wagon roads and were often nothing more than emigrant trails, ranch roads, and railroad service roads.

One of the first auto trails in Wyoming and northeastern Colorado was the Yellowstone Highway. Good roads clubs in Cody and Douglas, Wyoming, were instrumental in the promotion of this road which ran from Denver, Colorado, to Yellowstone National Park via Cody and the park's east entrance.

Two events in the summer of 1915 sparked the need for a well-marked, well-maintained highway between Denver and the park:

      1) Automobiles were allowed in Yellowstone National Park.

      2) Rocky Mountain National Park, northwest of Denver, was established.

The Yellowstone Highway would become the first section of the much longer National Park-to-Park Highway connecting all the National Parks of the Western United States. North of Denver, this highway ran through Estes Park, at the east entrance of Rocky Mountain National Park. North of Cheyenne, Wyoming, the Yellowstone Highway and National Park-to-Park Highway followed the same route.

To follow a particular auto trail, guide books and road markings were essential, for the traveler needed help in negotiating the many twists and turns of the primitive road. **The traveler on the Yellowstone Highway was forever on the lookout for a yellow painted rock with a large black "H."** In 1925, the Federal Government began assigning numbers to the major auto trails. Many of these highways evolved into our present interstate system.

This book attempts to tell the transportation history of the region traversed by the Yellowstone Highway. Emigrant trails, railroads, historical monuments and markers, and graves will be noted. **Much of this transportation history is missed by the interstate traveler.** The highway history concentrates on the time period from 1915 to 1930, from the year automobiles were allowed in Yellowstone to the start of the Great Depression, by which time most of the major highway route changes had been made. By 1930 the automobile was a much more reliable machine and tourist facilities were much more numerous, eliminating much of the true adventure of auto travel.

The book's guide section does not attempt to follow the original route of the Yellowstone Highway for, with the numerous highway changes and improvements, much of this route is lost. An attempt is made to avoid, wherever possible, Interstate 25 between Denver and Casper. Older sections of U.S. Highway 20 between Casper and Yellowstone will be followed. Side trips will lead to sites missed by the hurried traveler.

The book, using quotes from early travelers and guide books, hopefully will recapture some of the hardships and joys of early auto travel when "getting there was half the fun."

Enjoy, in your modern, air-conditioned automobile, this 21st Century trip along this early 20th Century "auto trail."

Acknowledgments

Old photographs, guide books, and diaries help bring back the excitement of early auto travel. But it is the people today, on and off the route of the Yellowstone Highway, that bring the story to life.

Landowners, shopkeepers, and early residents along the highway have helped point the way to the old highway and have shared stories of early travel. Individuals such as Jack and Irma Morison, Jim Ranninger, Duke Sumonia, Johnny Chasteen, William and Annie Gray, Doug Brickman, Lee Johnson, Harry Corl, Frank and Liz Kubiak, and Bob Richard.

Museums and libraries have much to offer on early auto travel.
The following have been very helpful in sharing this information: Cindy Brown, Wyoming State Archives; Jean Cerquoz, Chugwater Museum; Jeannie Cook, Park County Historical Archives; Frances Clymer, Buffalo Bill Historical Center; Kay Carlson and Diane Martin of the Hinckley Library at Northwest College in Powell, Wyoming.
Thanks to the staff and volunteers at the museums and libraries along the highway.

Thanks to Jim Krebs, of Krebs Imaging, for technical help with the photographs.

The following reviewed sections of the manuscript and made valuable additions and corrections: Carol Shively, Lee Whittlesey, Jeannie Cook, and Bob Edgar.

And special thanks to the following five individuals, who helped in many ways, including the review of the entire manuscript: Randy Wagner, Jane Whiteley, Vance Hester, Ed Bathke and Nancy Bathke.

When a man went hunting he took his time about it. The same was true when he went forth with scenery as his object. There was a desire to learn, to know; the person who could write an authentic book about an object of tourist curiosity was assured of a good sale, for the reason that before invading the district one learned everything possible about it. He wanted to know when and how it was discovered, and by whom. He desired all possible information about the scenic values and what they were, the cause of them, and their relation to the rest of the geological or natural history of the country. It was a journey of investigation and joyful curiosity, with the result that the questions prompted thereby furnished excellent material for wintertime story-telling. But now the stories are not so plentiful.

Ned Frost, 1929

Table of Contents

Travel, in the younger sort, is a part of education; in the elder, a part of experience. He that travelleth into a country before he hath some entrance into the language, goeth to school, and not to travel.

Francis Bacon, 1625

So it is in travelling; a man must carry knowledge with him, if he would bring home knowledge.

Samuel Johnson, 1778

Illustrations

Maps

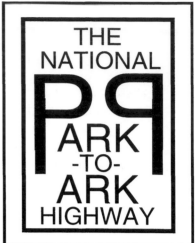

To Glacier, Mt. Rainier, and Crater Lake National Parks via the **National Park-to-Park Highway**

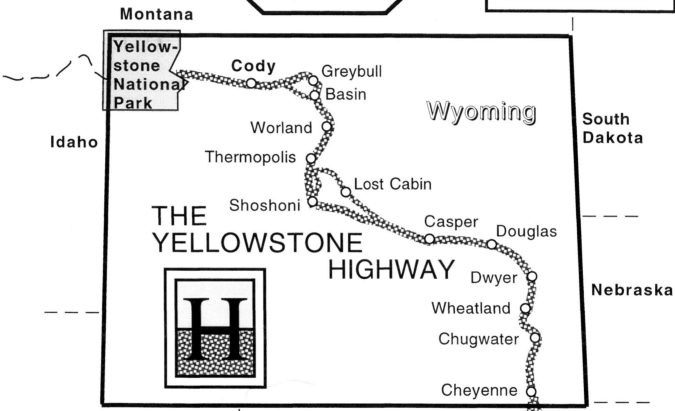

Montana

Yellowstone National Park

Cody
Greybull
Basin

Worland

Thermopolis

Shoshoni

Lost Cabin

Idaho

Wyoming

South Dakota

THE YELLOWSTONE HIGHWAY

Casper
Douglas

Dwyer

Wheatland

Chugwater

Nebraska

Cheyenne

Utah

Colorado

Fort Collins
Estes Park

Rocky Mountain National Park

Greeley

Boulder

Denver

To Mesa Verde, Grand Canyon, Zion, General Grant [Kings Canyon], Yosemite, and Lassen Volcanic National Parks via the **National Park-to-Park Highway**

I. Trails to Interstates

trail, trāl, *v.t.* . . . **3.** to follow the track, trail or scent of; track. **4.** to follow along behind (another) in a race . . . **6.** to tread down or make a path through (grass or the like) . . . **12.** to follow as if drawn along . . . **14.** to go slowly, lazily or wearily along . . . **23.** a path or track made across a wild region over rough country, or the like, by the passage of people or animals . . .

The 23rd definition of "trail" in the 1993 Random House Unabridged Dictionary accurately defines emigrant trails such as the Oregon-California Trail.

Early **"auto trails"** were little improved over the horse-drawn wagon trails they were slowly replacing. Auto trail associations and local businesses worked hard to improve the image and physical condition of their early "highways."

The Yellowstone Highway was the earliest "auto trail" between Denver and Yellowstone National Park. The "highway" and its routes are closely tied to the early exploration, trails, and railroads of the region. U.S. highways and the interstates evolved from the auto trails of the 1910s and 1920s. The Yellowstone Highway story is, therefore, a story of the transportation evolution of Wyoming and northeastern Colorado.

Trails followed waterways wherever possible: **waterways provided "wood, water, and grass."** Trail travelers were dependent on these items for comfort and survival for themselves and their animals. Waterways often followed the flattest terrain, which was often the best route for trails.

Railroads often followed the early trails, for railroads also needed the level terrain provided by waterways. Water was essential for the steam engines.

Early highways often followed the railroads, for along the railroads developed the major cities and towns of a region.

> Trails will ever be a part of the language of the westerner. The gypsy motorist unfolds his tent, as the Indian did decades ago, and sits by a campfire of windproof fuel and equipment. The romance of the West still lives, for, even in the mushroom cities of canvas there is the possibility that years before the Redman camped on that very spot. Who knows? Trails have a romantic appeal to the traveler. The name still sticks, but the mud doesn't. Permanent highways are replacing them.
>
> *Colorado Highways*, June 1923

> Trails they were called in pioneer days. The name still sticks, but the mud doesn't. Graveled highways and hard-surfaced stretches have taken the place of the beaten brushwood and rut-marked roads. And it's over these highways that the endless lines of auto tourists are pouring into the Sky-Land State [Colorado].
>
> *Colorado Highways*, June 1923

Until about five years ago Colorado had let the prospector and pioneer push his way in front of him. Today all that is changed. She opens the road and invites him to follow. And she does more. As if by way of apology, she has widened his old trail, reduced its grade and to insure against wash-outs, she has flung across it bridges of concrete as strong as the granite wall out of which the trail was often carved.

Mae Lacy Baggs in *Colorado, the Queen Jewel of the Rockies*, 1918

1920, unknown location.
Early day "auto trails" evolved from wagon roads.
Note the Casper, Wyoming, pennant on the rear of the stuck-in-the-mud auto.
A. G. Lucier photograph, courtesy of the Hinckley Library, Northwest College.

How to Maintain Dirt Roads.
The following ten suggestions are given. If these suggestions are followed the result will soon manifest itself in better roads:
1. Inspect the road for its entire length during a rainy day and locate all holes, which will be easily noted as they will be filled with water. . . .
Colorado Highways, November 1923

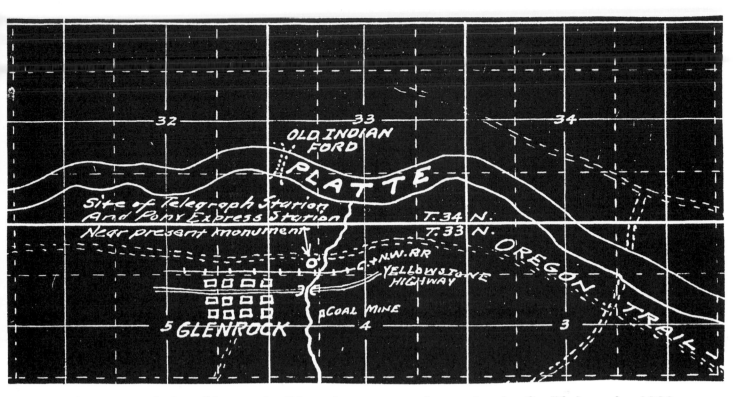

This map of the Glenrock, Wyoming, area, drawn by L. C. Bishop in 1933, illustrates the transportation evolution of the region.
Map courtesy of the Bishop family.

The **North Platte River** was followed by Native Americans, mountain men, and early military and survey expeditions.

The **Oregon-California Trail** was the primary emigrant wagon road west. The trail followed up the North Platte River and its tributary, Sweetwater River, to the easy Continental Divide crossing at South Pass. This route was also used by the Pony Express and the first transcontinental telegraph.

The **Chicago & Northwestern (C&NW) Railroad** was responsible for the establishment of several Wyoming towns along the North Platte River: Douglas in 1886, Glenrock in 1887, and Casper in 1888.

Auto trails which followed the North Platte River through Glenrock, coinciding with the **Yellowstone Highway** were the National Park-to-Park Highway, the Buffalo Highway, the Glacier to Gulf Highway, and the Atlantic Yellowstone Pacific Hiway.

In the mid 1910s the auto trail was designated **Wyoming Highway 11**.
In 1926, the highway was given the federal number, **U.S. Highway 20**, later joined by U.S. Highways 26 and 87.
To complete the transportation evolution of the Glenrock area, **Interstate 25** passes one and a half miles south of town.

Early Exploration

> "[Yellowstone] . . . the most interesting unexplored district in our widely expanded country."   William Raynolds, 1860

John Colter, former member of the Lewis & Clark expedition, was the first white to visit the Yellowstone area. While traveling along the east base of the Absaroka Mountains in 1807, he described the present-day DeMaris Springs west of Cody, Wyoming. From this discovery, the region received the name "Colter's Hell."

Major Stephen H. Long, while ascending the South Platte River in 1820, originally thought present-day Longs Peak to be Zebulon Pike's "highest peak" [Pikes Peak]. Members of the Long expedition were the first to climb Pikes Peak. Longs Peak is the major landmark in Rocky Mountain National Park.

Capt. Benjamin Bonneville, in 1832, brought the first wagons over South Pass to the Green River. He made a side trip to the Big Horn Basin and members of his expedition floated through the Wind River Canyon.

The **William Raynolds** expedition of 1860 was the first organized government <u>attempt</u> at exploration of the Yellowstone region. In May 1860, the expedition passed south, then west of the park. Because of weather and deep snow, they failed to penetrate the mountain barrier surrounding the park. Even guide Jim Bridger doubted that they could enter the park from the south. Capt. Raynolds quoted Bridger as saying "I told you you could not get through. *A bird cannot fly over that without taking a supply of grub along.*" Expedition member H. E. Maynadier's command passed east of the Yellowstone region.

Below: The Yellowstone region of the "**1878 Progress Map of the U.S. Geological Surveys West of the 100th Meridian.**" From Serial Set 1809, part 1.

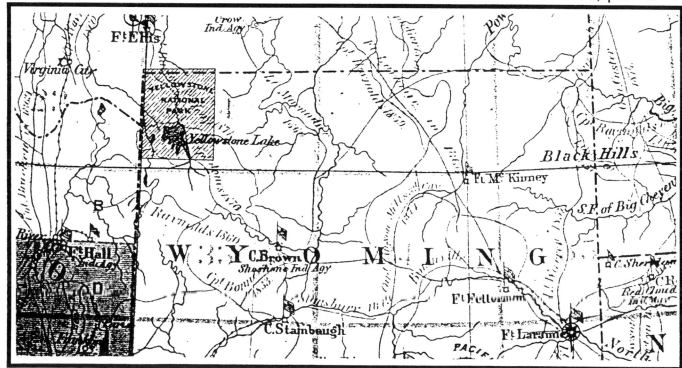

Expeditions to Yellowstone

"[Yellowstone] . . . I can conceive of no more wonderful and attractive region for the explorer."   Ferdinand Hayden, 1872

Early expeditions to Yellowstone were made from the north and northwest, from Montana, by one of two routes:

1. from Bozeman and Fort Ellis (two miles to the east), up the Yellowstone River.
2. from Virginia City, up the Madison River.

In 1869, the **Cook-Folsom-Peterson** expedition, a private enterprise, entered present-day Yellowstone from the north, up the Yellowstone River. After visiting the Canyon of the Yellowstone, Yellowstone Lake, and the major geyser basins, they exited by the Madison River to the northwest.

In 1870, the **Washburn-Langford-Doane** expedition took a similar route through the park. Nathaniel Langford presented lectures as part of a publicity program in the interests of the Northern Pacific Railway. It was one of his lectures that sparked Ferdinand Hayden's interest in the Yellowstone area.

In 1871, **Ferdinand Hayden** led the first U.S.-sponsored expedition to Yellowstone. He traveled by train to Ogden, Utah, then by stage to Fort Ellis. He also entered Yellowstone via the Yellowstone River. On the expedition were photographer William H. Jackson and artist Thomas Moran. Their reports, photographs, and paintings helped establish Yellowstone National Park, the world's first, in 1872. Hayden returned to Yellowstone in 1872 and 1878.

In 1873, **Capt. William Jones** traveled up the North Branch of the Shoshone River, west of present-day Cody, Wyoming, and was the first white to enter Yellowstone from the east. He entered the park by Jones Pass, six miles north-northwest of Sylvan Pass, the pass used by the present-day east entrance road. Jones exited the park to the south, over Togwotee Pass, used by present-day U.S. Highway 287. Capt. Jones, proud of his accomplishments, mentioned in his report previous failures in crossing the Absarokas:

> From the report for the year 1872 of N. P. Langford, superintendent of the Yellowstone National Park I extract the following: "The park is only accessible from Montana. *It is impossible to enter it from Wyoming.* Attempts to scale the vast ridge of mountains on the eastern and southern borders have been made by several expeditions . . ."
>
> As late as 1860, Captain Raynolds was foiled in repeated efforts to cross the barrier. . . .
>
> Dr. F. V. Hayden, in his report for 1871 says "The range of mountains on the east and south of the Yellowstone Basin seems to be entirely of volcanic origin; they are also among the ruggedest and most inaccessible ranges on the continent."

Arnold Hague conducted surveys in Yellowstone from 1883-1902. Many of Yellowstone's place names come from his mostly unpublished surveys.

Emigrant Trails

The Yellowstone Highway and the National Park-to-Park Highway closely follow several early emigrant trails. Most of the emigrant routes had as a common thread: **Gold**.

The **South Platte River Trail**, followed by Stephen H. Long in 1820, would become the most heavily traveled trail to Denver and the Colorado goldfields.

The **Cherokee Trail** connected William Bent's Old Fort on the Santa Fe Trail Mountain Branch, in southeastern Colorado, with Fort Bridger on the Oregon-California Trail, in southwestern Wyoming. The trail was named for Cherokee Indians who traveled from northeastern Oklahoma to the California goldfields in 1849 and 1850. The trail followed up the Front Range of the Rocky Mountains to take advantage of the lower Continental Divide crossing in southern Wyoming.

From the Orin Junction, Wyoming, area to Casper, the Yellowstone Highway followed the North Platte River and the **Oregon-California Trail**. This trail was the major emigrant trail to the West from 1843 until 1862. It was the primary route used by Mormon emigrants starting in 1847, and California-bound gold seekers, starting in 1849. This route was also used by the **Pony Express**, a short-lived mail service operated from April 1860 until October 1861. It was replaced by the first trans-continental telegraph which followed the Pony Express route through Wyoming. The Oregon Trail followed Idaho's Snake River into Oregon. The California Trail followed Nevada's Humboldt River to present-day western Nevada where branches led to California. In eastern and central Wyoming, the two trails were one and the same.

In 1862, much of the Oregon-California Trail traffic shifted south to Wyoming's Bridger Pass. In that year, Ben Holladay's Overland Stage Line began using this **Overland Trail** which used sections of the South Platte River and Cherokee Trails.

Opened in 1864, the **Bozeman Trail** branched off from several points on the Oregon-California Trail and ran northwest to the Montana goldfields. It traversed the Powder River Basin east of the Big Horn Mountains, favorite hunting grounds of the Sioux, Arapaho, and Cheyenne Indians.

West of Casper, the first route of the Yellowstone Highway followed closely the **Bridger Trail.** This trail, established by Jim Bridger in 1864, was an alternative to the more popular Bozeman Trail. The Bridger Trail crossed the east end of the Owl Mountains to the Bighorn River, then crossed the Big Horn Basin to Montana.

The **Nez Perce National Historic Trail** was the route used by the "non-treaty" Nez Perce in their failed effort to reach Canada in 1877. The trail passed through Yellowstone National Park. "Treaty" Nez Perce had ceded land to settlers and gold seekers who had overrun their land.

The Yellowstone Highway followed or crossed the major Emigrant Trails of Wyoming and northeastern Colorado

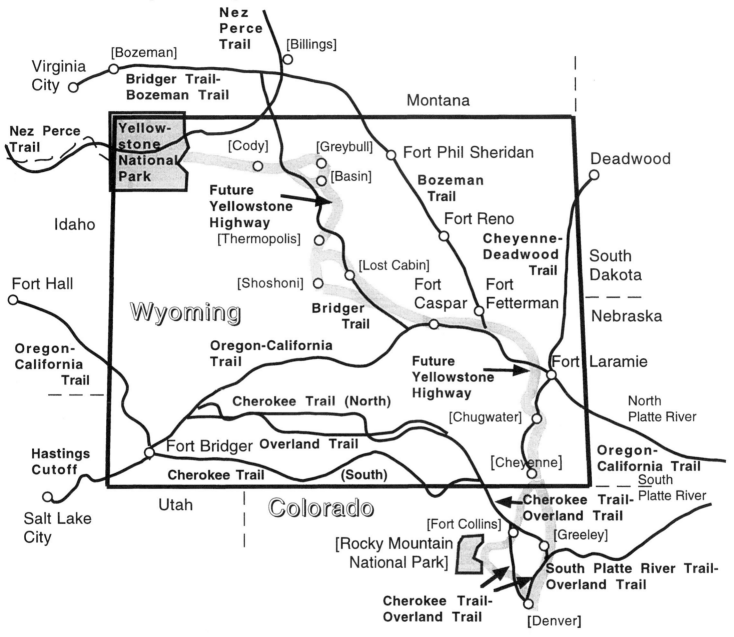

"Life has returned in the last decade to the overland trails of the forties and fifties. They were; they were not; and now, behold, they are again. History entombed them. They were glamerous with legend. Then came the automobile and resurrected them. To-day where the wagon ruts had faded out into sage brush and bunch grass, thousands of men labor yearly to reduce grades, flatten curves, improve surfaces so that the ever-increasing tide of motor cars bearing the modern counterpart of the pioneers may flow smoothly along these reincarnated highways, with profits to those who live beside them."

Frederic F. Van de Water, 1927

New Trails from Railroad Towns

Railroads decreased the need for most long-distance trails and freighting lines. But new trails developed from railroad towns and "end of track" to outlying areas. Sections of the following trails were later closely followed by sections of the Yellowstone Highway.

The **Cheyenne-Deadwood Trail** ran north from the Union Pacific town of Cheyenne to the new goldfields in the Black Hills of South Dakota. Beginning in 1876, the Cheyenne and Black Hills Stage and Express route ran north via Fort Laramie. The use of the trail declined as the Cheyenne & Northern Railroad built north from Cheyenne, beginning in 1887. The southern terminus of the stage advanced north as the tracks reached Chugwater, Bordeaux, and then Wendover.

The Chicago & Northwestern Railroad reached Casper in 1888. From here a new stage and freight line ran northwest to Thermopolis and the Big Horn Basin. This route closely followed the old **Bridger Trail** to Montana. Much of this route, through present-day Arminto and Lost Cabin, was the first route of the Yellowstone Highway between Casper and Thermopolis.

When the Chicago & Northwestern was extended from Casper to Shoshoni in 1906, a shorter trail to the Big Horn Basin was established. This route over **Birdseye Pass** was east of the roadless Wind River Canyon. This stage and freight business provided a link between the Chicago & Northwestern at Shoshoni and the Burlington Railroad at Kirby. In 1913, the Burlington completed its tracks through the Wind River Canyon. The Birdseye Pass route was the second route of the Yellowstone Highway, used until 1924, when the road through the Wind River Canyon was completed.

Below: Bureau of Land Management **1993 map**, Chugwater, Wyoming. The **Cheyenne-Deadwood Trail** curves northeast from Bordeaux to Fort Laramie (off the map). The Burlington Railroad was originally the **Cheyenne & Northern**.

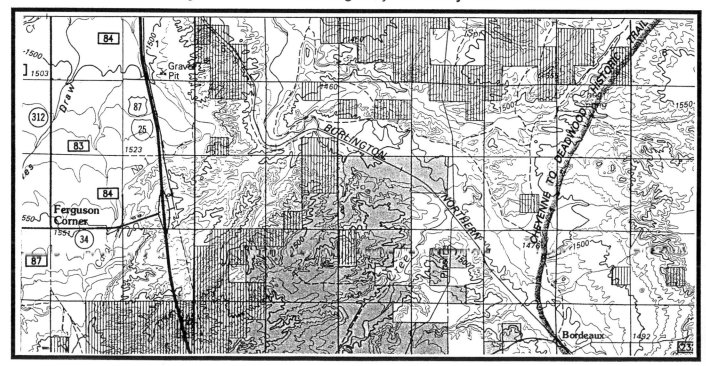

8

Railroads to the Yellowstone National Park Region

"Railway termini. They are our gates to the glorious and the unknown. Through them we pass out into adventure and sunshine, to them, alas! we return."　　　　　　　　　　　　　　E. M. Forster

The Union Pacific-Central Pacific was the first transcontinental route across the country, completed in May 1869. Cheyenne was the Union Pacific "end of track" during the winter of 1867-1868. In December 1867, the *Helena Herald* made the following prediction of travel to Yellowstone:

A few years more and the U. P. Railroad will bring thousands of pleasure seekers, sightseers and invalids from every part of the globe, to see this land of surpassing wonders.

But it was the Northern Pacific Railroad which brought the first railroad to the edge of Yellowstone National Park. The railroad also played an important role in the establishment of the park. It was Jay Cooke, financial advisor to the railroad, who publicized the 1870 Washburn-Langford-Doane expedition to the park. This publicity led to the official U.S. survey of the park by Ferdinand Hayden in 1871. His reports, and the photographs by William Henry Jackson and paintings by Thomas Moran, led to the establishment, in 1872, of Yellowstone National Park, the world's first.

The Northern Pacific completed its transcontinental line in 1883. A spur line, the "Park Branch," was built south from Livingston to Cinnabar, a few miles north of Gardiner, Montana. The line was extended to Gardiner, at the north entrance to the park, in 1903. **Tourism was the railroad's primary goal**. As with most early trails and expeditions to the park, the first railroad approached the park from the north. This would be the route of the later National Park-to-Park Highway north of Yellowstone.

The **Utah & Northern**, later part of the Union Pacific system, ran north from Ogden, Utah, to Beaver Canyon (now Spencer, Idaho) and Monida, Montana. From these points, stagecoaches carried tourists to Yellowstone via the west entrance.

The **Chicago Burlington & Quincy** completed its 131-mile spur line from Toluca, Montana, east of Billings, to Cody, Wyoming, in November 1901. This line hastened the development of the "Cody Road" to the east entrance of Yellowstone and the Sylvan Pass road within the park.

With the acquisition of the Colorado & Southern system in 1908 and the completion of the railroad's line through Wind River Canyon in 1913, the Burlington system extended from the Pacific Northwest to the Gulf Coast. The Burlington Railroad promoted travel from Denver to Yellowstone. Its 1928 time-table noted:

Over the Inter-mountain route, the Burlington operates through trains daily between Denver and the famous Cody Gateway to Yellowstone National Park. It is the shortest route and by far the quickest time (24 hours) between Colorado and Yellowstone. IF YOU DON'T SEE THE CODY ROAD YOU DON'T SEE YELLOWSTONE PARK.

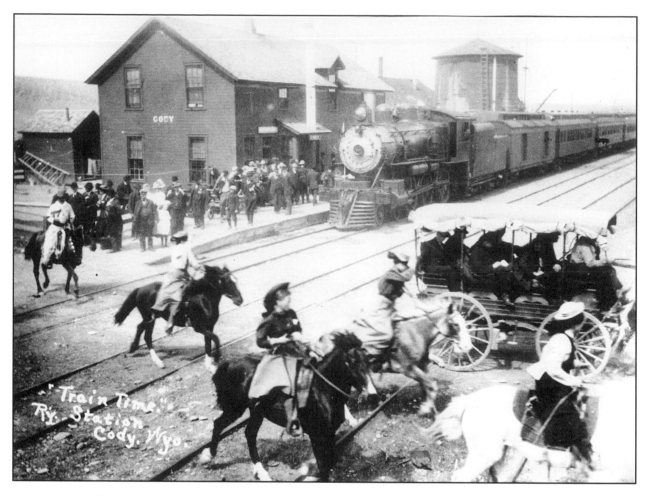

"Train Time." The Cody Railroad Depot. Courtesy of the
Buffalo Bill Historical Center, Cody, WY. Jack Richard Collection, photo P.89.1085.

The **Union Pacific** Railroad's Oregon Short Line reached West Yellowstone in
1908. An ad for the Oregon Short Line stated:

> . . . from Salt Lake City, Ogden and Pocatello to the
> YELLOWSTONE NATIONAL PARK Connecting with TransContinental
> Trains from ALL POINTS EAST AND WEST

F. Dumont Smith said of the Denver to Yellowstone travel on the Union Pacific
Railroad in 1909:

> To arrive at the Yellowstone . . . . you go to Ogden and turn to the
> right. You can not lose your way, because it is the first turn to the right,
> and then you go till they tell you to get off. This will be at the western
> entrance of the Park, where the railroad stops.

The **Chicago Milwaukee & St. Paul Railway** reached Three Rivers,
Montana, in 1926, providing access to Yellowstone via the "Gallatin Gateway." Its
slogan: "GALLATIN - The greatest Gateway to the Greatest National Park!"
The motor route led to West Yellowstone, Montana, at the west entrance to the park.
The **Chicago & Northwestern Railroad** reached Lander, Wyoming, from
Casper, in 1906. The railroad arranged for bus transportation to Yellowstone National
Park via the south entrance. The route followed the old Rocky Mountain Highway,
present-day U.S. Highway 287, over Togwotee Pass.

53 54

Everywhere West

Denver-Cheyenne-Casper-Thermopolis-Cody-Billings Lines

Burlington Route

Table No. 13

READ DOWN — READ UP

23 Daily	31 Daily	29 Daily	Mls.	Colorado & Southern Ry.	Mls.	30 Daily	22 Daily	32 Daily	
PM	AM	PM		*Mountain Time*		AM	AM	PM	
3.00	8.00	6.00	0	Lv....1,4 **Denver** 12....Ar	670	8.55	10.40	5.55	
3.12	f 8.12	6.12	3	Utah Junction	669	8.40	10.27	5.43	
f 3.18	f 8.20		6	Westminster	666		f10.21	f 5.37	
f 3.24	f 8.27		9	Semper	663		f10.15	f 5.31	
3.33	8.36		14	Broomfield	658		f10.06	f 5.23	
	f 8.38		14	Burns Junction	657			f 5.21	
f 3.38	f 8.42		16	**Coalton**	655		f10.00	f 5.18	
f 3.44	8.51		20	Superior	651		f 9.53	f 5.12	
f 3.52	f 9.00		24	Marshall	647		f 9.44	f 5.03	
f 4.00	f 9.08		28	University	643		f 9.34	f 4.54	
4.12	9.17	7.08	29	**Boulder** (Rocky Mt. Nat'l Park) Union Station	642	7.50	9.30	4.50	
	f 9.20		31	Ara	640				
4.30	f 9.33		38	Niwot	633		9.08	4.30	
4.41	9.45	7.37	43	**Longmont** (Ry. Mt. Nat'l-Estes Park)	628	7.16	8.59	4.20	
f 4.45	f 9.49		45	Grenfell	626		f 8.53		
			47	Morey	624			f 4.12	
f 4.51	f 9.55		49	Highland	622		f 8.47	f 4.09	
5.01	10.05	7.58	54	Berthoud	619	6.56	8.38	4.00	
f 5.06	f10.10		57	Campion	616		f 8.32	f 3.53	
5.15	10.19	8.13	60	**Loveland** (Ry. Mt. Nat'l-Estes Park)	613	6.42	8.26	3.47	
f 5.21	f10.25		64	Marion	609		f 8.17		
f 5.27	f10.31		68	Trilby	605		f 8.11		
f 5.30	f10.34		69	McClelland's	604		f 8.08	f 3.29	
f 5.34	f10.38		71	Drakes	602		f 8.05	f 3.25	
f	f		73	Agricultural College	600		f	f	
5.40	10.40	8.40	74	Ar...**Fort Collins** 87...Lv	599	6.18	8.00	3.20	
6.50	12.05		99	Ar.... **Greeley** 87 Lv			6.50	2.05	
PM	10.50	8.50	74	Lv...**Fort Collins** 87...Ar	599	6.18	AM	3.15	
	f11.01		79	Giddings	594			f 3.02	
	f11.04		81	Whittaker	592			f 3.00	
	f11.06		82	Barnett	591			f 2.58	
	11.12	9.13	85	**Wellington**	588	5.50		2.53	
	f11.15		87	Dixon	586			f 2.48	
	f11.24		91	Bulger	582			f 2.41	
	f11.36		96	Heston	577			f 2.33	
	f11.48		102	Crouse, Colo	571			f 2.23	
	f11.58		107	Warrenton, Wyo	566			f 2.14	32 Daily
	f12.10		112	Speer	561			f 2.06	PM
	12.30	10.35	120	Ar . **Cheyenne** 11, 75 . Lv	553	4.45		1.45	
	1.30	11.00	120	Lv . **Cheyenne** 11, 75 . Ar	553	4.25		PM	11.25
		e	120	Camp Carlin	552	e			
	f 1.41	e	120	Fort Russell	552	e			f11.10
		e	121	Northfield	551	e			
		e	123	Ware	549	e			
	f 2 03	e	131	Silver Crown	541	e			f10.49
	2.20	e	139	Federal	533	e			f10.34
	f 2.28	e	143	Islay	529	e			f10.27
	2 44	e	151	Horse Creek	521	e			f10.12
	f 2.47	e	153	Murke	519	e			f10.08
	f 2.57	e	157	Altus	515	e			f10.01
	3.09	e	162	Farthing	510	e			9 51
	f	e	167	Underwood	505	e			f
	f	e	169	Jordan	503	e			f
		e	170	Lambert	502	e			
	f	e	176	McDonald's Ranch	496	e			f
	f 3 39	e	177	Diamond	495	e			f 9.20
	f 3 50	e	183	Brinton	489	e			f 9.09
	4.04	1.33	188	Chugwater	484	1.33			9 00
	f 4.16	e	194	Swan	478	e			f 8 45
	4.22	e	197	Slater	475	e			f 8.40
	f 4.31	e	202	Bordeaux	470	e			f 8.31
	f 4 48	e	211	Gibson	461	e			f 8.14
	4.57	2.30	214	**Wheatland**	458	12.35			8.08
	f	e	216	Curtis	456	e			f
	f 5.11	e	221	Uva	451	e			f 7.53
	5.30	e	231	Dwyer	441	e			7.34
	f 5.41	e	237	Walker	435	e			f 7.23
	‖ 5.55	3.30	241	Ar....**Wendover**, 11....Lv	429	11.35			7.15
	PM	AM				PM			PM

Over this inter-mountain route, the Burlington operates through trains daily between Denver and the famous Cody Gateway to Yellowstone National Park. It is the shortest route and by far the quickest time (24 hours) between Colorado and Yellowstone.

IF YOU DON'T SEE THE CODY ROAD
YOU DON'T SEE YELLOWSTONE PARK

READ DOWN — READ UP

Frt. Tu. Th. Sa.	31 Daily	29 Daily	Mls.	Burlington Route	Mls.	30 Daily	32 Daily	Frt. Mo. We. Fr.
	PM	AM		*Mountain Time*		PM	PM	
	7.45		251	Ar..... *Guernsey*, 11 Lv	0		*5.25*	
	12.45		380	Ar.... 8, 12 *Alliance*, 11 Lv	⊙		*1.25*	
	1.25		⊙	Lv.... 8, 12 *Alliance*, 11 ....Ar	566		12.45	
	5.25		0	Lv..... *Guernsey*, 11 .....Ar	438		7.45	
	‖ 6.15	3.35	241	Lv..... **Wendover**, 11 .....Ar	429	11 30	‖ 6.55	
	f 6.35	f 3.55	249	Cassa	421	f11.06	f 6.35	
	6.46	4.06	257	Glendo, 11	413	10.45	6.20	
	f 7.05		266	Bona	404	f10.25	f 6 03	
	f 7.09	f 4.29	268	McKinley	402	f10.20	f 5.58	
	7.15	4.35	272	Orin, 11	398	10.15	5.53	
				Natural Bridge				
	7.45	5.10	287	Douglas, 11	383	9.45	5.25	
	f 7.55	f 5.19	292	Arnold	378	f 9.30	f 5.13	
	f 8.04	f 5.28	297	Orpha	373	f 9.20	f 5.05	
	f 8.14	f 5.37	302	Alberta	368	f 9.09	f 4.57	
	f 8.19	f 5.42	305	Carey, 11	365	f 9.02	f 4.52	
	f 8.26	f 5.49	309	Clayton, 11	361	f 8.53	f 4.46	
	8.40	6.03	316	Glenrock, 11	354	8.40	4.36	
	f 8.55	f 6.16	323	Lockett	347	f 8.26	f 4.26	
	f 9.05	f 6.28	330	Fry	340	f 8.16	f 4 16	
	9.25	6.50	340	Ar .... **Casper**, 11 Lv	330	8.00	4.00	
	PM	7.10	340	Lv .... **Casper**, 11 .... Ar	330	7.30	PM	
		f 7.28	351	Bishop	319	f 7.10		
		7.36	355	Illco	315	f 7.02		
		f 7.47	362	Bucknum	308	f 6.51		
		f 7.56	368	Petrie	302	f 6 42		
		f 8.05	373	Sodium	297	f 6.34		
		f 8.15	379	Powder River	291	f 6.25		
		f 8.32	390	Lox	280	f 6.05		
		8.45	398	Arminto	272	5.50		
		f 9.07	412	Madden	258	f 5.20		
		9.25	422	Lysite	248	5.00		
		f 9.40	429	Schoening	241	f 4.42		
		10.15	443	Bonneville	227	4.10		
		f10.30	454	Emery	216	f 3.53		
		f10 38	458	Boysen	212	f 3.45		
				← WIND RIVER CANON →				
		f10.52	465	Dornick	205	f 3.30		
		f11.04	470	Minnesela	200	f 3.17		
		11.10	475	Thermopolis	195	3.10		
		f11.30	482	Lucerne	188	f 2.48		
		11.40	487	Kirby	183	2.38		
		f11.49	492	Chatham	178	f 2.16		
		f11.59	499	Neiber	171	f 2.02		
		f12.05	502	Colter	168	f 1.55		
		12 20	507	Worland	163	1.45		
		f12.33	515	Durkee	155	f 1.30		
		f12.43	520	Rairden	150	f 1.20		
		1.05	526	Manderson	144	1.05		
		1.25	535	Basin	135	12.47		
		1 45	543	Ar ...... **Greybull** Lv	127	12.30		
		2.00	543	Lv ...... **Greybull** ...... Ar	127	12.15		
		f 2.24	554	Spence	116	f11.52		
		f 2 37	561	Himes	109	f11.36		
		2.53	570	Kane	100	11.16		
		3 08	580	Lovell	90	10.57		
		3 23	586	Cowley	84	10.44		
		3 35	592	Deaver	78	10.32		
		3.50	598	Ar .... **Frannie** Lv	72	10.02		
		† *4.05*	598	Lv .... *Frannie*, 84 .... Ar	⊙	† *9 50*		
		† *5.45*	640	Ar .... *Cody*, 8, 84 Lv	⊙	† *8.20*		
		† *2 30*		Lv .... *Cody*, 8, 84 .... Ar	⊙	†*12.10*		
		† *3.35*		Ar .... *Frannie*, 84 Lv	⊙	†*10.30*		
		4 05	598	Lv .... Frannie .... Ar	72	10.02		
		4 22	603	Warren	67	9.49		
		f 4.33	610	Duff	60	f 9.35		
		f 4.41	615	Wade	55	f 9.23		
		f 4.50	621	Tyndell	49	f 9.11		
		5.00	626	East Bridger	44	9.01		
		5.20	632	Fromberg	38	8.45		
		f 5.33	638	Edgar	32	f 8.42		
		5 48	645	Silesia	25	8.25		
		6.15	655	Laurel	15	8.05		
			658	Mossmain	12			
		6.40	670	Ar...... **Billings** 8, 12 Lv	0	7.30		
		PM				AM		

Guernsey to Casper. Consult agent for time.

Additional Service—Freight trains provide additional service between Casper and Laurel. Consult local agent for time.

Passengers on Nos. 29 and 30 get off at special platform here for 10 minutes' sightseeing.

For local time between Frannie and Cody see Table 84

Casper to Guernsey. Consult agent for time.

Time from 12.01 midnight to 12.00 noon is shown by LIGHT faced figures, and time from 12.01 noon to 12.00 midnight by HEAVY faced figures.

Reference Marks:

⊙ Connection. ‖ Meal stop. †Daily except Sunday.

e Stops only to take on passengers for or let off passengers from points north of Casper and south of Wellington.

f Flag stop.

For equipment of these trains, see page 28.

1928 Chicago Burlington & Quincy Railroad Timetable

Many of the cities, towns, and stations along the route will be mentioned in the telling of the Yellowstone and National Park-to-Park Highway story. Courtesy of the Denver Public Library, Western History Collection.

Yellowstone: Stagecoaches to Automobiles

The railroads catered to the "carriage trade," offering package deals, which included railroad transportation, stagecoach transportation, hotels, and meals within the park.

Railroads brought tourists <u>to</u> the park. Stagecoaches, also referred to as "observation coaches," transported them <u>within</u> the park.

In 1883, the U.S. Army Corps of Engineers began the systematic construction of the "Grand Loop Road" in Yellowstone. The loop road was completed in 1905. The roads within the park were narrow, only wide enough for coaches. Most roads were one-way only. They were engineered for maximum speeds of eight miles per hour.

Many were satisfied with this slow pace.

"Remember, that one cannot really enjoy fine scenery when traveling at a rate of 15 or 20 or 25 miles an hour."
British Ambassador
Lord James Bryce

Baggage stickers courtesy of the National Park Service, Yellowstone National Park.

In 1908, William Cody and the people of the town of Cody petitioned the government to allow automobiles in Yellowstone via the east entrance:

Automobiles for the Park. A law was passed years ago prohibiting the entrance of steam vehicles to the park.

At that time automobiles were unknown, but the law was so drawn that it prohibits all such power vehicles, when the idea really was to prevent the construction of railways in the Park.

When the beautiful lake above the Shoshone canyon dam is filled with water and the road from Cody to the Park is completed along its banks to connect with the Forest Reserve road, it will make the most romantic and scenic auto boulevard in the United States, and the passage of an amendment to the present law so as to allow autos to be used in a trip from Cody to the Park and around the circle would greatly increase the pleasure of tourists and make this town a favorite gateway to Nature's Wonderland. *Basin Republican*, January 10, 1908

The request was denied, but the admission of automobiles to the park was inevitable, for they were allowed in Mount Rainier National Park in 1908, Glacier in 1912, Sequoia and Yosemite in 1913, and Mesa Verde in 1914.

A U.S. Senate resolution in April of 1912 stated:
> *Resolved*, That the Secretary of War be, and is hereby, directed to submit to the Senate, as early as practical, an estimate of the cost of construction of new roads, or changes in the present roads, in the Yellowstone National Park, in order to permit the use of autos and motor cycles therein without interfering with the present mode of travel in vehicles drawn by horses and other animals.

"Just as the motor car has speeded up life in every other phase, so has it speeded up tourist travel. . . . while more distance is covered, much less is really seen, and certainly a great deal less is learned of the scenery, the condition of the country, the romance and history that once was known."
Ned Frost, 1929

The three major transportation companies in the park were asked to respond to the 1912 Senate resolution, not on whether to allow autos in, but <u>how</u> to accommodate them. The three companies accounted for 70% of visitor transportation within the park and all used horse-drawn stages. All three recommended that a separate and distinct road system be built for use by automobiles. All were concerned about the confrontation between horses and automobiles. One company stated: "It is safe to say there isn't over one horse in a hundred of the three main transportation companies' horses that ever saw an automobile. These companies own and use about 2,000 head each season."

But the small independent Frost and Richard Camping Company, user of the east entrance road from Cody, stated:
> . . . we would like to direct your attention to the present inadequacy of that part of the road which lies between the park line on the east and Yellowstone Lake, and particularly between the soldiers quarters and Sylvan Pass, as compared with the road on the circle.

For the past three years there has been a steadily increasing automobile traffic between Cody, Holm Lodge, and Pahaska. This road, especially in the Shoshone Canyon, is narrow. There is a tacit understanding between all drivers that the automobiles always give the teams the inside of the road. There has not yet been a serious accident due to the meeting of teams and autos.

If this understanding held good in the park and the machines were limited as to their speed, we think that a separate road would be entirely unnecessary.

The Army Corp of Engineers recommended that the road system in Yellowstone be reconstructed "in order to provide a single system of roads for automobiles, motor cycles, and vehicles drawn by horses or other animals." The report also stated "The eastern approach road is not now of sufficient importance to require more than widening of the road to a width sufficient to provide for both classes of traffic."

Yellowstone road work from 1913 to 1915 was geared toward the admission of automobiles.

A "pathfinding" trip along the Yellowstone Highway was made in July 1913. On the trip was a representative of the Blue Book Publishing Company, a leading tour book company. The Yellowstone Highway Association said of this trip:

This party made the trip to the Eastern entrance of the [Yellowstone] Park, but for the reason that the Park was closed to automobiles, could not enter. However, this knocking at the door of the Park has its place in the program of preliminary movements to secure the opening of the Park to rubber tires.

Richard Bartlett, in *Yellowstone: a Wilderness Besieged*, relates the following story:

. . . the western manager of the American Automobile Association, Mr. A. L. Westgard, made an annual pilgrimage to one of the park entrances, climbed out of his car and shook his fist at the soldiers on duty there, climbed aboard and drove away until another year rolled by.

Automobiles were allowed in the park on August 1, 1915. Motorcycles were not initially allowed in the park. For the first two years, during the transition from wagon roads to auto roads, the two shared the road.

It was soon obvious that autos and horse-drawn vehicles could <u>not</u> share the same road. In 1916, almost one half of Yellowstone visitors arrived by automobile, compared to less than 7% in 1915. By 1917, the major public transportation concessionaires in Yellowstone had changed to motorized vehicles. And they were transporting more tourists than ever.

One season's operation of the automobile regulations demonstrated to the powers that be that the average motorist is a saner and more reasonable being than was at first supposed; as a consequence, there has been a considerable downward revision of the rules governing his actions.   Charles J. Belden, 1918

The first Official Yellowstone "Auto Rules and Regulations" appeared in the *Park County Enterprise* (Cody) July 21, 1915.

The chart shows the restrictions placed on the automobile. **The times were to accommodate both auto and horse team traffic on the same road.** Below are rules 7 and 8:

7. Speeds. -- Speeds must be limited to 12 miles per hour ascending and 10 miles per hour descending steep grades, and to 8 miles per hour when approaching sharp curves. On good roads with straight stretches, and when no team is nearer than 200 yards, the speed may be increased to 30 miles per hour. Horns must be sounded at all curves where the road cannot be seen for at least 200 yards ahead, and when approaching teams or riding animals.

8. Teams. -- When teams, saddle horses, or pack trains approach, automobiles will take the outer edge of the roadway, regardless of the direction in which they may be going, taking care that sufficient room is left on the inside for the passage of vehicles and animals. Teams have the right of way, and automobiles will be backed or otherwise handled as may be necessary so as to enable teams to pass with safety. In no case must automobiles pass animals on the road at a greater speed than 8 miles per hour.

15

(Note—First two columns are Schedule A; second two columns Schedule B. The words "not earlier than" should precede the hour stated in all cases. First column gives mileage.)

GARDINER TO NORRIS

		Schedule A		Schedule B	
Lv. Gardiner Entrance	0	7.00 a. m.	6.30 a. m.	2.30 p. m.	3.00 p. m.
Ar. Mammoth Hot Springs	5	6.30 a. m.	7.00 a. m.	3.00 p. m.	3.00 p. m.
Lv. Mammoth Hotel	0	6.45 a. m.	7.15 a. m.		
Lv. 8-mile Post	8		8.00 a. m.		
Ar. Norris	20	8.30 a. m.	9.00 a. m.		

NORRIS TO WEST ENTRANCE

Lv. Norris	0			4.00 p. m.	4.30 p. m.
Ar. West Entrance	37			6.00 p. m.	6.30 p. m.

(For Gallatin Station Entrance see Note 1)

NORRIS TO FOUNTAIN

		8.45 a. m.	9.15 a. m.	4.00 p. m.	4.30 p. m.
Lv. Norris	0				
		(Via Mesa Road)		(Via Mesa Road or Madison Junction)	
Lv. Firehole Cascades	14.7		10.00 a. m.		
Ar. Fountain Hotel	20	10.30 a. m.	11.00 a. m.	5.45 p. m.	6.15 p. m.

(For Gallatin Station Entrance see Note 1.)

WESTERN ENTRANCE TO FOUNTAIN HOTEL

		6.45 a. m.	7.15 a. m.		
Lv. West Entrance	0				
Ar. Fountain Hotel	21	8.30 a. m.	9.00 a. m.		

FOUNTAIN HOTEL TO THUMB

		10.30 a. m.	11.00 a. m.	5.45 p. m.	6.15 p. m.
Lv. Fountain Hotel	0				
Ar. Upper Basin (Old Faithful Inn)	9	12.00 m.	12.30 p. m.	6.45 p. m.	7.00 p. m.
Lv. Upper Basin (Old Faithful Inn)	0	2.30 p. m.	3.00 p. m.	7.00 a. m.	7.30 a. m.
Ar. Thumb Station	19	4.30 p. m.	5.00 p. m.	9.00 a. m.	9.30 a. h.

(For South Entrance see No. 1)

THUMB TO LAKE HOTEL

		4.30 p. m.	5.00 p. m.	9.00 a. m.	9.30 a. m.
Lv. Thumb Station	0				
Ar. Lake Hotel	15	4.45 p. m.	6.15 p. m.	10.30 a. m.	11.30 a. m.

LAKE HOTEL TO EAST BOUNDARY

		7.00 a. m.	7.30 a. m.	2.00 p. m.	2.30 p. m.
Lv. Lake Hotel	0				
Ar. East Boundary	28	9.30 a. m.	10.30 a. m.	4.30 p. m.	5.30 p. m.

EAST BOUNDARY TO LAKE HOTEL

		3.15 p. m.	3.45 p. m.	7.30 a. m.	8.00 a. m.
Lv. East Boundary	0				
Ar. Lake Hotel	28	5.45 p. m.	6.15 p. m.	10.00 a. m.	11.00 a. m.

LAKE HOTEL TO CANYON HOTEL

		7.00 a. m.	7.30 a. m.	2.00 p. m.	2.30 p. m.
Lv. Lake Hotel	0				
Lv. Canyon Station	16	9.00 a. m.	10.00 a. m.		
		(See Note 2.)			
Ar. Canyon Hotel	17	9.10 a. m.	10.10 a. m.	3.15 p. m.	3.45 p. m.

CANYON TO NORRIS

		2.15 p. m.	2.30 p. m.		
Lv. Canyon Hotel	0				
Ar. Norris	12	3.15 p. m.	3.30 p. m.		

(For schedules from Norris to Fountain, Upper Basin, and West Entrance, see page 3.)

CANYON TO TOWER FALLS

		1.30 p. m.	2.00 p. m.	7.00 a. m.	7.30 a. m.
Lv. Canyon Hotel	0				
Arrive Tower Falls:					
Via Dunraven Pass	16	3.15 p. m.	3.45 p. m.	8.45 a. m.	9.15 a. m.
Via Mount Washburn	19	4.15 p. m.	4.45 p. m.	9.45 a. m.	10.15 a. m.

(For Cooke City Entrance see No. 1.)

TOWER FALLS TO GARDINER

		3.15 p. m.	4.45 p. m.	9.15 a. m.	10.15 a.m.
Lv. Tower Falls	0				
Ar. Mammoth Hot Springs	20	5.30 p. m.	6.45 p. m.	11.15 a. m.	12.15 p. m.
Lv. Mammoth Hot Springs (via Main Road)	0	7.00 a. m.	7.30 a. m.	2.30 p. m.	3.00 p. m.
Ar. Gardiner Entrance	5	7.30 a. m.	8.00 a. m.	3.00 p. m.	3.30 p. m.

MAMMOTH HOT SPRINGS TO GARDINER

		8.45 a. m.	9.00 a. m.	11.45 a. m.	1.00 p. m.
Lv. Mammoth Hot Springs (via Old Road)	0				
Ar. Gardiner Entrance	0	9.30 a. m.	9.45 a. m.	12.15 p. m.	1.45 p. m.

The Acting Superintendent of the park has authority to change these schedules if necessary.

Note 1.—Owing to scarcity of travel on the roads named, automobiles will be permitted to travel without schedule on the roads between the South Entrance and the Thumb; between the Northeast or Cooke City Entrance and Tower Falls Station; and between the West Entrance (Yellowstone, Montana,) and the Northwest or Gallatin Station Entrance. Upon entering the main roads at the Thumb, Tower Falls, and the West Entrance, however, automobiles must conform to the regular schedules.

Note 2.—Automobiles making the morning trip from the Lake to the Canyon will be permitted to make this side trip to Artist Point, provided they keep within the schedule upon passing Canyon Station.

"Good Roads Clubs"

"Auto Trails" were descriptive names given to early automobile roads. The concept of a named highway connecting various points was promoted by businesses and local "Good Roads Clubs" along the route. The auto trail association promoted the route, printed tour guides, and helped improve and maintain the roads. This was before state and federal involvement in highway funding and maintenance.

Railroads endorsed <u>early</u> good road efforts for improved highways enabled farmers better access to the railroad stations.

Clubs would hold "Good Roads Day" when businesses would close and men volunteered their services. They improved bad sections of road and repaired bridges and culverts. Members would carry bags of sand in their auto, ready to fill the first pothole they encountered. **Road improvements were necessary.**

> Highways, as we know them, were non-existent in those days. Roads? Yes. The state had plenty of roads, such as they were, but most of them for long and frequent stretches, were worse than none. Deep ruts; high centers; rocks, loose and solid; steep grades; washouts and gullies; stumps; sage brush roots; unbridged streams; sand; alkali dust; gumbo; and plain mud, were some of the more common abominations the cross-country traveler had to contend with.
>
> Calvin W. Williams, describing 1909 Wyoming roads.

In 1902, 42 Denver automobile owners formed the **Colorado Auto Club**. The same year, the **American Automobile Association** (AAA) was formed. In 1905, the Colorado Good Roads Association was formed.

> Whoop for good roads and get into the band wagon. You may own an automobile some day and then you'll realize the joyousness of beautiful highways over which to travel from one end of the state to the other. . . . The good roads movement is on in the United States and Colorado steps officially into the procession today. There will be a permanent organization formed and the work taken up systematically.
>
> *Rocky Mountain News*, July 27, 1905

The Colorado Highway Commission was established in 1909, followed by the Colorado Highway Department in 1910. Tom Tully, one of the first named to the commission, stated in *Colorado Highways*, April 1929:

> started out in 1910 . . . to go over the state and map out a system of state highways. . . . Every community wanted to be on the main highways we sought to map out. . . . we found bridges we did not dare cross in a car, encountered mud that stuck us, found grades we managed to crawl up at a speed a snail could best, and roads that were never meant for anything but a horse drawn vehicle.

The Home of the Club That Is Making Douglas Famous.
WHERE WILL BE HELD

GOOD ROADS CLUB

MORSCH & SON

THE FIRST AUTOMOBILE SHOW IN WYOMING
SEPTEMBER 28, 29, 30 AND OCTOBER 1, 2, 3, 1914
DURING WYOMING STATE FAIR

"THE FIRST AUTOMOBILE SHOW IN WYOMING"
1914 postcard of the Morsch and Sons Garage in Douglas.
The sign on the roof noted: "GOOD ROADS CLUB   200 MEMBERS."

The Douglas, Wyoming, Good Roads Club was incorporated in 1910. The club evolved into a local organization dedicated to improving and promoting the Converse County road system. The club voted to become the Douglas Chamber of Commerce and one of its first projects was financial support of the Yellowstone Highway.

The way to get good roads is for the government to present every intelligent man with a Ford. . . . The owners of cars are our best road builders, and let a man buy a machine and he is ready at any time to get out and work for highways that are a credit to the state.
J. B. Okie, *Northern Wyoming Herald*, August 20, 1915

The Rocky Mountain Telephone Company is this year installing what is known as the Daily Telephone Road Directory. This is a means of informing the traveler by daily reports to hotels, garages and other public places, the condition of the roads. . . . The information thus posted by the Telephone Company is received by the local road boosters and is calculated to furnish accurate information.
Yellowstone Highway in Wyoming and Colorado, 1916

Road Improvements

Gone are the days when "any road" would do.
Gone are the days when oxen pulled 'em thru.
Gone are the days when devilish Fords were few.
I hear those voices loudly calling:
"Build GOOD Roads."
Gone are the days when mud was right in style.
Gone are the days when three hours meant a mile.
Gone are the days when "highways" were on trial.
I hear those voices loudly calling:
"Build GOOD Roads."

Colorado Highways, May 1924

Wyoming Department of Transportation road work. Unknown location.
A. G. Lucier photograph, courtesy of the Hinckley Library, Northwest College.

"The tourist follows the paved road where he can."

Colorado Highways, October 1924

On and on it goes, the shortest possible highway distance between two points. If a hill has stood in its way, the hill has been blasted out, leaving the raw cut a scar against the landscape. Graded fills arise, ungrassed, ugly; straight stretches protrude before one with no other object than to get a car from one place to another in the shortest possible time. It wasn't like that with the old wagon road.   Ned Frost, 1929

18

Auto road construction did not keep pace with the improved reliability of the automobiles themselves. The higher speeds of the automobile dictated changes in the layout of roads. In agricultural areas, early roads followed section lines, for private land ownership dictated where public roads were located. This alignment is illustrated by the following **directions from the 1915 *Automobile Blue Book*:**

62.2 [miles from Denver] Eaton. 4-corners beyond RR. crossing, straight thru.
62.4 4-corners; turn right around brick school house, across RR. 62.9 - 63.3.
64.2 4-corners; turn left with cross-lines of poles. Cross RR. 67.0 into
67.1 Ault. 4-corners, straight thru.
67.2 4-corners, armory on left; turn right.
68.2 End of road, turn left.
69.0 4-corners, large school on far left; turn right, crossing RR. 71.4 into
71.7 Pierce. 4-corners, straight thru.
71.9 End of road, turn right across RR. and left beyond.
75.6 Irregular 4-corners, turn left with travel.
76.7 End of road, turn right with travel.
77.1 Left-hand road beyond wood bridge, turn left across RR. into
77.4 Nunn. 4-corners at lumber yard, straight thru. Turn right 78.0

15.2 miles of travel: Seven railroad crossings; 12 right-angle turns.
Railroad crossing accidents killed more people than any other form of accident.

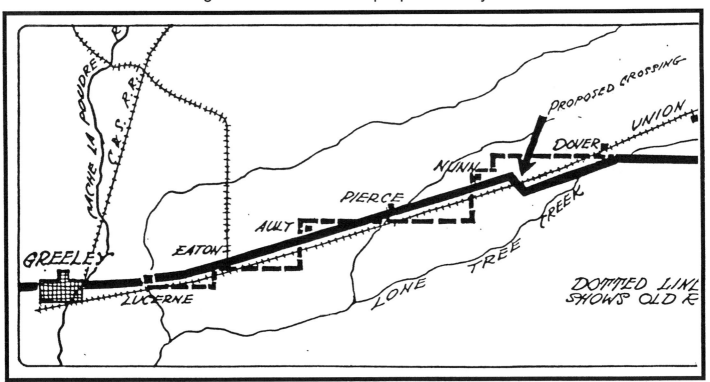

This map, from the **May 1924** issue of *Colorado Highways*, shows how seven railroad grade crossings were eliminated between Greeley and Dover. By also eliminating right-angle turns, the distance traveled was reduced by seven miles.
Map courtesy of the Colorado Department of Transportation.

GOOD ROADS BUREAU

LITTLE USED ROUTE TO ESTES PARK LEADS INTO HEART OF MOUNTAINS ALONG STREAMS AND THRU GROVES

Motorists Who Desire to Revel in Delightful Scenery But Who Care Little for Speed Will Find This Journey Full of Quaint Charm.

If you're looking for a new route to Estes park, a road which takes you into the heart of mountains, along streams, thru canons and trees, take the Allen park road from Lyons.

This road leads almost due west from Lyons for twenty-two miles, thru Middle St. Vrain canon; thence north to Copeland lake, on the North St. Vrain up to Long's Peak, thence into Estes Park on the North St. Vrain up to Long's Peak inn, thence into Estes Park by way of a gently sloping, typically mountain highway.

GOOD ROADS BUREAU

DENVER-YELLOWSTONE PARK ROAD LOGGED AND IN GOOD CONDITION THRU WYOMING, DECLARE EXPERTS

Hotel Accommodations Along Route Are Satisfactory, And Highway to Be Improved by Counties—The Roads in Colorado Are Excellent.

A road which, while it may not be a boulevard, will rank as a first-class highway, is promised by Gus Holm's and L. L. Newton of Cody, Wyo., officials of the Yellowstone Highway association, to all motorists who drive from Denver to Yellowstone park over the newly logged auto road. The road is much better than one would expect to find in a state so thinly settled as is Wyoming, according to the two men. They say that a motorist can make twenty miles an hour comfortably and stop at good hotels every night.

The *Denver Post* ran a daily "Good Roads Bureau" column from July to December, 1915. It featured articles on new road construction, road maintenance, and auto travel hints. The column also included current road conditions around the region.

Above left: September 13   **Above right:** November 5
Below left: November 17   **Below right:** August 12

POST ROAD BUREAU

Information concerning the condition of all the main highways of Colorado may be obtained from The Post Good Roads bureau on any week day between 8 a. m. and 6 p. m. By an arrangement with the Mountain States Telephone and Telegraph company, which receives daily reports on all roads, The Post is enabled to give accurate information concerning any route.

GOOD ROADS BUREAU

CHUCK HOLE CLUBS FOR AUTOISTS URGED AS SCHEME TO PROCURE BETTER ROADS THRUOUT NATION

Each Motorist Is Asked to Carry a Shovel and Make Temporary Repairs, Then Report Bad Spots to Proper Officials—Plan Permits Civil Action.

C. A. English of Los Angeles, Cal., has suggested that motorists thruout the country form "chuck hole clubs," the purpose being to enlist the aid of automobile owners and drivers in the work of improving the roads. English's plan is for each motorist to stow away some place in the car a shovel. When a bad hole was discovered in the road the autoist would be expected to fill it up temporarily and to report it to the proper officials as soon as possible.

GOOD ROADS BUREAU

MOTORISTS CAN HELP SAVE ROADS BY NOT DRIVING CARS IN THE RUTS AND CUT STATE HIGHWAY REPAIRS

Teams and Autos Following Ruts After Rain and Storm Create Discomfort for Themselves and Tear Up Roads They Drive Over.

Motorists touring the state can do a great deal towards keeping the roads in good condition by not driving their cars in the ruts. In many states and communities the automobile and good roads organizations carry on a campaign urging all autoists to keep out of ruts in the roads, especially after each rain or storm.

Auto Camps

"The automobile and the municipal camps have so cheapened travel that the wonders of the West's national parks today are accessible to hundreds of thousands."   *Sunset Magazine*, 1924

Auto camps appealed to those with small amounts of cash, extra time, and a love of freedom. Cities and towns were quick to realize the economic benefit of providing free municipal camps to the new visitor, the motorist.

"Sagebrushers" were park travelers who camped out instead of patronizing the hotels.
Note the "fee-paid" stickers on the windshield. The car has 1923 California plates.
Photograph courtesy of the National Park Service, Yellowstone National Park.

Free auto camps were established in Yellowstone in 1916 at Mammoth Hot Springs, Old Faithful, Canyon, and Lake. **By 1919, two-thirds of the park visitors were prepared to camp out**. Other facilities for the Yellowstone Highway auto traveler to the Lake area included:

> 1916 - Hamilton opened a general store at Lake, in the former Yellowstone Park Boat Company store.
> 1920 - store established at Fishing Bridge to service the auto campground.
> 1921 - "modern" auto camp established at Fishing Bridge. Facilities included bathhouses, toilets, washrooms, and cooking spits.
> 1926 - Cafeteria established at Fishing Bridge.

Auto Trails

"Auto Trails" were early automobile roads mapped, maintained, and promoted by local businesses and "Good Roads Clubs." About 450 auto trails crisscrossed the country from 1911 through the 1920s. Some auto trails were relatively short, others crossed the continent.

Each auto trail had a distinctive name.
Some names reflect the primary points, landmarks, or destination of the highway:
> The Yellowstone Highway ran from Denver to Yellowstone National Park.
> The National Park-to-Park Highway connected the National Parks of the West.
> Other highways: Banff-Grand Canyon, Custer Battlefield, Plains to Mountain, Denver-Deadwood, Utah-Idaho Yellowstone, Dallas-Canadian (Texas)-Denver, Gulf Plains and Canada, Colorado to Gulf, Glacier to Gulf, Pikes Peak Ocean to Ocean ("O to O"), Texas-Oklahoma-Colorado.
> Many auto trail names carried a patriotic theme: George Washington National, Jefferson, Lincoln, Jefferson Davis, Lee, Theodore Roosevelt International, Uncle Sam, Victory, and International Peace.
> Highways were named after earlier trails and railroads: Spanish Trail, Old Santa Fe Trail, New Santa Fe Trail, Old Oregon Trail (not well-defined in Wyoming), National Old Trails Road, and Union Pacific Highway.
> Some names were just fun: Rainbow Route, Ben Hur Highway, Teepee Highway, Scenic Highway, Bee Line, and Ayr Line.

Each auto trail had a distinctive symbol or "pole marking." This symbol would be placed on poles, posts, and bridges along the highway and would help guide the traveler. Other methods of marking the route were used. The Yellowstone Highway route (pole marking at right) was marked with yellow-painted rocks with a large black H.

Most auto trails had an association which published a guide book or brochure for the highway. Besides maps and mileages, information was provided on garages, gasoline suppliers, restaurants, hotels, and auto-camps. The guide would often offer tips for the motorist:
> "To keep your windshield clear of mist on rainy days, rub a sliced onion over the glass with an up-and-down motion."
> "Pure vinegar will clean celluloid windows in the curtains of your car."
> "Don't forget the colored goggles. In driving west you face the sun all afternoon, and the glare is hard on the eyes."
> "Don't wear new shoes."

The Federal Government began assigning <u>numbers</u> to the major highways in 1925. But auto trail names remain, in the form of short sections of roads, businesses, and historical organizations.

Transcontinental Auto Trails. Several coast-to-coast auto trails provided access to the Yellowstone Highway and National Park-to-Park Highway.

The **Theodore Roosevelt International Highway** ran from Portland, Maine, to Portland, Oregon. It connected with the National Park-to-Park Highway at Browning, Montana.

North of Yellowstone National Park, the **Yellowstone <u>Trail</u>** (not <u>Highway</u>) ran from Boston to Seattle and advertised itself as "A GOOD ROAD from PLYMOUTH ROCK to PUGET SOUND." The idea for this highway began in 1911 when members of the Minnesota Automobile Association worked out a route from Minneapolis to Yellowstone, a route closely followed today by U.S. Highway 10. (They returned east on the railroad.) From Livingston, Montana, a branch line ran south to Gardiner, Montana, at the north entrance to Yellowstone.

South of Yellowstone, the **Lincoln Highway** ran from New York City to San Francisco. It passed through southern Wyoming, intersecting the Yellowstone Highway at Cheyenne. The first transcontinental <u>bus</u> route (1925) used the highway.

The 1924 *A Complete Official Road Guide of the Lincoln Highway* noted:
> The drive from the Lincoln Highway to the Yellowstone Park over the Yellowstone Highway offers the tourist a splendid view of the scenic wonders of the state of Wyoming as well as an insight into the great progress made in the agricultural development of the state.

John Faris, in *Roaming American Highways*, set out in 1931 to travel the length of the Lincoln Highway. He noted:
> Cheyenne is another danger-point for those who wish to push on to the West. For they may be tempted to take the road that leads to the Cody entrance to Yellowstone Park, more than five hundred miles to the Northwest. That will be found an unforgettable trip, for it leads across the wonderful mountains about Thermopolis. Those who take the journey are able to tell of a great mountain trip that is so different from other western trips that there will be no difficulty in speaking of it.

An early <u>branch</u> of the Lincoln Highway ran up the South Platte River from Big Springs, Nebraska, to Denver; then north, through Longmont, Loveland, and Fort Collins (all in Colorado) to the main highway at Cheyenne. The highway was not fully sanctioned by the national organization but appeared on Colorado maps for years.

The **Pikes Peak Ocean to Ocean ("O to O") Highway** ran from New York to San Francisco intersecting the National Park-to-Park Highway in Colorado Springs.

The **National Old Trails Road** ran from Washington D.C. to Los Angeles. It followed the Santa Fe Trail (Mountain Branch) through Colorado. The National Park-to-Park Highway followed this road between Gallup, New Mexico, and Los Angeles.

The Yellowstone Highway

". . . it is such a big and healthy infant that its growth cannot be stopped."
Thermopolis Record, January 25, 1912

The term "Yellowstone Highway" was coined in 1912. The following appeared in the *Thermopolis Record*, January 25, 1912:

STATE ROAD IS NAMED "YELLOWSTONE HIGHWAY"

      Ezra Emery, the father of the good roads movement in Laramie county, was before the state officials yesterday and succeeded in having "Yellowstone Highway" officially born, and according to Ezra's statement, it is such a big and healthy infant that its growth cannot be stopped.

A pathfinding trip along the proposed Yellowstone Highway was made in July 1913. Along on the trip was a representative of the Blue Book Publishing Company, the leading road guide publisher in the country.

Two events in the summer of 1915 solidified the need for a well-marked, well-maintained road between Denver and Yellowstone National Park:

1. Automobiles were allowed in Yellowstone beginning August 1.

2. Rocky Mountain National Park was created September 4.

Also in September of 1915, good roads clubs, with the backing of the federal government, began planning for a longer, grander highway, one which would connect all the National Parks of the West.

AUTO ROAD PLANNED TO LINK PARKS. Assistant Secretary Mather Backs Highway to Connect Denver With Yellowstone.

      . . . With such a permanent highway it is believed that practically all automobile tourist travel between the East and the West could be diverted over this route, as the scenery would be unsurpassed and excellent hotel accommodations naturally would follow the building of such a highway. It would induce thousands of automobilists to pass thru Denver, thence thru the Rocky Mountain National parks to Yellowstone, via the Cody entrance, and out thru the Gardiner entrance of Yellowstone into the Glacier National park.

Rocky Mountain News, September 4, 1915

The Yellowstone Highway <u>Association</u> was organized in Douglas, Wyoming, in September 1915. The first and only *Yellowstone Highway in Wyoming and Colorado* guidebook was published in 1916. It stated:

      This association assumes the responsibility of placing and keeping in good condition for automobile tourist travel the road to the East Entrance of the Yellowstone Park and is co-operating with the Lincoln Highway and all other roads entering Yellowstone Park. . . .

      In addition to being the leading road in the State of Wyoming, the

YELLOWSTONE HIGHWAY
MENU

"Strive mightily, but eat and drink as friends."—Shakespeare.

Cody OYSTER COCKTAIL

"He was a bold man that first eat an oyster."—Swift.

Thermopolis Sulphur CREAM SOUP
Laramie SOUR PICKLES   Wiley SWEET PICKLES
Ilo OLIVES

Eat, drink and be merry, for tomorrow we build good roads.

ROAST CHICKEN with Casper Crude Oil GRAVY
Moneta JELLY   Newcastle KETCHUP
BOILED PORK a la Cheyenne   Ft. Russell CELERY
Denver TOBASCO SAUCE
Wheatland SLAW and IRISH FRUIT
Meeteetse SANDWICHES   Douglas Harmony SALAD

"For I look upon it, that he who does not mind his belly will hardly mind anything else."—Johnson.

Chugwater ICE CREAM
Wolton, Powder River, Cadoma, Inez, Orin and Uva
ASSORTED CAKES
Shoshoni SALTED ALMONDS

Our Highway, our whole Highway, and nothing but our Highway!

Big Muddy COFFEE
CIGARS, Careyhurst Alfalfa Filler

"Thus far shalt thou go, and no further" (?).

1912 Banquet Menu
From *Pages From Converse County's Past*
Published by the Wyoming Pioneer Association, 1986

Yellowstone Highway is destined to become the first link in the proposed Park to Park Highway, a Highway being promoted pursuant to a suggestion made by Hon. Steven T. Mather, Assistant to the Secretary of the Interior, to the effect that the Federal Government be asked to build and maintain a good Highway connecting all of the National Parks in the Western part of the United States.

Little work was done on promoting "auto trails" during World War I.

The first chairman of the Yellowstone Highway Association was Gus Holm's of Cody, Wyoming (he spelled his name with the apostrophe). He was also president of the Cody Club, a local civic organization which started in 1900 as a sportsman's club. The Cody Club was active in promoting the town and their road to Yellowstone.

"YELLOWSTONE ROAD COMPLETELY MARKED

Gus Holm's field secretary of the Yellowstone Highway association, returned to Cody from the round trip from Yellowstone park to the Colorado line over the Yellowstone highway having completely relogged the road and placed over a thousand yellow and gray markers along the entire length to guide the traveller diagonally across the state."

Wyoming State Tribune, June 9, 1920

Yellowstone Highway yellow painted rock (the black "H" has worn off), auto trails map, and Goodrich Tires highway sign.
Display at the Wyoming Pioneer Museum in Douglas, Wyoming.

Although the idea and early organizational work of forming the Yellowstone Highway Association was done in Wyoming, the highway itself extended south to Denver, Colorado. The association was well aware of the large population center of Denver and the popularity of the nearby Rocky Mountain National Park.

"THE YELLOWSTONE HIGHWAY was organized some years ago in Douglas, Wyoming, at a meeting called by the Douglas Good Roads Club, which has the distinction of being the first Club organized for the purpose of forwarding and promoting better roads in Wyoming. . . .
The Highway extends down into Colorado for two reasons: First, upon invitation from Colorado; second, because Wyoming is a sister State to Colorado and in selecting a mountain trip, both states should be considered. We extend to the Colorado traveler our most cordial welcome."
Yellowstone Highway in Wyoming and Colorado, 1916

Right: from *Yellowstone Highway in Wyoming and Colorado,* 1916

This Association is affiliated with the National Highway Association, the American Automobile Association and co-operating with all other associations promoting

and developing roads leading to the four sides of YELLOWSTONE NATIONAL PARK.

THE YELLOWSTONE HIGHWAY is the first, and the Wyoming link, in the proposed United States National Park Highway connecting all National Parks in the Rocky Mountains and on Pacific Coast. This association assumes the responsibility of placing and keeping in good condition for automobile tourist travel the road to the East Entrance of the Yellowstone Park and is co-operating with the Lincoln Highway and all other roads entering Yellowstone Park.

It will heartily support any constructive movement for good roads everywhere and invites correspondence with the officers or the commissioners nearest the place where the proposed road enters WYOMING.

Price 25c

All proceeds accruing from the sale of this book are maintained in the Yellowstone Highway Association fund.

The National Park-to-Park Highway

"The greatest natural wonders of the world will remain obscure and of no value as an asset until made easy to reach - a paradise on a poor highway can never become popular."

Colorado Highways, May 1926

At the **Yellowstone Highway Association** meeting held in Casper, August 2, 1919, a resolution was passed that **endorsed the National Park-to-Park Highway Association** and its plan to connect the National Parks of the West. In 1919, the executive offices of both the highway organizations were headquartered in Cody, Wyoming. Gus Holm's was Chairman and L. L. Newton was Secretary of the National Park-to-Park Highway Association. For the Yellowstone Highway Association, Newton was President, and Holm's was Executive Secretary. Both were from Cody.

It was only natural that the route of the two "auto trails" coincided exactly from Cheyenne to Yellowstone. In Colorado, the National Park-to-Park Highway ran through Fort Collins and Loveland to Estes Park (at the east entrance to Rocky Mountain Park), then to Denver. From Denver, the National Park-to-Park Highway ran southwest to Mesa Verde National Park.

Other towns sought the National Park-to-Park Highway route in Wyoming. A Saratoga-Rawlins-Yellowstone National Park south entrance route was considered, but Yellowstone's east entrance road through Cody won out. The south entrance route would become the Rocky Mountain Highway.

AAA pathfinding tour

A. L. Westgard, scout for the American Automobile Association (AAA), mapped out the complete route of the National Park-to-Park Highway for AAA and the National Park Service. He drove the route, connecting the National Parks of the West, starting from Denver June 28, 1920, arriving back in Denver August 22.

Dedication Tour

The National Park-to-Park Highway was officially dedicated August 26, 1920, at ceremonies at Overland Park in Denver. The dedication ceremonies kicked off a sixty-day tour of the highway.

The tour will be educational in character, urging the various communities to improve the roads comprising the highway in their respective localities, until congress can be prevailed upon permanently to improve the course. *The Denver Post*, August 22, 1920

The educational tour includes a campaign of bringing before the people of America, the need for at least one continuous motor way that will insure economy in motor travel and provide for greater accessibility of the national playgrounds to tourists.

The Rocky Mountain News, August 25, 1920

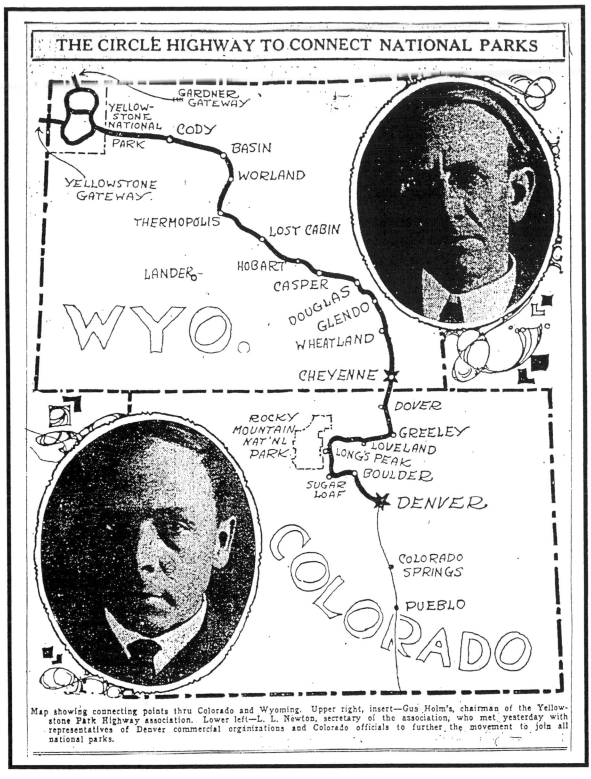

THE CIRCLE HIGHWAY TO CONNECT NATIONAL PARKS

Map showing connecting points thru Colorado and Wyoming. Upper right, insert—Gus Holm's, chairman of the Yellowstone Park Highway association. Lower left—L. L. Newton, secretary of the association, who met yesterday with representatives of Denver commercial organizations and Colorado officials to further the movement to join all national parks.

From the *Rocky Mountain News*, November 2, 1915.

The idea for a "park to park" highway was addressed in Denver during the dedication of Rocky Mountain National Park. The route of the highway was later changed to pass through Fort Collins, not Greeley and Dover. Gus Holm's (upper right) and L. L. Newton (lower left) would become officers in both the Yellowstone Highway and National Park-to-Park Highway Associations.

The National Park-to-Park Highway dedication tour left Overland Park in Denver on August 26, 1920.
A. G. Lucier photograph, courtesy of the Hinckley Library, Northwest College.

From the *National Park-to-Park Highway Guide, Wyoming Edition*, 1924

Denver, the Gateway

"Twelve major federal playgrounds in the West, as well as many national monuments and forests, have been lassoed by a scenic running noose, in the master motor road of the country, known as the National Park-to-Park Highway. . . . The master highway begins, lariat fashion, any place in Maine, Virginia, Florida, Illinois or Louisiana, wherever the automobile tourist lives. Other cities on the route may be used but Denver is the logical gateway to these twelve national parks. . . . The connecting park highway touches every main transcontinental trail . . . crossing and using them in part to make a continuous thorofare."

The Fort Collins Courier,
August 28, 1920

Completion of the Dedication Tour

Commenting on the completion of the dedication tour, Stephen Mather, director of the National Park Service, noted:

The circle tour of the national parks of the West by a large caravan, traveling on a predetermined schedule without regard to weather-conditions, has demonstrated these wonderful regions belonging to the people may be visited by motorists from all parts of the country, particularly those carrying camping equipment and living out-of-doors, without fear of finding long stretches which would break up their trip as they journey from park to park.

I believe the opening of the National Park-to-Park highway will greatly stimulate automobile travel to the West next summer. Aside from demonstrating that good roads connect all the parks, it also aroused Western communities to the need of providing comfortable automobile camps for visitors, not only as a matter of hospitality, but as an investment, for such tourists necessarily spend much money in the towns they visit, and mean new population in that some of them decide to settle. The national park service stands ready to assist the growing travel movement by making the national parks the most attractive vacation spots in the world, and by furnishing information to all who may ask.

Rocky Mountain News, November 10, 1920

This highway offers to the tourist the most satisfactory routing between Rocky Mountain and the Yellowstone National Parks, as well as to and through the principal cities and towns in Wyoming. This portion of the Master Scenic Highway of America is known locally as the Yellowstone Highway, which was once marked with its own markings but now replaced by the state highway markings through Wyoming.   *National Park-to-Park Highway* guide, 1924

National Park-to-Park Highway. There is something wrong when American citizens, who have never been west of the Middle States, can be induced to go to foreign countries year after year in search of scenic attractions and recreation. The only answer is: That the West is solely to blame. We have the attractions; we have the hotels; and now we have the highways and the railroads; but we have not the cooperative spirit in our publicity. . . . The National Park-to-Park Highway Association is working in close harmony and co-operation with the National Park Service, and the Department of Interior, as well as with all other legitimate agencies in a combined effort to draw these European vacationists into the great playground of our own West. . . . The greatest natural wonders of the world will remain obscure and of no value as an asset until made easy to reach - a paradise on a poor highway can never become popular.   *Colorado Highways*, May 1926

The National Park-to-Park Highway Association headquarters were in Denver at 1608 Broadway. Gus Holm's moved to Denver from Cody to head the organization. **The Yellowstone Highway and it's association lost much of its identity with the incorporation of the highway's route into the larger National Park-to-Park Highway system.**

31

Other Auto Trails

The following auto trails coincided with sections of, or intersected with, the Yellowstone Highway and/or National Park-to-Park Highway.

White

Red

White

The **National Parks Highway** ran from Milwaukee, through Fargo and Bismarck, North Dakota, to Livingston, Montana. Here, a branch ran south along the Yellowstone River to Yellowstone National Park. From Livingston, the highway continued west through Butte, Montana, to Seattle and Mt. Rainier National Park in Washington.

Yellow

Black

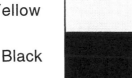

The **Yellowstone-Glacier Bee Line Highway** became the route of the National Park-to-Park Highway between Yellowstone and Glacier National Parks. It passed through Livingston, White Sulphur Springs, Great Falls, and Choteau to Glacier National Park. The route closely followed present-day U.S. Highway 89.

White
Yellow
White

The **Billings-Cody Way** ran southwest from the Yellowstone Trail at Billings, Montana, to Cody, Wyoming, and the Yellowstone Highway. It passed through Bridger, Montana, and Frannie and Powell, Wyoming.

Black

Yellow

Black

The **Black and Yellow Trail** started in Milwaukee and ran west through Pierre and Rapid City, South Dakota. It passed through the Black Hills, then through Buffalo, Wyoming, to Worland, where it merged with the Yellowstone Highway.

Color?

The **George Washington National Highway** ran from Chicago, through Sioux Falls and Rapid City, South Dakota, to Worland, where it also merged with the Yellowstone Highway. The highway then continued west to Spokane and Seattle, Washington.

Yellow

Black

Yellow

The **Grant Highway** entered Wyoming from the Black Hills of South Dakota. It passed through Lusk and Lost Springs, Wyoming, to Douglas, Casper, and Shoshoni. At Shoshoni, it left the route of the Yellowstone Highway and ran to the south entrance of Yellowstone via Riverton and Dubois.

The **Short-Cut West Highway** ran through Waterton and Belle Fourche, South Dakota (present-day U.S. Highway 212). In Wyoming the highway passed through Dundance, Gillette, Spotted Horse, and Buffalo, merging with the Yellowstone Highway at Worland. The highway followed the early Yellowstone Highway route through Otto and Burlington.

Black

Yellow

Black

The **Atlantic Yellowstone Pacific Hiway** (APY) was a late arrival. It crossed Wyoming, passing through Lusk, then coincided with the Yellowstone Highway from Orin Junction west to Shoshoni. The highway then followed the Grant Highway route to the south entrance of Yellowstone. Its motto: "East to West, It is the Best."

Red

White

In direct competition with the Yellowstone Highway was the **Rocky Mountain Highway**. This auto trail ran from Denver to the south entrance of Yellowstone National Park, following much of the route of present-day U.S. Highway 287. From Laramie, Wyoming, the highway ran southwest to pass through the north edge of North Park in Colorado, then turned northwest to pass through the Wyoming towns of Encampment, Saratoga, Rawlins, Lander, and Dubois.

White

Green letters

The east-west **Victory Highway** and **Midland Trail** passed through Denver, funneling traffic to the Yellowstone Highway. The **Detroit-Lincoln-Denver Highway** and the **Denver-Black Hills Highway** entered Denver from the northeast.

Black

White

Black

Several auto trails ran along the Front Range of the Rocky Mountains, in places, coinciding with the Yellowstone and National Park-to-Park Highways. They included the **Powder River Trail, Buffalo Highway**, **and Glacier to Gulf Highway**.

White
Black
White
Black
White

White

Brown

Black

White

Black

The **Glacier to Gulf Highway** was a late-comer in the auto trail field. It was mapped and promoted by Canadian interests beginning in 1925. It ran from Calgary, Alberta, Canada, to Tampico, Mexico. The route passed through Great Falls and Billings, Montana, then followed the Yellowstone Highway route to Denver. It continued south, passing through Colorado Springs and Pueblo, Colorado.

State Highway Numbers

State highway commissions assigned numbers to many of their main highways in the mid 1910s, well before Federally assigned highway numbers.

In Wyoming, the Yellowstone Highway and the National Park-to-Park Highway would follow, for the most part, Wyoming Highway 11 from the Wyoming border to Greybull. Wyoming Highway 26 ran west from Greybull, through Cody, to the east entrance of Yellowstone National Park.

An April 1920 letter from the Wyoming State Highway Department to the Yellowstone Highway Association stated:

> To avoid future complications, the State Highway Commission does not desire that we determine for any highway association the route they may desire to advertise to tourist travel.

> Our State Highway No. 11 will be laid out however, to provide for travel from the state line south of Cheyenne to the Montana line north of Deaver, and I presume you will desire to mark this as the Yellowstone Highway as far as Greybull or Basin and from there to the Park either the Basin-Burlington road or the Greybull-Germania [now Emblem] road. . . .

> Between Casper and Thermopolis, we will lay out our State Highway via Shoshoni and Birdseye Pass, while you possibly may desire to maintain your old route via Lost Cabin.

Several days later, the Yellowstone Highway Association's response to the State Highway Department:

> We are endeavoring to have the Yellowstone Highway follow exactly the routes laid out by the State Highway Commission and to that end we are routing our people this year to Shoshoni over Birds Eye Pass into Thermopolis as well as following your lead from Basin to Greybull, Greybull to Germania and to Cody.

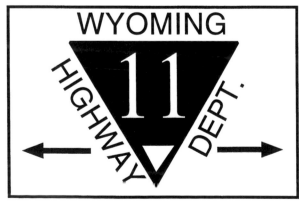

Wyoming State Highway
"Pole Marking"
Black and white

Colorado State Highway
"Pole Marking"
Black on orange

34

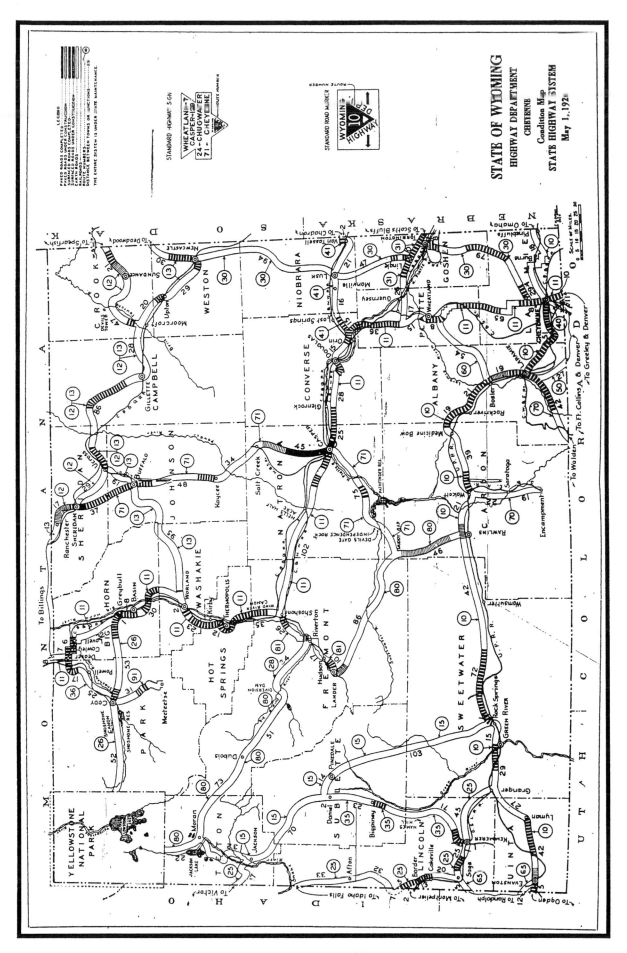

Wyoming map from *Wyoming Roads*, May 1926
showing the state highway numbers (circled).

The next issue replaced most state numbers with the new Federal highway numbers.

Northern Colorado Map

from the 1916 *Yellowstone Highway in Wyoming and Colorado.*

The Yellowstone Highway Association was formed in Wyoming and most of the highway markings were done in that state.

Their 1916 map of Colorado stated that, from Denver, the traveler could use either the road through Greeley or Fort Collins to reach the Yellowstone Highway in Cheyenne.

The map labeled the highway from Greeley south to Denver and from Denver north through Fort Collins, the Lincoln Highway. This branch of the famed transcontinental highway was not fully sanctioned by the national organization.

The 1922 *Automobile Blue Book* labeled the highway from Denver through Greeley to Cheyenne, the Yellowstone Highway.

From Denver, the National Park-to-Park Highway would pass through Boulder, Estes Park (at the east entrance to Rocky Mountain National Park), Loveland, and Fort Collins.

North of Cheyenne, the Yellowstone and National Park-to-Park Highway would follow the exact same route.

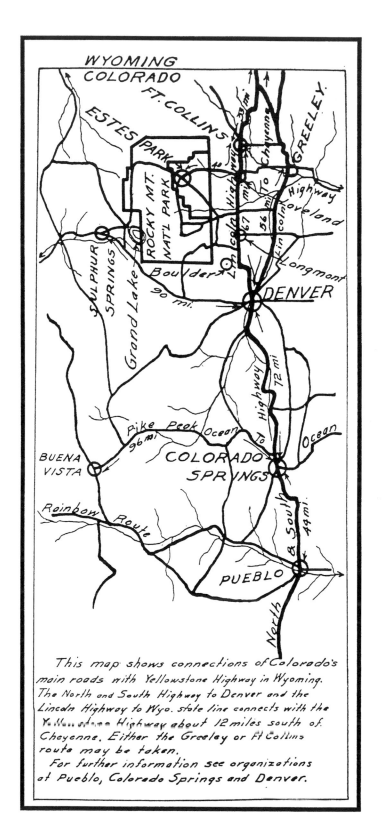

This map shows connections of Colorado's main roads with Yellowstone Highway in Wyoming. The North and South Highway to Denver and the Lincoln Highway to Wyo. state line connects with the Yellowstone Highway about 12 miles south of Cheyenne. Either the Greeley or Ft Collins route may be taken.

For further information see organizations at Pueblo, Colorado Springs and Denver.

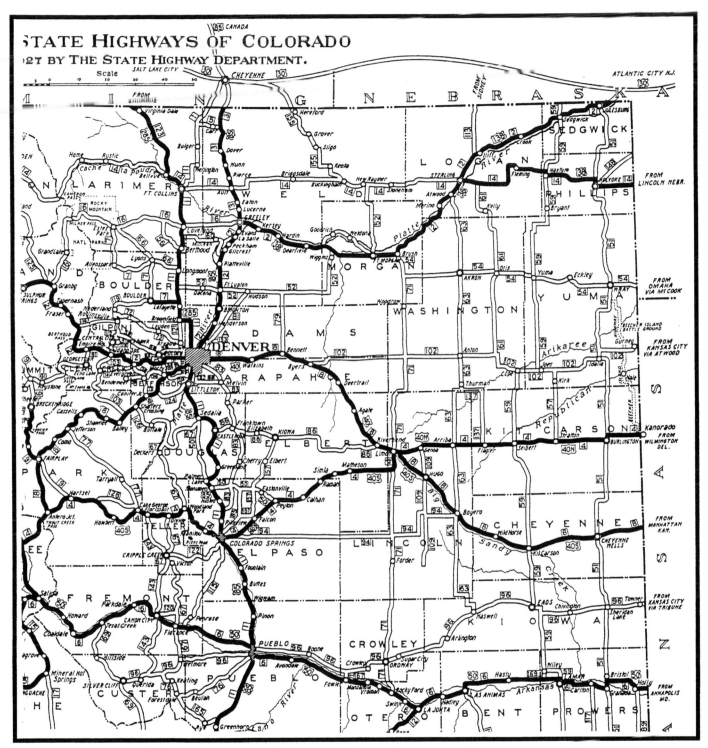

1927 map of Northeastern Colorado from *Colorado Highways*, February 1928.
Colorado highway numbers in rectangles.
Map courtesy of the Colorado Department of Transportation

Colorado Highway 1 ran from New Mexico to Wyoming along the Front Range of the Rocky Mountains. The Yellowstone Highway would become **Colorado Highway 2** from Denver to Greeley, then **Colorado Highway 3** north of Greeley to the Wyoming border. The National Park-to-Park Highway route would become **Colorado Highway 7** from Lafayette to Estes Park.

37

Federal Highways

The 7% Road System
　　The 1921 Federal Aid Highway Act directed federal funds to the states for highway maintenance. Each state selected 7% of its road system for this Federal Aid program. These roads would link all the county seats and made real the idea of a national "interstate" road system.

Federal Highway Numbering System
　　In late 1925, the Federal Government began assigning numbers to the nation's major highways. These highways were usually the major named "Auto Trails." Odd numbered highways run north-south, beginning with U.S. Highway 1 on the east coast to U.S. 101 on the west coast. Even numbered highways run east-west with U.S. 2 to the north and U.S. 70 to the south.
　　U.S. 2 closely followed the route of the Theodore Roosevelt International Highway.
　　U.S. 10 approximated the Yellowstone <u>Trail</u> west of Miles City, Montana.
　　U.S. 20 followed the Yellowstone and National Park-to-Park Highway from Orin Junction, Wyoming, to Yellowstone.
　　U.S. 30 followed the Lincoln Highway across southern Wyoming to Granger. U.S. 30S [South] continued to Salt Lake City with the Lincoln Highway. U.S. 30N [North] branched northwest into Idaho.
　　U.S. 40 passes through Denver.

　　In Colorado, **U.S. 85** was assigned to the major north-south highway along the Front Range of the Rocky Mountains. North of Denver, it followed the route of the Yellowstone Highway to Cheyenne, via Greeley.
　　U.S. 285 [present-day U.S. 287] ran north from Denver, through Fort Collins to Laramie, Wyoming. The National Park-to-Park Highway route from Fort Collins to Cheyenne was not originally given a federal number. In 1934, the Denver to Cheyenne highway through Fort Collins was designated U.S. 87. The highway from Fort Collins to Laramie became U.S. 287.

　　In Wyoming, **U.S. 30** was attached to most of the Lincoln Highway route.
　　U.S. 185 ran north from Cheyenne to Orin Junction. Later this route became U.S. 87.
　　In Wyoming, **U.S. Highways 16**, **20**, and **26**, all assigned in 1926, retain these numbers today.

　　1956 was a year of major changes in the Yellowstone Highway story.
　　The Interstate Highway System was authorized.
　　The National Park's "Mission 66" project started.
　　Passenger rail service to Cody ended.

Interstate Highway System

The Interstate Highway System was authorized by the Federal-Aid Highway Act of 1956 under the Eisenhower administration. It was envisioned and developed as a military road system. But the main benefit was economic. "Things would move better."

Odd numbered north-south interstates begin with I-5 on the West Coast to I-95 on the East Coast. Interstate 10 runs along the southern tier of states; I-90 to the north.

Interstate 25 follows up the Front Range of the Rocky Mountains, through Denver, Cheyenne, and Casper to Buffalo, Wyoming.

Interstate 80 replaced much of the Lincoln Highway and U.S. Highway 30 through southern Wyoming.

Mission 66

Begun in 1956, **"Mission 66" was an effort to upgrade National Park services, roads, trails, and utilities**. The upgrades were directed at improving services to the public by the year 1966. Over half the mission's money was spent on improving roads and trails.

Below: "Illustration of the need for standard system of highway signs"
From *Wyoming Roads*, April 1926.

—Courtesy A. A. A.

Illustration of the need for standard system of highway signs

The Yellowstone Highway
Time Line

Some of the transportation events along the route of the Yellowstone (and National Park-to-Park) Highway:

1807   **John Colter** visits Yellowstone and present-day Cody, Wyoming, area.
1820   **Stephen H. Long** expedition to the base of the Rocky Mountains.
1832   **Capt. Benjamin Bonneville** takes wagons over South Pass.
1843   **Oregon emigrants** travel Oregon Trail.
1847   **Mormons** emigrate to Salt Lake Valley via Oregon Trail-Hastings Cutoff.
1849   **California gold rush** increased usage of Oregon-California Trail.
          Cherokee Trail used by wagons of California-bound gold seekers.
1859   **Colorado gold rush**, South Platte River Trail heavily used.
1860   **Pony Express** established along portions of the Oregon-California Trail.
          William Raynolds expedition circles Yellowstone region.
1862   **Ben Holladay** moves his Overland Stage Line south to the South Platte
          River Trail-Cherokee Trail-Bridger Pass route.
1864   **Bozeman Trail** to Montana goldfields opened.
          Bridger Trail to Montana goldfields opened.
1867   **Cheyenne** established with the arrival of the Union Pacific Railroad.
1869   **Cook-Folsom-Peterson** expedition to Yellowstone.
          Union Pacific-Central Pacific transcontinental railroad completed.
1870   **Washburn-Langford-Doane** expedition to Yellowstone.
          Denver Pacific Railroad from Cheyenne to Denver completed.
1871   **Ferdinand Hayden** expedition to Yellowstone.
1872   **Yellowstone National Park** established.
1873   **Capt. William Jones** expedition crosses Absaroka Range to Yellowstone.
1876   **Cheyenne to Black Hills Stage Line** established.
1877   **Nez Perce** pass through Yellowstone on their failed attempt to reach
          Canada.
1881   **Sylvan Pass** in Yellowstone discovered by Philetus Norris.
1883   **Northern Pacific Railroad** reaches Cinnabar, MT, north of Yellowstone.
          Yellowstone's Grand Loop Road construction assumed by the U.S.
          Army Corp of Engineers.
1884   **Lost Cabin**, Wyoming, established by J. B. Okie.
1886   **Wyoming Central** (Chicago & Northwestern Railroad) builds west to
          Douglas, Wyoming.
1887   **Cheyenne & Northern Railroad** builds north from Cheyenne to
          Wendover, Wyoming.
1888   **Chicago & Northwestern** extended west to Casper.
1890   **Casper to Thermopolis** stage and freight line via Lost Cabin established.
1891   **Lake Hotel** opens.
1901   **Chicago Burlington & Quincy Railroad** completes line to Cody.
          Yellowstone East Entrance road construction begins.

1902	**American Automobile Association** established.
	Colorado Automobile Club organized.
	Irma Hotel in Cody opened by William Cody.
1000	**Yellowstone's East Entrance road** opened.
	Fishing Bridge completed but not named as such until 1914.
	Roosevelt Arch at Yellowstone's north entrance dedicated.
1904	**Pahaska Tepee** opened by William Cody.
1905	**Yellowstone's Grand Loop Road** and Mt. Washburn road completed.
	Corkscrew Bridge completed east of Sylvan Pass.
1906	**Chicago & Northwestern Railroad** completed to Shoshoni and Lander.
	Stage line operates over Birdseye Pass.
1907	**Burlington Railroad** extended south to Kirby, Wyoming.
1908	**Union Pacific Railroad** builds to West Yellowstone.
1910	**Douglas "Good Roads Club"** organized.
	Shoshone Dam (Buffalo Bill Dam) completed; road through Shoshone Canyon opened to public.
1912	**"Yellowstone Highway"** name approved.
1913	**Yellowstone road construction** geared towards use by automobiles.
	Burlington Railroad completes line south through Wind River Canyon.
1915	**Automobiles** allowed in Yellowstone National Park.
	Rocky Mountain National Park established.
	National Park-to-Park Highway idea conceived.
1916	**Yellowstone Highway Association** guide book issued.
	First Federal-Aid Highway bill.
1918	**Road maintenance** in Yellowstone transferred to the newly-formed National Park Service.
1919	**Corkscrew Bridge** improved with rock fill and concrete overpass.
1920	**National Park-to-Park Highway** route established; dedication tour; Denver made headquarters of the organization.
	Fall River Road in Rocky Mountain National Park opened.
1921	**Federal-Aid** directed to 7% of state roads.
	Lake Lodge construction started.
	Modern auto camp established at Fishing Bridge.
1923	**Road west of Cody** changed, Hayden Arch Bridge opened.
1924	**Wind River Canyon road** completed.
1925	**Federal Highway numbering** system initiated.
1926	**Bureau of Public Roads** begin major improvements to Yellowstone's road system.
1931	**Present-day Sylvan Pass Road** completed.
	Fishing Bridge Visitor Center opens, one of four "Trailside Museums."
1932	**Trail Ridge Road** in Rocky Mountain Park opened.
1956	**Interstate Highway System** authorized.
	"Mission 66" project to improve National Park services begins.
	Burlington Railroad ends passenger service to Cody.
1961	**Present-day Shoshone Canyon Road** opened.
	Last passenger train service to Yellowstone.

II. The Drive Guide

Rules of the Road

All roads described in the following "drive guide" are public roads. Most are paved, some are good gravel, none are "4-wheel" or "high-clearance vehicles only" roads. The described tour does not stray far from an interstate or U.S. highway. **Extra film will probably be the only extra provision necessary**.

Some described roads <u>lead</u> <u>to</u> gates, fences, and roads no longer maintained. Do not be tempted to go beyond the <u>view</u> <u>only</u> points.
Respect private property.

The use of the words 'CAUTION' or 'DANGER' has been avoided with studious care in this book; where they do appear there is real reason for their use. Too many log books are so liberally sprinkled with them that the effect of their use is soon lost. Common sense and reasonable care are necessary in driving a motor car anywhere.
Midland Trail Tour Guide, 1915

While you may not believe in signs, it is safe to assume that 'Caution' and 'Danger' warnings are not erected for the mere amusement of those who took the trouble to put them up.
Rand McNally Auto Road Atlas, 1926

Mileages in this book are approximate. **Most highway milepost references in the book reflect the posted highway mile markers**. Highway mileposts are used by law enforcement, other government agencies, and the traveling public.
When highway mileposts are not present, use your vehicle's odometer to measure the miles. The prompt will be ***"Reset mile 0.0."***

<u>**Underscored**</u> <u>**bold**</u> <u>**highway**</u> <u>**names**</u> are primary road names to be followed as part of the Yellowstone Highway and National Park-to-Park Highway tour.

[Highways, towns, and directions in **brackets** are informational only, not part of the Yellowstone Highway tour].

<u>**Side**</u> <u>**trip**</u>: describes optional trips off the primary route. The side trip may leave the primary route, then return to the same point; or may parallel the primary route.

Since the earliest "auto trails" were little more than wagon roads, much of the original route is not drivable by public roads today. Road improvements and route changes are an ongoing process.

Following are the primary references cited in this book:

1915 - *Official Automobile Blue Book.* Detailed guidebook published by the Automobile Blue Books, Inc. of New York and Chicago. Often referred to as simply the "Blue Book" or "the blue bible" by some early tourists.

1916 - *Yellowstone Highway in Wyoming and Colorado.* Official route book of the Yellowstone Highway Association. The guide contained maps, city and county descriptions, and business advertisements, but no mile-by-mile guide.

1918 - *Goodrich Tour #2255.* A Denver to Yellowstone National Park guide, including mile-by-mile directions. Signs were put along the route in the summer of 1915. Published by the B. F. Goodrich Touring Service.

1920 - **Newspaper accounts of the National Park-to-Park Highway dedication tour.** The tour left Denver August 26th for Yellowstone and other National Parks of the West. **A. G. Lucier** of Powell, Wyoming, was the official photographer. His photographs are now housed at the Hinckley Library, Northwest College, in Powell.

1922 - *Official Automobile Blue Book.* By 1922, several volumes were issued, each one representing a different region of the country.

1924 - *National Park-to-Park Highway Guide.* Wyoming edition of the National Park-to-Park Highway Association publication.

1926 - **Blanche Johnston Diary.** Describes in detail her nine day trip from Boulder to Yellowstone and back. Diary from the Carnegie Branch Library for Local History, Boulder, Colorado.

The book's drive guide from Denver to Yellowstone National Park is divided into 8 sections. Each is rather unique in type of terrain and history.

Two routes from Denver to Cheyenne, Wyoming, are included:
1. **The Yellowstone Highway** route through Brighton and Greeley.
2. **The National Park-to-Park Highway** route through Boulder, Lyons, Estes Park, Loveland, and Fort Collins.

North of Cheyenne, the Yellowstone and Park-to-Park highways coincide.

1922 *Automobile Blue Book*:

Denver to Yellowstone Park - 674 Miles

Via Cheyenne, Douglas, Casper, Thermopolis, Basin and Cody

This is a section of the Yellowstone highway, connecting two of the nation's greatest playgrounds. That part from Cheyenne to Yellowstone park is used a great deal as a section of one of the main roads from the east to Yellowstone park. Motorists from points east of Cheyenne use the Lincoln highway or other transcontinental routes to this point and then follow this route across Wyoming to Yellowstone park. The roads are dirt practically the entire distance and are bad in wet or extremely dry weather. Their condition will depend upon the amount of dragging and grading they receive during the touring season. The worst stretch is usually between Casper and Thermopolis, this often being very badly worn and rutted on account of the heavy traffic thru the oil fields.

Denver
"Gateway to the National Park-to-Park Highway"

The intersection of Colfax Ave. and Broadway St. in Denver is the center of the city. Highway mileages were, and still are, measured from this intersection. Nearby are the State Capitol, City and County Building, U.S. Mint, Denver Public Library, Colorado Historical Museum, and the Denver Art Museum.

Postcard of the Pioneer Monument at the corner of Broadway and Colfax.
The monument was dedicated June 24, 1911.
At left is the former Denver Public Library, in use from 1910-1956.

Colfax Ave. (U.S. 40) is the longest commercial street in the country and is the major east-west street through the Denver metropolitan area. This 26-mile-long "concrete river" was the route used by the Victory Highway and Midland Trail.
Broadway is the main non-interstate north-south road through Denver. Old U.S. 85-87 to Colorado Springs and Pueblo ran south on Broadway to Mexico Ave., west to Santa Fe Drive, then south on Santa Fe Drive. This was the route of the Buffalo Highway, Glacier to Gulf Highway, and the National Park-to-Park Highway.

At Mexico Ave. and Santa Fe Drive is located **Overland Park.** Denver opened its main municipal "auto camp" here in 1920. It had 800 spaces, each with an electric light. It also had a 24-room clubhouse with a restaurant, store, barber shop, and billiard room. Now a golf course, Overland Park also had an automobile racetrack.

Before the completion of Interstate 25, two primary highways led north from Denver to Cheyenne.

1. The Yellowstone Highway and its successor, U.S. Highway 85, passed through Brighton and Greeley.

The 1915 *Automobile Blue Book*:

"northwest on 17th St. with trolley; Champa St.; turn right, leaving trolley . . . left on Downing St. and right around store on 33rd St. . . . left on Lafayette St. . . . . curve left on 38th St.; across RR [railroad] . . . right on Wewatta St., across RR . . . cross trolley . . . cemetery [Riverside] on left . . . Brighton . . ."

In 1921, this route was simplified when Broadway was extended north and the new Broadway Viaduct crossed the many sets of railroad tracks. The viaduct connected with Wewatta St., whose name was changed to Brighton Blvd. in 1924. An alternate route to Brighton Blvd. was described in the 1922 *Automobile Blue Book*:

"Broadway & Colfax Av., at state capitol. North on Broadway . . . right on Welton St. . . . right on 29th Av. . . . York St.; left . . . End of road at RR; right. . . . Henderson . . ."

2. The National Park-to-Park Highway, later used in part by U.S. Highway 285 (later renumbered 287) and U.S. 87, ran through Lafayette, Loveland, and Fort Collins. U.S. 87 continued north to Cheyenne.

The 1915 *Blue Book*:

"Broadway & Colfax Ave. From monument on right go west on Colfax. Bear diagonally right on 14th St. . . . curve left into W. 27th St.; . . . bear right into West Lake Place . . . right on Boulevard F. . . . Lafayette . . ."

The highway crossed the old 14th St. Viaduct, which was renamed Speer Viaduct in 1927. West Lake was also renamed that year, becoming an extension of Speer Blvd. Boulevard F was renamed Federal Blvd. in 1912.

Right: 1922 *Automobile Blue Book* **map of Denver.** "Speer" and "Wewatta" are misspelled. Map courtesy of the Denver Public Library, Western History Collection.

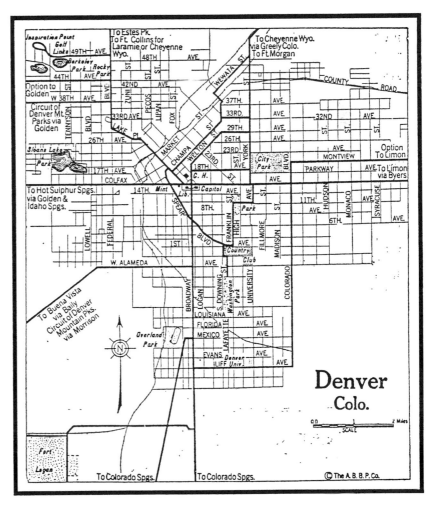

45

Denver, North to the Colorado-Wyoming Border
United States Geological Survey map, State of Colorado, 1980
The drive guide routes have been enhanced:
The Yellowstone Highway route via Greeley.
The National Park-to-Park Highway route via Estes Park.
Both routes lead to Cheyenne, Wyoming.

Cheyenne
Estes Park
Greeley
Denver

Colorado

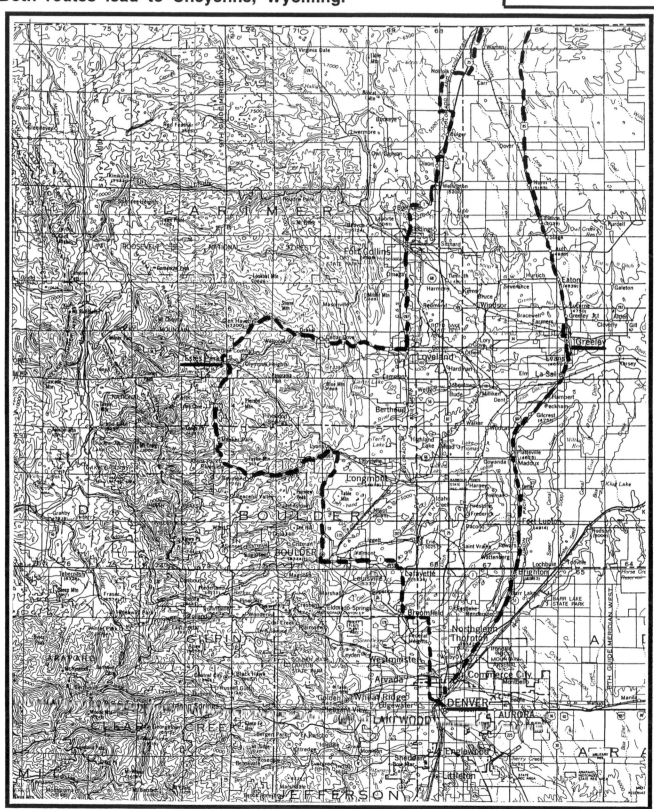

46

Denver to Cheyenne

The Yellowstone Highway via Greeley.
The National Park-to-Park Highway
via Estes Park and Fort Collins.

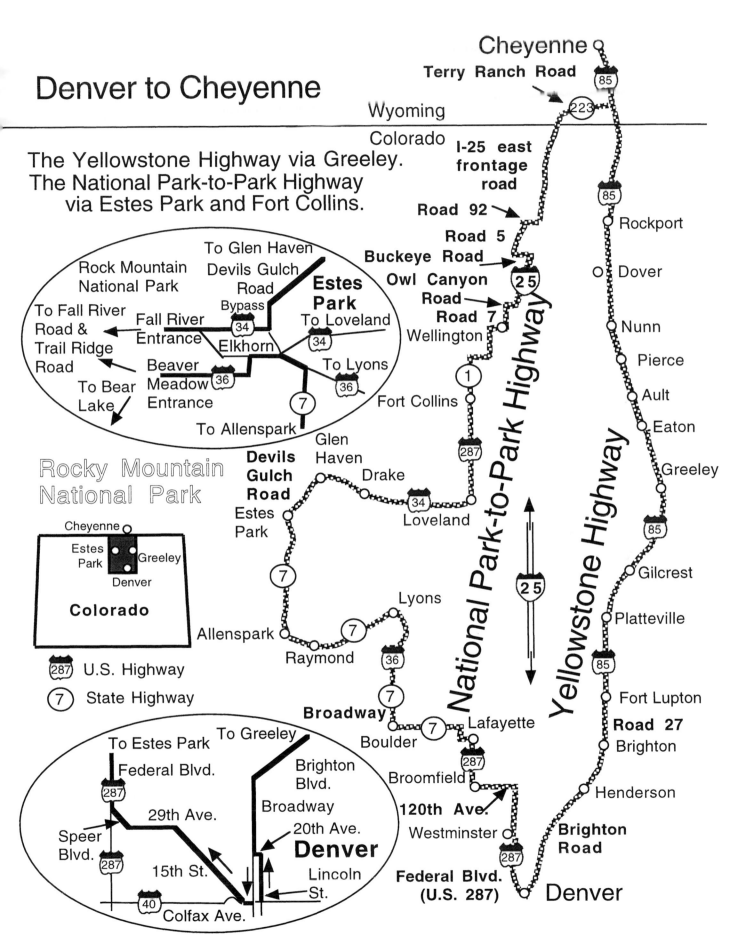

Cheyenne

Terry Ranch Road

Wyoming

Colorado

I-25 east frontage road

Road 92

Road 5

Buckeye Road

Owl Canyon Road

Road 7

Wellington

Rockport

Dover

Nunn

Pierce

Ault

Eaton

Greeley

Gilcrest

Platteville

Fort Lupton

Road 27

Brighton

Henderson

Brighton Road

Fort Collins

Glen Haven

Drake

Loveland

Lyons

Raymond

Broadway

Boulder

Lafayette

Broomfield

120th Ave.

Westminster

Federal Blvd. (U.S. 287)

Denver

Devils Gulch Road

Estes Park

Allenspark

Rocky Mountain National Park

Rock Mountain National Park

To Glen Haven

Devils Gulch Road

Bypass

Estes Park

To Loveland

Fall River Entrance

Elkhorn

To Lyons

Beaver Meadow Entrance

To Fall River Road & Trail Ridge Road

To Bear Lake

To Allenspark

Colorado

Cheyenne

Estes Park

Greeley

Denver

287 U.S. Highway

7 State Highway

To Estes Park

To Greeley

Federal Blvd.

Brighton Blvd.

Broadway

29th Ave.

20th Ave.

Denver

Speer Blvd.

15th St.

Lincoln St.

Colfax Ave.

47

Denver to Cheyenne via Greeley

The Yellowstone Highway Route:

Waterways: The route follows down the South Platte River from Denver to Greeley. After crossing the Cache la Poudre River, the highway ascends Lone Tree Creek and traverses the high plains of northeastern Colorado.

Trails: The South Platte River Trail was used by Stephen H. Long's 1820 expedition and was the primary emigrant trail to the Colorado goldfields. The Denver to Greeley section of this trail was also the route of: the Trappers Trail, connecting Taos with Fort Laramie; the 1849 branch of the Cherokee Trail; the Latham (southeast of Greeley) to Denver branch of Ben Holladay's Overland Trail.

Railroads: The Yellowstone Highway closely follows the route of the Denver Pacific Railroad, the first to reach Denver. It is now part of the Union Pacific system.

Auto Trails: The Denver-Black Hills Highway coincided with the Yellowstone Highway from Denver north to Ault, where it branched northeast to pass through Pine Bluff, Wyoming. An <u>early</u> <u>branch</u> (not long sanctioned by the national organization) of the Lincoln Highway followed the South Platte River to Denver.

State Highways: The Denver to Greeley road was designated State Highway 2. Highway 3 ran north from Greeley to the Wyoming border.

U.S. Highway: U.S. 85 was the original number assigned to the highway.

Today: From Denver, Interstate 76 whisks one to U.S. Highway 85, 10 miles south of Brighton. A more historic route is Brighton Blvd. and Brighton Road from Denver to Brighton, the original Yellowstone Highway and U.S. 85 route.

1915 *Automobile Blue Book*:

    Denver, Colo., to Cheyenne, Wyo. - 109.7 m.

      First 85 miles good gravel, balance almost perfect hard graded road. Marked as a section of the Lincoln Highway from Denver into Greeley.

1922 *Automobile Blue Book*:

    Denver, Colo., to Cheyenne, Wyo. - 114.7 m.

      Via Greeley. First few miles concrete; balance gravel and dirt. The greater of this route thru northern Colorado's agricultural district. This is the best and most popular route between these terminals. This is a section of the Yellowstone highway.

Yellow
Black H
Gray

Yellowstone Highway

THE HOBO
LETS HIS
WHISKERS SPROUT
ITS TRAINS-NOT GIRLS
THAT HE TAKES OUT
Burma-Shave

Black
White
Black

Denver-Black Hills Highway

Left and right: auto trail "pole markings."
Center: Burma-Shave roadside rhyme (see page 94).

Note: Brighton Blvd. north of Denver passes through a highly industrialized section of town, with possible heavy traffic. Interstate 76 may be taken northeast to 96th Ave. (exit 11), where Brighton Road takes on a more rural atmosphere.

Reset mile 0.0.

Downtown Denver, Colfax Ave. and Lincoln St. (One block east of Broadway, which is one-way southbound).

Mile 0.0: North from Colfax on **Lincoln St**.

Mile 0.5: Jog west on **20th St.** for one block.

Mile 0.6: North on **Broadway**.

Mile 1.5: Pass underneath the Union Pacific Railroad tracks. The Broadway Viaduct, which took one over the tracks, was torn down in 1999. Broadway jogs north to become **Brighton Blvd**.

Mile 3.1: Pass the Denver Coliseum and National Western Stock Show complex. The stock show began in 1906 and is the largest show of its kind in the world. South of the Coliseum is the new home of the Forney Transportation Museum.

Mile 3.2: Brighton Blvd. passes beneath Interstate 70.

Mile 3.9: **Riverside Cemetery**. Oldest operating cemetery in Denver. Resting place for many of Colorado's trail and transportation pioneers.

Mile 4.2: At the corner of Brighton Blvd. and York St. stands a marker:
> COMMEMORATING THE ROUTE OF THE **PLATTE RIVER TRAIL**   PRINCIPAL ROUTE OF COLORADO PIONEERS; TRAIL OF MAJOR S. H. LONG IN 1820; TRAPPERS TRAIL 1830 AND 1840; THE 1858-9 ROUTE OF GOLD SEEKERS WITH PICK AND PAN; HOME-SEEKERS IN COVERED WAGONS; BULL WHACKERS WITH OX-TEAMS; STAGE COACHES WITH TREASURE AND MAIL - THE PATH THAT BECAME AN EMPIRE.

Mile 4.4: Pass beneath the **Union Pacific Railroad** tracks. This is the route of the Denver Pacific, first railroad to Denver, completed in 1870. It connected with the transcontinental route at Cheyenne. Continue north on Brighton Blvd.

Mile 5.6: Pass beneath Interstate 270.

Mile 6.1: 64th Ave. Site of an old filling station and recently demolished tourist cabins. 1918 *Goodrich Tour* guide: "pass Hiawatha Resort on left."

Mile 6.8: 69th Ave. Jog north on **Dahlia St**. to **70th St**., then east one block, back to **Brighton Blvd**.

Mile 8.0: 77th Ave. East across present-day U.S. 6-85.

Mile 8.1: North on **Brighton Road**.

Mile 8.7: 82nd Ave. Unincorporated town of Dupont.

Mile 10.8: **96th Ave**. Turn west, passing under Interstate 76 at exit 11. The interstate was originally designated Interstate 80 South, but was changed in 1976, a century after Colorado became a state.

Mile 11.0: North on **Brighton Road** which now takes on a more rural appearance.

Mile 14.8: Town of **Henderson**. [West on 124th Ave. for one mile to the Adams County Museum, with its reconstructed Conoco filling station.]

Mile 15.5: To the west is the site of the **Pierson Ranch**, a stage station on the South Platte River Trail-Overland Trail. An 1887 ranch house was moved in 2000 from the Pierson site to the grounds of the Adams County Museum.

Mile 19.0: **Bromley Lane** in Brighton. Turn east to cross present-day U.S. 85, then north at the first intersection, onto **Main Street**.

Mile 20.3: Downtown **Brighton**, Main Street and Bridge Street.

Reset mile 0.0.

North on Main Street (**Weld County Road 27**). The road continues north to Fort Lupton and is the Yellowstone Highway and old U.S. 85 route.

Mile 0.7: Former Great Western sugar beet factory.

Mile 0.9: Business U.S. 85 to left, continue north.

Mile 6.4: **Fort Lupton**. Continue north through downtown Fort Lupton on Denver Ave.

Mile 7.4: Left on **17th St**. (Weld County Road 14 1/2).

Mile 7.5: U.S. 85 (at U.S. 85 milepost 242.8). **North on U.S. Highway 85**.

Highway mileposts now reflect U.S. 85 mileage.

Mile 242.8: North on **U.S. 85**.

Mile 242.9: A marker on the west side of U.S. 85 (0.1 mile north of the 17th St. intersection) reads:

> DUE WEST 1/4 MILE IS THE SITE OF **FORT LUPTON**   ESTABLISHED IN 1836 BY LANCASTER P. LUPTON   A RENDEZVOUS OF THE EARLY FUR TRADERS VISITED BY FREMONT AND KIT CARSON IN 1843   FARMING BEGAN HERE IN THE EARLY FORTIES   OVERLAND STAGE STATION AND REFUGE FROM INDIANS IN THE SIXTIES

The South Platte Valley Historical Society is in the process of reconstructing Fort Lupton.

Mile 249.5: **Fort Vasquez**. Reconstructed in the 1930s by the WPA (Work Projects Administration). The property and museum are operated by the Colorado Historical Society. A marker here reads:

> **FORT VASQUEZ**   ESTABLISHED IN 1837 BY LOUIS VASQUEZ AND ANDREW W. SUBLETTE   MAINTAINED UNTIL 1842 AS A POST FOR TRADE IN BUFFALO ROBES AND BEAVER SKINS WITH THE ARAPAHOES AND CHEYENNES. RENDEZVOUS OF EARLY TRAPPERS.   EMIGRANT STATION ON THE PLATTE RIVER TRAIL AFTER GOLD RUSH OF 1859.

Mile 251: **Platteville**. Founded in 1871 on land purchased from the railroad.

Mile 255.9: **Side trip**: West on Weld County Road 40 for 4.0 miles to the site of Fort St. Vrain. A marker at the fort site.

> **FORT ST. VRAIN**   BUILT ABOUT 1837 BY COL. CERAN ST. VRAIN   GEN. FREMONT REORGANIZED HIS HISTORIC EXPLORING EXPEDITION HERE ON JULY 23, 1843.   THIS FORT WAS ALSO VISITED BY FRANCIS PARKMAN AND KIT CARSON.

Mile 256.3: **Gilcrest**.

Mile 262.5: **LaSalle**. Junction of the Union Pacific line to Cheyenne and the its former line from Julesburg, Colorado.

Mile 263.8: Cross the South Platte River. It runs northeast to join the North Platte River at North Platte, Nebraska. We now leave the South Platte River Trail-Overland Trail.

Mile 265.2: **Evans**. Named for Colorado Territorial Governor John Evans, one of the promoters of the Denver Pacific Railroad.

Mile 265.5: **Greeley**. Continue north on U.S. 85 (not the bypass), passing beneath U.S. 34 and onto Greeley's **8th Ave**. The 5.7-mile route through downtown Greeley will rejoin U.S. Highway 85 at milepost 271.2.

North on 8th Avenue, the route of the Yellowstone Highway. Pass the campus of the University of Northern Colorado, formerly Colorado Teacher's College (many a Denver-area teacher knows well the "Greeley Road" from Denver).

West on **7th St**., leaving U.S. 85. Public Library to the north.

Jog south, then west on **8th St**. Pass the old Greeley High School.

North on **11th Ave**.

[West on A St. to **Centennial Village Museum** at 1475 A St.]

[**Island Grove Park**, west on D St. Site of the **Greeley Stampede**, largest Fourth of July rodeo in the United States.]

Cross the Cache la Poudre River. The 1849 branch of the Cherokee Trail ran west along the north bank of the river. It crossed the South Platte River east of Greeley, below the Cache la Poudre confluence.

Rejoin U.S. 85 at milepost 271.2. **North on U.S. Highway 85**.

Mile 272.5: **Lucerne.**

Mile 275.6: **Eaton**, follow Oak St. (U.S. 85) through downtown. Sugar beet factory to the east. Eaton is the eastern terminus of the mostly abandoned Great Western Railway which ran southwest to Loveland and Longmont. The railroad supported the sugar beet industry of the area.

Mile 279.8: **Ault**. A Unique Little Town. Ault is the western end of the Pawnee Pioneer Trails Scenic and Historic Byway which runs east to Sterling. This route passes through the Pawnee National Grasslands and by Pawnee Buttes. The area was the setting for James Michener's Venneford Ranch in *Centennial*. Interpretive sign in Caboose Park: "Weld County Irrigation."

Mile 283.6: **Pierce**.

Mile 288.4: **Nunn**.

Mile 289.0: Interpretive sign on the Denver Pacific Railway, first railroad to Denver, connecting the city with the transcontinental route at Cheyenne.

Mile 291.0: Overpass over the tracks of the Denver Pacific, now Union Pacific Railroad.

Mile 293.1: [West one mile, then north 0.7 miles to the site of **Dover**, on the Denver Pacific Railroad and the early Yellowstone Highway.]

Little remains at the site of Dover.
The town was a stop on the Denver Pacific (now Union Pacific) Railroad.

Mile 296.0: Pawnee Grasslands to the east.
Mile 298.5: Note the old roadbed to the west.
Mile 301.9: Interpretive sign: "Majestic Plains."
Mile 302.2: **Rockport**. Dating from the late 1920s, Rockport had a large dance floor and hosted the "Big Bands" in the 1930s. It now does a large business in Colorado Lottery sales, being the closest outlet to Cheyenne.
Mile 303.9: "Twin Bridges" and the old roadbed of the earlier highway to the northeast.

Mile 309.6: **Colorado-Wyoming border**, 309.6 miles from the New Mexico border via old U.S. 85.

Highway mileposts now reflect U.S. 85 mileage north of the Colorado state line.
Mile 4.1: Wyoming Highway 223 (Terry Ranch Road) merges from the west. This was old U.S. 87 from Fort Collins. The combined U.S. 85-87 continued north to Cheyenne.
Mile 4.5: Old Denver Pacific railroad grade visible to the east.
Mile 6.2: Enter Cheyenne via South Greeley Highway.
Mile 8.5: Pass beneath Interstate 80.
Mile 8.8: The old Yellowstone Highway "strip" is Central Ave., the west frontage road between 3rd and 10th St.
Mile 9.2: Cross the viaduct over the busy tracks of the Union Pacific Railroad into downtown **Cheyenne**.
Mile 9.5: Lincolnway (16th Avenue), the old **Lincoln Highway**.

Denver to Cheyenne via Rocky Mountain National Park

The National Park-to-Park Highway Route:

Waterways: The route crosses the South Platte River at Denver, then follows north along the Front Range of the Rocky Mountains. The highway enters the Rocky Mountains via South St. Vrain Creek and exits the mountains further north via Big Thompson River. After crossing the Cache la Poudre River at Fort Collins, the highway traverses a divide to Crow Creek at Cheyenne.

Trails: From Denver to Lafayette and from Loveland to Fort Collins, the highway followed the route of the 1850 branch of the Cherokee Trail. Beginning in 1864 this route was used by Ben Holladay's Overland Stage Line.

Railroads: The Colorado & Southern, now part of the Burlington Northern Santa Fe system, follows most of the route, except for the highway's loop west through Estes Park.

Auto Trails: The Buffalo Highway, Glacier to Gulf Highway, and Powder River Trail followed the Front Range of the Rocky Mountains north to Cheyenne. The Rocky Mountain Highway followed the same route to Fort Collins, then branched northwest to Laramie. An early branch of the Lincoln Highway ran from Denver to Cheyenne.

State Highways: The route from Denver to the Wyoming border was designated Colorado Highway 1. Lafayette to Estes Park was and still is Colorado Highway 7. The highway from Estes Park to Loveland was Colorado Highway 16.

U.S. Highways: Present-day U.S. Highway 287 from Denver to Laramie via Fort Collins was originally designated U.S. 285. The road from Fort Collins to Cheyenne was not designated a U.S. Highway in 1926. In 1934, the Denver to Fort Collins to Cheyenne highway was designated U.S. 87.

Today: Interstate 25 is now the major highway along Colorado's Front Range. U.S. 36, which includes the Denver-Boulder Turnpike, leads directly to Estes Park and Rocky Mountain National Park. The Turnpike opened as a toll road in 1952 and became a freeway in 1967. U.S. Highway 34 runs west from Loveland to Estes Park, then through Rocky Mountain National Park via Trail Ridge Road.

1915 *Automobile Blue Book*:

Denver to Estes Park, Colo. - 71.3 m.

A very scenic trip over good roads all the way. Extreme Caution should be used for numerous sharp turns on steep grades.

THE NATIONAL **Pꟼ** ARK -to- ARK HIGHWAY	White, black letters	CATTLE CROSSING MEANS GO SLOW THAT OLD BULL IS SOME COW'S BEAU *Burma-Shave*	GLACIER TO GULF	Black White, black letters Black
The National Park-to-Park Highway			**Glacier to Gulf Highway**	

Reset mile 0.0. **Downtown Denver**, Colfax and Broadway. West on **Colfax Ave**.

Mile 0.1: Right onto **15th St**. (14th St., the old route, is one-way, southeast-bound).

Mile 1.1: Union Station to the northeast, Cherry Creek to the southwest. At one time seven railroad bridges crossed **Cherry Creek**. Five remain today.

Mile 1.2: Pass underneath the two remaining active railroad tracks.

Mile 1.5: Cross the **South Platte River**. To the south is the confluence of the river with Cherry Creek. Here is the 1850 Cherokee Trail crossing of the South Platte.

Mile 1.7: Cross Interstate 25.

Mile 1.8: Jog left onto **29th Ave**.

Mile 2.3: Right on **Speer Blvd**.

Mile 2.5: North on **Federal Blvd., U.S. 287** (at U.S. 287 milepost 284.0). Federal was the main street of the community of Highlands. From 1897-1912 the street was called Boulevard F.

Highway mileposts now reflect U.S. 287 mileage.

Mile 285.6 (W. 48th Ave.): Cross Interstate 70.

Mile 286.7 (W. 57th Ave.): Cross Interstate 76.

Mile 287.1 (W. 60th Ave.): Cross **Clear Creek**. In the 1860s Jim Baker, famed mountain man, operated a store and ferry upstream 0.5 miles, at the Cherokee Trail -Overland Trail crossing of the creek.

Mile 288.2 (W. 69th Ave.): Cross the Burlington Railroad tracks. The railroad will be crossed many times as we follow it to Greybull, Wyoming.

Mile 288.6 (W. 72nd Ave.): West to the original section of the town of **Westminster**.

Mile 289.2 (77th Ave.): Cross U.S. 36 (Denver-Boulder Turnpike).

Mile 289.8 (W. 82nd Ave.): West of the highway is Belleview College, formerly Westminster University, a Presbyterian school founded in 1892.

Mile 293.4 (W. 110th Ave.): Old water tower, used by the Savery Savory Mushroom Company, in operation from the 1920s to 1935. Foundations remain of some of the 40 buildings used by Joseph Savery.

Mile 294.6 (W. 120th Ave.): Cozy Corner. A filling station and garage were located to the southwest. Turn west with **U.S. 287** (West 120th Ave.).

Mile 298.1: U.S. 287 turns north. **Broomfield** was a stop on the Burlington Railroad. It was named for the broom straw grown in the area.

Mile 298.6: Memorial in the roadside park on the southeast corner of 6th Ave.:
> BLUE STAR MEMORIAL HIGHWAY.   A tribute to the Armed Forces that have defended the United States of America.   Sponsored by the Broomfield Garden Club and Mrs. Aster's Garden Club.

Along Colorado's Blue Star Memorial Highway are 14 roadside parks, from Raton Pass on the New Mexico border to "Natural Fort" near the Wyoming border.

Mile 300.8: Dillon Road. On the southeast corner was Johnson's Corner, a filling station and a restaurant noted for their ice cream.

Mile 302.2: **South Public Road**. North 1 7 miles to downtown **Lafayette**, "Where Coal is King" (many coal mines were located in the region). Old Lafayette is along E. Simpson St. Present-day U.S. 287 bypasses the downtown area.

West 0.6 miles on **Baseline Road** to rejoin **U.S. 287** at milepost 304.3.

Mile 304.3: U.S. 287 and Baseline Road. On the northeast corner is another Blue Star Memorial Highway monument:

BLUE STAR MEMORIAL HIGHWAY   In tribute to all Men and Women living or dead who have served, are serving or will serve in the Armed Forces of the United States of America.   Dedicated 1998   VFW Post 1771 and Ladies Auxiliary.

Also located northeast of the intersection were a filling station, picnic tables, fireplace, and outhouses.

Mile 305.3: Ninemile Corner. A filling station once stood on the northwest corner. The intersection was also known as the "Boulder Gateway." Turn west on **Colorado Highway 7** (Arapahoe Ave.). **We now leave U.S. 287** and the route of the 1850 branch of the Cherokee Trail. We start our loop road west to Estes Park and Rocky Mountain National Park. We will rejoin U.S. 287 at Loveland, 30 miles north.

Entrance gates to the "Road of Remembrance" at Ninemile Corner.
From *Colorado Highways*, October 1929.
Courtesy of the Colorado Department of Transportation.

Highway mileposts now reflect Colorado Highway 7 mileage.
Mile 60.8 (just west of U.S. 287): **Entrance gates**. Erected by the Lion's Club of Boulder, the gates mark the beginning of the **"Road of Remembrance."**

With the present great transition from rail to motor traffic, it is unnecessary to point out the possibilities roads present for creating a favorable impression upon the traveler . . . Recognizing that roads comprise a powerful agency of appeal, the city of Boulder is preparing to beautify its principal approach road for a distance of nine miles from the city limits. . . . The road will be officially known as the "Road of Remembrance," dedicated to the 11,000 men and women of Boulder county who served in the World War. The whole plan is being sponsored by Boulder Post No. 10, American Legion. Figuring a tree every 50 feet, there will be over 1,000 over the whole line . . .

Colorado Highways, August 1927

Mile 56.2: Panoramic views of Boulder and the Rocky Mountains from Legion Park, north of the highway.

Mile 52.5: [Cross 28th St. (U.S. 36). Present-day Colorado Highway 7 jogs north, then west on Canyon Blvd.] Continue west on Arapahoe Ave.

Mile 51.4: Arapahoe Ave. and Broadway. **University of Colorado** to the southeast. The school opened in 1877 with 44 students.
North on <u>Broadway</u>. At Canyon Blvd. rejoin Colorado Highway 7.

Mile 51.3: Broadway and Canyon Blvd. The Colorado & Northwestern Railway Locomotive #30 sits in Central Park southeast of the intersection. The railroad ran from Boulder to Ward and Lake Eldora from 1897-1919. It was called the "Switzerland Trail of America." The engine was used on other railroads until 1952, then was donated to the city in 1953.

Mile 51.2: Cross the Pearl St. pedestrian mall, the heart of downtown **Boulder**. The Boulder Chautauqua was started in 1898 by Texas teachers. The city operated its streetcar system, the Boulder Street Railway Company, from 1899-1931.

HOTEL BOULDERADO.   BOULDER, COLO.

Postcard of the **Hotel Boulderado**, located at 13th & Spruce St.
Opened in 1909, the name is a combination of Boulder and Colorado.
The owners wanted guests to not forget where they had been.

1920 Park-to-Park Highway dedication tour: August 26th, guests of the Commercial Association at the Chautauqua Cafeteria.

1926 Blanche Johnston diary:
"Friday, August 27, 1926

Three o'clock P.M. and at last we are off -- Miss Fenton, Cicely and myself -- for Yellowstone Park on our first trip of more than one day's duration in our own car, Chiquita.

We had intended starting at 1:30 but there were many things to look after at the last -- such as buying a wrench & having the extra tire securely fastened."

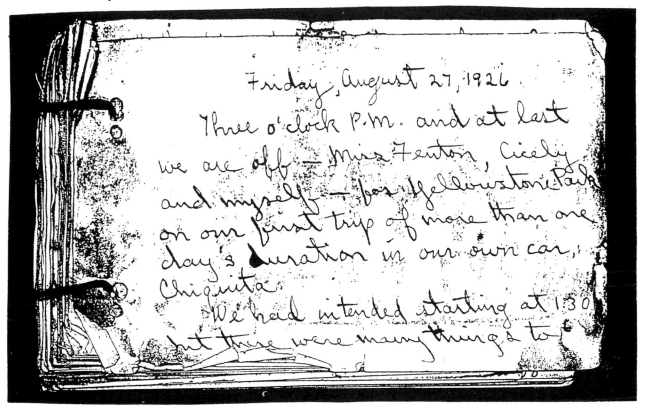

First page of Blanche Johnston's 1926 diary of her trip to Yellowstone.
Johnston, a Boulder librarian, kept a detailed journal of her nine-day trip.
Pasted into her diary were maps, road regulations, guide book pages,
souvenir postcards, and expense and mileage summaries.
Courtesy of the Carnegie Branch Library for Local History, Boulder, Colorado.

From downtown Boulder, continue north on Broadway (Colorado Highway 7) for 3.5 miles.
Mile 47.7: Merge with U.S. 36 (Foothills Highway) at U.S. 36 mile marker 32.5.
North on U.S. 36 (and Colorado Highway 7).

Highway mileposts now reflect U.S. 36 mileage.
Mile 27.7: Altona. The early town hoped to be the center of toll roads extending west to the mining districts. Boulder won out, with better roads and the railroad.
Mile 21.7: Turn west, merging with Colorado Highway 66. The highway now follows St. Vrain Creek and the Burlington Railroad west to Lyons.

Mile 20.3: **Lyons**. The Denver Utah & Pacific Railroad was completed to Lyons in 1884. It later became part of the Burlington system. Stagecoaches, then automobiles provided transportation from the railroad to Estes Park and Rocky Mountain National Park. The restored railroad depot is a block south of Main St.

At the west end of Main St. was located an entrance arch noting Lyons as the "Double Gateway to the Rocky Mountain National Parks." Here one had a choice of following either North St. Vrain Creek (present-day U.S. 36) or South St. Vrain Creek (Colorado Highway 7).

LYONS   DOUBLE GATEWAY TO ROCKY MOUNTAIN NATIONAL PARK
The pillars advertised the various lodges along the Colorado Highway 7 route.
Photograph courtesy of Fran Brackett

Turn southwest to follow <u>Colorado Highway 7</u> to Estes Park via South St. Vrain Creek. This was the original National Park-to-Park Highway route. South St. Vrain Road opened as a toll road in 1892, acquired by Boulder County in 1910.

Highway mileposts now reflect Colorado Highway 7 mileage.
Mile 32.6 (0.5 miles southwest of downtown Lyons): **Side trip**. Left on Old South St. Vrain Road to follow 1.5 miles of the older road, on the south side of South St. Vrain Creek. Rejoin Colorado Highway 7 at Mile 31.2. Continue west.
Mile 30.0: Little Narrows.
Mile 27.8: Big Narrows.

Mile 21.4: **Side trip**: Left on Riverside Drive to follow the pre-1952 road 2.2 miles through **Rivoroide** to **Raymond**. Here was the junction with the old north-south Peak to Peak Highway. Turn north at the Raymond Store to ascend Stanley Hill, for 0.6 miles, rejoining Colorado Highway 7 at mile 19.7. Continue west.

Mile 19.3: **Side trip**: Left to follow the older highway for 0.2 miles. Along this old section of road is the **"Glacier View" pullout** with a wonderful view to the southwest of Arapaho Peaks and Arapaho Glacier. Here also was a small refreshment and souvenir stand (the chipmunks are still here). Rejoin Colorado Highway 7 at mile 19.2.

Mile 19.1: Merge with Colorado Highway 72 and the present-day **Peak to Peak Scenic Byway**. [South to Ward, Black Hawk, Central City, and U.S. 6.] The Byway received scenic designation in 1989.

Mile 18.7: Bunce School to the west. The school was opened in 1888, closed in 1940, and restored in 1998. Here was the pre-1920 junction with the "Ward to Estes Park Road." The Colorado & Northwestern Railway arrived in Ward (eight miles south of Raymond) from Boulder in 1898.

Mile 16.5: **Peak to Peak Highway interpretive sign**. This designated scenic highway runs north from Black Hawk to Estes Park. Originally the Peak to Peak Highway ran from Colorado Springs, at the base of Pikes Peak, north past Mount Evans and Longs Peak to Estes Park. Manitou Springs, Woodland Park, Deckers, Buffalo, Evergreen, Idaho Springs, and Central City were all on this highway.

Mile 16.1: **Side trip**: Left on "Highway 7 Business Route" to pass through the towns of **Ferncliff** and **Allenspark**. North of Ferncliff is the Fawn Brook Inn. A mile north of Ferncliff is Allenspark. The Crystal Springs Lodge was opened in 1912 by Burns Will. He hosted the 1920 Park-to-Park dedication tour on August 26. The Allens Park Lodge, formerly Isle's Trading Post, was opened in 1933.
Rejoin Colorado Highway 7 at mile 14.9. Continue north.

Mile 13.6: **Side trip**: 1.6 miles of the old highway run west of the present-day highway (Boulder County Road 84W). The site of the **Copeland Lake Lodge**, opened in 1914 by Burns Will, is 1.3 miles down the old highway. With 11 rooms and five cottages, the lodge was later named Wild Basin Lodge. It burned in 1980 and was rebuilt across the highway in 1988. Rejoin Colorado Highway 7 at mile 12.8.

Mile 11.8: Meeker Park. The Meeker Park Lodge was opened in 1934. Cabins date from the 1920s.

Mile 10.9: **St. Catherine Chapel**, built in 1934, is part of the St. Malo Camp, established in 1916.

Mile 9.9: Eagle Plume's. Opened as a tea room in 1920, it was later called Perkins Trading Post. Today, the post offers arts and crafts by American Indian people.

Mile 9.0: [West to the Longs Peak trailhead and ranger station. Up this road was the Hewes-Kirkwood "Hotel," a collection of rustic cabins opened in 1914, now the Rocky Ridge Music Center.]

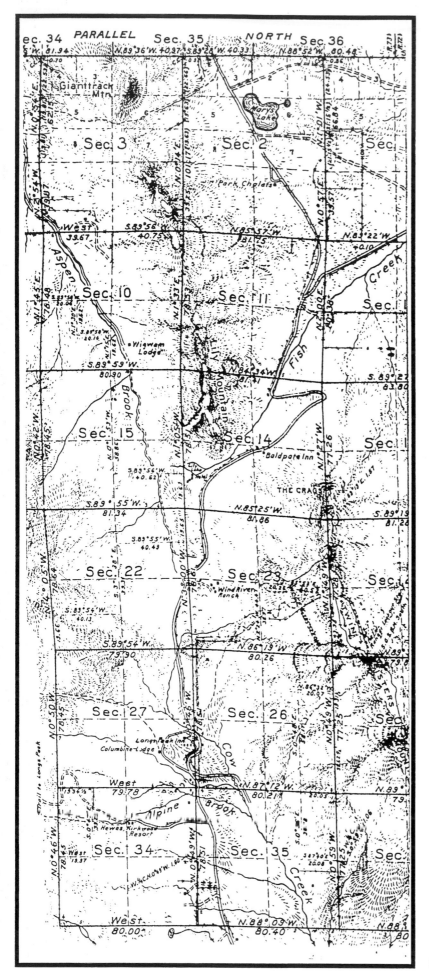

Old Colorado Highway 7 to Estes Park passed to the west of **Marys Lake**.

Colorado Highway 7 continued south to Raymond (off the map), then turned east to Lyons and Boulder. Continuing south from Raymond was the "Peak to Peak Highway."

The highway ran in front of the **Baldpate Inn**. The present-day highway passes west of the inn.

1926 Land Plat, showing The National Park-to-Park Highway (Colorado Highway 7) south of Estes Park.
    Map from the Bureau of Land Management, Lakewood, Colorado.

The **Longs Peak Inn** was owned by naturalist Enos Mills. The inn burned in 1949.

Note the **"Trail to Longs Peak"** west of the Hewes-Kirkwood Resort.

Mile 8.4: Enos Mills monument, east of the highway. Marker text:
      Enos A. Mills   Father of Rocky Mountain National Park.
Internationally known naturalist, author, guide, lecturer, and nature guide.
Homesteaded on this site 1885.   Erected by Namaqua Chapter,
Daughters of the American Revolution 1982.

Mile 8.4: West of the highway is the site of the **Longs Peak Inn**, purchased by Enos
    Mills in 1902. The original inn burned in 1906 and was immediately rebuilt. The
    second inn burned in 1949. Current buildings are owned by the Salvation Army.

Longs Peak Inn, owned by naturalist Enos Mills.
A small sign over the doorway reads "Ice Cream."
Courtesy of the Denver Public Library, Western History Collection. Photo MCC-2320.

Mile 8.1: East of the highway is the 1885 **Enos Mills homestead cabin**. Since
    1968, the cabin has housed a museum with mementos of his life.

Mile 6.3: **Side trip**: Right to the **Baldpate Inn**, opened in 1917. Named after the
    novel *The Seven Keys of Baldpate*, the inn has a collection of several thousand
    keys. The first key was donated by famed lawyer Clarence Darrow in 1923. Old
    Colorado Highway 7 ran in front of the inn. This road was opened in 1877 as the
    "Longs Peak Toll Road."

Mile 3.5: [The Marys Lake Road, to the west, was the original route of the National
    Park-to-Park Highway and Colorado Highway 7. The old road ran south of the lake
    and joins U.S. 36, 1.4 miles southwest of downtown Estes Park.]

Mile 0.0: **U.S. 36**. End of Colorado Highway 7 and the Peak to Peak Scenic Byway.
    [East on U.S. 36 to Lyons.] West on U.S. 36 to Estes Park. In 0.2 miles, intersect
    U.S. 34 from Loveland. West on Elkhorn Avenue to the heart of Estes Park.

Estes Park. "Gem of the Rockies." The valley was settled shortly after the Colorado gold rush of 1859. Abner Sprague, early resort owner noted:

> The hotel business was forced on us . . . We came here for small ranch operations, but guests and visitors became so numerous, at first wanting eggs, milk and other provisions, then wanting lodging, and finally demanding full accommodations, that we had to go into the hotel business or go bankrupt from keeping free company.
>
> Quoted in *This Blue Hollow*, by James Pickering

William Byers, publisher of the *Rocky Mountain News* and the first to climb Mt. Meeker, named the valley. He stated in his newspaper September 23, 1864:

> . . . eventually this park will become a favorite pleasure resort. Probably by another season the road will be so improved that a carriage can go from Denver directly to the foot of the snowy range, and the drive will be but a day and a half to reach such magnificent prospects and surroundings as the imagination can hardly paint.

The Stanley Hotel was opened in 1909 by Freelan O. Stanley. He ran a fleet of Stanley Steamers to his hotel from Loveland.

Elkhorn Ave. in Estes Park about 1921.
Signs: "Ice Cream Cones, Hot Coffee, Near Beer, Cigars"
"Cigarettes, Cigars, Tobacco"
"Coney Island Red Hot Sandwiches"
"Ice Cream Cones, Soda Pop"
"Lunches, Ice Cream and Soft Drinks"
Courtesy of the Denver Public Library, Western History Collection. Photo X-8298.

Time was when Estes Park was in the wilderness, and to reach it was an adventure. Today it still touches with one hand the wilderness of the National Park, while with the other it grasps civilization.

Yellowstone Highway in Wyoming and Colorado, 1916.

Estes Park in the 1920s. Looking west to Rocky Mountain National Park. Courtesy of the Denver Public Library, Western History Collection. Photo X-8268.

1916 *Yellowstone Highway* ads:
Estes Park Hotel	"We Never Close"
The Hupp Hotel	"Situated in the Village - Good Home Cooking"
Elkhorn Lodge	"A Hotel of High Standards"
The Lewiston	"Open all the Year"
Longs Peak Inn	"The best of food by the best of women cooks"
Fall River Ranch and Lodge	"Located at the entrance to the Rocky Mountain National Park on the new Fall River Road"

From *The Rocky Mountain News*, September 3, 1915.
The headlines stated:
**"Colorado Is to Be Made Official Playground of the Nation
WORLD WILL BE TOLD OF STATE'S WONDER"**

Rocky Mountain National Park was established just 34 days
after automobiles were first allowed in Yellowstone National Park.

Side trip: **Rocky Mountain National Park**, the nation's 10th national park, was established September 4, 1915. From downtown Estes Park, at Elkhorn Ave. and Moraine Ave, a quick tour of the park can be made year round.

Reset 0.0. U.S. 36 (Moraine Ave.): southwest to the Beaver Meadows entrance.

Mile 1.4: Marys Lake Road, old Colorado Highway 7.

Mile 2.4: Visitors Center and Park Headquarters.

Mile 3.6: Beaver Meadows entrance.

Mile 3.8: [Side road to Moraine Park and Bear Lake.]

Mile 6.7: Deer Ridge Junction. U.S. 34-36 junction. Northeast on U.S. 34.
   [West on U.S. 34 to **Trail Ridge Road**. Closed in winter, it is the highest continuous paved road in the world. The highway opened in 1932.]

Mile 8.5: Fall River Junction. Continue east to Estes Park. [West at Fall River Junction to the old **Fall River Road**, the first road through the park to Grand Lake. Opened in 1920, it is now an eleven-mile-long, one-way road, connecting with Trail Ridge Road at Fall River Pass. Closed in winter.]

Mile 10.6: Fall River entrance to the Park.

Mile 13.9: U.S. 34 Bypass straight ahead. [U.S. 34 to downtown to the right.]

Mile 15.1: Devils Gulch Road. The **Stanley Hotel** is east of the Devils Gulch Road-U.S. 34 Bypass intersection. **North on Devils Gulch Road.**

White Touring cars negotiating a snowdrift at the upper end of **Fall River Road.**
Courtesy of the Colorado Historical Society, photograph # X499.

Reset mile 0.0. **North on the** <u>Devils</u> <u>Gulch</u> <u>Road</u> (Larimer County Road 43). The road will join U.S. 34 at Drake, east of Estes Park.

Mile 0.8: **MacGregor Ranch** to the west. Alexander MacGregor homesteaded here in 1873. In 1875, he opened a toll road from Lyons, following the North St. Vrain Creek and Little Thompson River, approximating present-day U.S. Highway 36.

Mile 3.8: [Larimer County Road 61 leads northeast to the site of Shep Husted's Rustic Hotel, opened in 1902. Later renamed Lester's, it is now a youth hostel.]

Mile 4.7: Head of **Devils Gulch**. The pre-1910 road did not have the present-day switchbacks. Logs were laid side by side to form a "corduroy" road, which kept the very steep road from washing away.

Mile 7.0: **Glen Haven**. "Colorado's oldest summer colony." The general store opened in 1921 and the Glen Haven Inn opened in the early 1930s.

Mile 14.8: **Drake**. Originally called The Forks.

Forks Hotel at present-day Drake. The hotel opened in 1905 and had 23 rooms. The east end of the present-day River Forks Inn is the original section.
Courtesy of the Denver Public Library, Western History Collection. Photo MMC-997.

At Drake, **merge with** <u>U.S.</u> <u>34</u> at milepost 75.6. Continue east down the **Big Thompson Canyon**. This was the site of the Big Thompson Flood of 1976.

Highway mileposts now reflect U.S. 34 mileage.
Mile 81.9: Cross the **Big Thompson River** in "The Narrows." The pre-1930s roadbed crossed the river several times in The Narrows.

Mile 83.3: Exit Big Thompson Canyon. The **Dam Store** opened in the 1930s when the present day road alignment was completed. The original Dam Store was opened in 1900 at the old Loveland Dam [reached via the narrow old road, now Larimer County Road 22H, just east of the Dam Store parking lot].

Mile 85.7: Intersect Laramie County Road 27 (Buckhorn Road). This road north was the route of the Glacier to Gulf Highway which passed through Masonville before entering Fort Collins.

Mile 89.4: Namaqua Rd. South 0.3 miles to the Cherokee Trail-Overland Trail crossing of the Big Thompson River. Here, at **Namaqua**, Mariano Medina operated a ferry.

Mile 92.0: **Loveland**. Rejoin U.S. 287 (North Lincoln Ave.) at U.S. 287 milepost 334. We have now completed our loop west of Estes Park. Loveland was the site of the first Great Western sugar beet factory, opened in 1901.

Highway mileposts now reflect U.S. 287 mileage.

North on <u>U.S.</u> <u>287</u>, rejoining the route of the Buffalo Highway, Powder River Trail, Rocky Mountain Highway, and an <u>early</u> <u>branch</u> of the Lincoln Highway. We left the route of these "auto trails" at Ninemile Corner, north of Lafayette.

Mile 340.1: "Trimby Corner."

Old gas station on Harmony Road in Fort Collins.
Longs Peak in the background.
A 1994 photograph, taken before developments to the southwest.

Mile 343.1: Horsetooth Road. The intersection was known as Spans Corner. Continue north on U.S. 287 (College Ave). Pass **Colorado State University**, originally called Colorado State College of Agriculture and Mechanic Arts.

Mile 346.5: Mountain Ave. Center of **Fort Collins.** Here the Glacier to Gulf Highway from Masonville rejoined the National Park-to-Park Highway.

Mile 346.6: College Ave. and Walnut St. Here is the **Northern Hotel**, known as the "Pearl of Northern Colorado." The hotel was originally called the Commercial Hotel, but was renamed after major renovation in 1905. Across the street is the Silver Grill Cafe which opened as the Uneeda-Lunch Cafe in 1912. The original section is at 212 Walnut St.

1920 Park-to-Park Highway dedication tour: August 27, lunch at the Northern Hotel.

North of Fort Collins, several routes led north to Wellington. Most followed section lines through this mostly agricultural region.

The 1915 *Blue Book*:

"Fort Collins; College & Mountain Aves. & Linden St.

Turn diagonally right with one line of trolley on Linden St.

0.8 [miles] End of street beyond RR crossing, turn right with trolley.

0.5 [additional miles] 4-corners; turn left with trolley . . . "

From downtown Fort Collins, continue north on U.S. 287 (College Avenue).

Mile 347.0: Cross the Cache la Poudre River.

Mile 348.5: Colorado Highway 1 (Terry Lake Road) to Wellington. We now leave U.S. 287 and the route of the Cherokee Trail-Overland Trail and the Rocky Mountain Highway "auto trail." They turn northwest to the Laramie, Wyoming, area.

Highway mileposts now reflect Colorado Highway 1 mileage.

Mile 0.0: North on **Colorado Highway 1**.

Mile 1.8: "Kenyon Corner."

Mile 6.3: "Meyers Corner."

Mile 9.3: Cross the Burlington Railroad tracks (originally the Colorado & Southern).

Mile 9.5: **Wellington**. Incorporated in 1905.

Mile 9.7: **North 6th St**. (0.2 miles west of I-25 exit 278 and the end of Colorado Highway 1.)

Reset mile 0.0.

Mile 0.0: North on **Larimer County Road 7** (North 6th St., **old U.S. 87**).

Mile 3.5: East on **Owl Canyon Road** (Larimer County Road 70).

[Old U.S. 87 continued northeast.]

Mile 3.8: I-25 exit 281 (Owl Canyon exit).

Highway mileposts now reflect I-25 mileage.

North on Interstate 25 from I-25 exit 281 to exit 288.

I-25 milepost 282.5: The interstate follows the old route of U.S. 87 and the Colorado & Southern Railroad.

I-25 milepost 288.5: Old U.S. 87 and railroad tracks veer north, away from I-25. I-25 exit 288 (Buckeye Road exit). **Exit the interstate.**

Reset mile 0.0.

Mile 0.0: West on **Buckeye Road** (Larimer County Road 82).

Mile 0.3: Cross old U.S. 87, which followed the east side of the railroad.

Mile 0.7: North on **Larimer County Road 5**.

Mile 5.4: Norfork railroad siding.

Mile 5.8: East on **Larimer County Road 92**, crossing railroad tracks.

Mile 6.8: Cross old U.S. 87.

   South: Old asphalt roadbed to fence line.

   North: Private road.

Mile 7.4: I-25 exit 293 (Carr exit). [East 4.5 miles to Carr; 9.0 miles to Rockport and U.S. Highway 85.]

Reset mile 0.0.

Mile 0.0: North on the **I-25 East Frontage Road**. Old U.S. 87, now a private road, runs 0.5 miles west of the interstate for six miles.

Mile 2.3: Old U.S. 87 bridge visible 0.5 miles to the west.

Mile 3.0: **Natural Fort**, rock formations and former I-25 rest stop. Blue Star Memorial Highway monument:

A TRIBUTE TO THE NATION'S ARMED FORCES WHO SERVED IN WORLD WAR II

COLORADO FEDERATION OF GARDEN CLUBS

THE STATE HIGHWAY DEPARTMENT

Mile 4.2: Good view of old U.S. 87 following the power poles west of the interstate.

Mile 6.3: **Colorado-Wyoming state line**. Billboards abundant here.

"Beneath this slab
John Brown is stowed.
He watched the ads,
And not the road."
Ogden Nash, 1942

   Old U.S. 87 and the Colorado & Southern Railroad approach I-25 from the southwest. The railroad and the very early National Park-to-Park Highway route continued north, entering Cheyenne from the southwest.

Mile 6.6: Terry Bison Ranch. Tourist facilities and one of the largest Bison herds in the state.

Mile 9.0: I-25 exit 2 (Terry Ranch Road).

Reset mile 0.0.

Northeast on Wyoming Highway 223 (Terry Ranch Road), old U.S. 87.

Mile 5.4: Merge with U.S. Highway 85. (See page 52, the Denver to Cheyenne via Greeley chapter, to continue travel **north to Cheyenne**.)

Darkness fell quickly and we seemed to have lost Cheyenne, we saw
its lights many times but the city itself was very elusive. . . .
Blanche Johnston, 1926

From the *Rocky Mountain Weekly News*, November 4, 1915

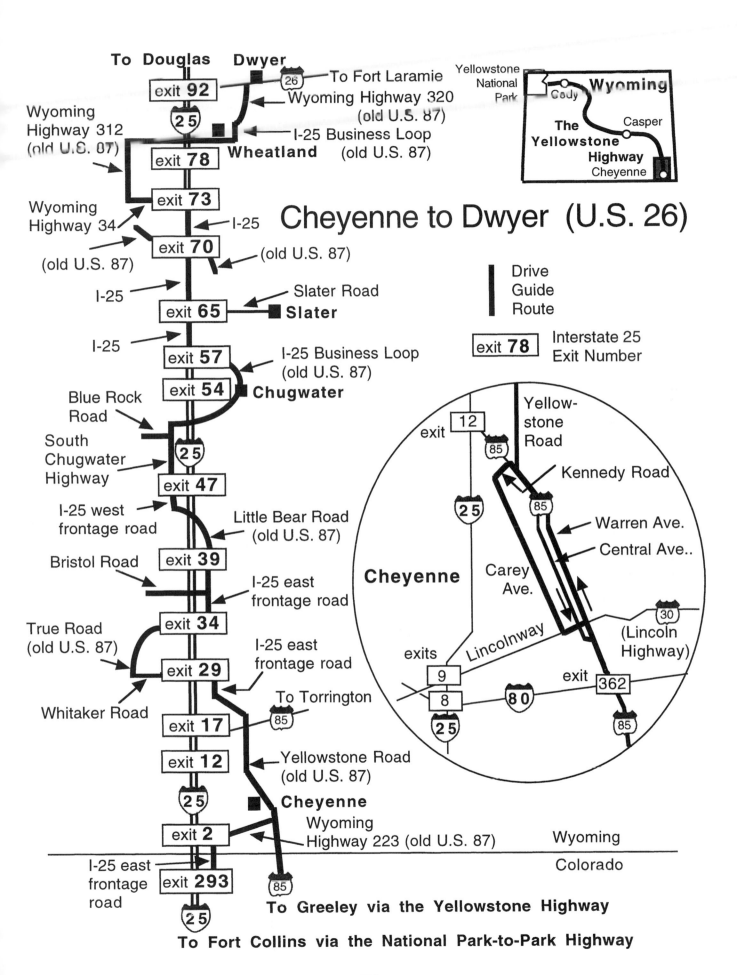

Cheyenne to Dwyer (U.S. 26)

To Douglas   Dwyer

exit 92

To Fort Laramie

Wyoming Highway 320 (old U.S. 87)

I-25 Business Loop (old U.S. 87)

Wheatland

Wyoming Highway 312 (old U.S. 87)

exit 78

exit 73

I-25 (old U.S. 87)

Wyoming Highway 34

exit 70

(old U.S. 87)

(old U.S. 87)

I-25

Slater Road

Slater

exit 65

I-25

exit 57

I-25 Business Loop (old U.S. 87)

exit 54

Chugwater

Blue Rock Road

South Chugwater Highway

exit 47

I-25 west frontage road

Little Bear Road (old U.S. 87)

Bristol Road

exit 39

I-25 east frontage road

True Road (old U.S. 87)

exit 34

exit 29

I-25 east frontage road

Whitaker Road

To Torrington

exit 17

exit 12

Yellowstone Road (old U.S. 87)

Cheyenne

exit 2

Wyoming Highway 223 (old U.S. 87)

I-25 east frontage road

exit 293

Wyoming

Colorado

To Greeley via the Yellowstone Highway

To Fort Collins via the National Park-to-Park Highway

Yellowstone National Park

Wyoming

Cody

Casper

The Yellowstone Highway

Cheyenne

Drive Guide Route

exit 78   Interstate 25 Exit Number

Yellowstone Road

exit 12

Kennedy Road

Warren Ave.

Central Ave.

Cheyenne

Carey Ave.

Lincolnway

(Lincoln Highway)

exits 9

exit 8

exit 362

71

Cheyenne. Established in 1867 with the arrival of the Union Pacific, the first transcontinental railroad. Cheyenne was "end of track" during the winter of 1867-68. Rapid growth and sudden wealth earned the city the nickname "Magic City of the Plains." **Fort D. A. Russell, predecessor of Francis Warren Air Force Base**, was also established in 1867 and was, at one time, America's largest cavalry outpost.

Through Cheyenne passed the **Lincoln Highway, first transcontinental "auto trail."** It funneled traffic from the east onto the Yellowstone Highway.

902 VIADUCT, CHEYENNE, WYO.

MAIN OUTLET FOR MOTOR TRAFFIC TO THE SOUTH
5548-29

The Yellowstone Highway entered Cheyenne via this old viaduct.
Passing over the railroad yards, it led into Central Ave.
where the present-day southbound U.S. 85 viaduct is located.
All U.S. Highway 85 and 87 traffic used the viaduct.

Plains Hotel. "Grand Old Lady of the Plains" was opened in 1911 with 200 rooms. It served travelers on the Yellowstone and Lincoln Highways. It was refurbished in the 1980s.

The **Capitol Building** has been in use since 1888. Murals in the Senate and House chambers depict scenes from Wyoming's history. The murals were painted by Allen True of Littloton, Colorado. He also designed the cowboy and bucking horse (named Steamboat) on the Wyoming license plates. They first appeared on plates in 1936.

The **Atlas Theater**, at 211 W. 16th St. (Lincolnway), opened in 1887.

Dinneen Auto Dealership is located at 400 W. 16th St. The dealership opened in 1913 across the street from the Bon Ton Stables which had "carriages for all occasions." The present building was opened in 1928. The 1916 *Yellowstone Highway* guide noted its sales of Hudson and Reo automobiles.

Union Pacific #4004, one of a series of 25 "Big Boys," largest steam locomotive ever built. Used on the Cheyenne to Ogden, Utah, run. It is on permanent display in Holliday Park, 0.5 miles east of downtown, on East Lincolnway.

991   THE TRANSPORTATION CENTER OF CHEYENNE, WYOMING

Postcard of Cheyenne's Union Pacific Depot, built in 1886.
It was the largest between Omaha and San Francisco. It is now being restored and houses the Wyoming Transportation Museum and Learning Center. On the left is the Burlington Depot, now a parking lot. Note the old U.S. 85-87 viaduct entrance ramp.

1916 *Yellowstone Highway* ad:
> "**Cheyenne** Offers You   GOOD ROADS to Drive Over   GOOD PARKS to rest in
> GOOD PLAYHOUSES for Amusement   GOOD TROUT FISHING in Mountain Streams
> GOOD WATER From the Mountains   GOOD GARAGES For Your Supplies
> GOOD HOTELS   AND A WELCOME
> It is the heart center of the Lincoln Highway and the Yellowstone
> Highway, two of the best roads for the tourist in America."

1920 Park-to-Park Highway dedication tour: August 27. Tour delayed by a rain and hailstorm near the Colorado-Wyoming border. Dinner at the Masonic Temple.

1922 *Blue Book* ad: Dildine Garage: 315 W. 19th St.
> "Tourist Trade a Specialty. Daily Road Reports. Ask us about Roads."

Cheyenne to Dwyer (U.S. 26)

The Yellowstone Highway Route:

Waterways: The Yellowstone Highway followed no major waterway as it traversed the high plains east of the Laramie Mountains. The highway crossed Lodgepole Creek, tributary of the South Platte River; then crossed a divide to the North Platte River drainage. Crossed were Horse Creek, Bear Creek, Chugwater Creek, and the south and north fork of the Laramie River.

Trails: The highway follows the general path of the Cheyenne-Deadwood Trail, used by the Cheyenne and Black Hills Stage and Express.

Railroads: The Cheyenne Northern Railroad was built from Cheyenne to Orin Junction, beginning in 1887. The railroad was later the Colorado & Southern, now the Burlington Northern Santa Fe. From Cheyenne, the tracks led northwest to pass near the base of the Laramie Mountains. From Chugwater, the original Yellowstone Highway followed the railroad through Wheatland, Uva, Dwyer, and Wendover.

Auto Trails: Sharing the route of the Yellowstone and National Park-to-Park Highways were the Buffalo Highway, Powder River Trail, and the Glacier to Gulf Highway.

State Highways: Wyoming Highway 11 was the original number given to the Yellowstone Highway route.

U.S. Highways: U.S. Highway 185 was the original number given to the Cheyenne to Orin Junction road. The number was later changed to U.S. Highway 87. U.S. Highway 85 branches northeast, passing through Torrington and Lusk.

Today: Interstate 25 whisks the traveler north from Cheyenne.

1915 *Automobile Blue Book*:
> **Cheyenne to Douglas, Wyo. - 148.8 m.**
> Via Wheatland. Fair to good natural roads all the way.

1922 *Automobile Blue Book*:
> **Cheyenne to Douglas, Wyo. - 151.7 m.**
> Via Chugwater, Wheatland and Glendo. Dirt roads all the way. Thru a rolling, grassy prairie, with some hilly sections and a stretch of about 12 miles of irrigated farm land of which Wheatland is the center. This is a section of the Yellowstone highway.

Brown & white

Buffalo Highway

A PEACH
LOOKS GOOD
WITH LOTS OF FUZZ
BUT MAN'S NO PEACH
AND NEVER WUZ
Burma-Shave

White
Black
White
Black
White

Powder River Trail

Colorado-Wyoming border north through Chugwater

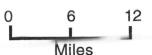

0   6   12

Miles

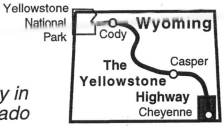

Yellowstone National Park

Wyoming

Cody

The Yellowstone Highway

Casper

Cheyenne

United States Geological Survey map
State of Wyoming, 1980

1916 map from the
*Yellowstone Highway in
Wyoming and Colorado*

Present-day highways with
the drive guide route enhanced

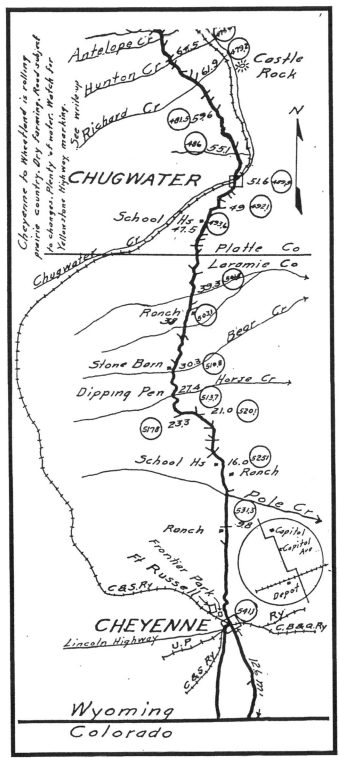

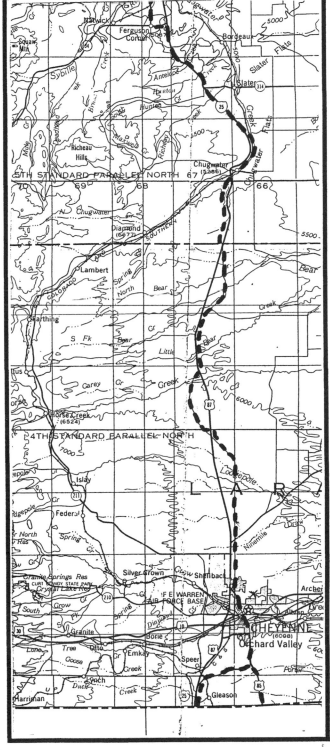

75

"Preparing for a Fishing Trip Up the Platte River," 1912.
Photographer Joseph Stimson (right) at his studio near Wyoming's Capitol.
Photograph courtesy of the Wyoming Division of Cultural Resources.

Over the years, various routes have led north out of Cheyenne.

1915 *Blue Book*:

"From 16th & Carey, north with trolley on Carey Ave., left on 26th St., with trolley, enter Fort Russell Reservation, pass the railroad water tank. . . . follow poles across prairie."

1920s route:

This route can be followed today. From Lincolnway and Carey, proceed northwest on **Carey Ave**. Enter **Frontier Park**, site of the Cheyenne Frontier Days Rodeo. First held in 1897, "The Daddy of 'em all" is the world's largest outdoor rodeo. It is Wyoming's largest annual event, held the last full week of July. Also in Frontier Park is the **Cheyenne Frontier Days Old West Museum** with its large collection of horse-drawn vehicles.

Carey dead-ends at Kennedy Road. At this intersection, on the grounds of the Municipal Golf Course, is a Fort Laramie Trail marker:

> **FORT LARAMIE TRAIL.** THIS STONE MARKS THAT ROAD OF ROMANCE AND ADVENTURE TRAVELED BY TRAPPERS, TRADERS, AND TROOPS TO FORT LARAMIE, THE MOST HISTORIC SPOT IN THE WEST   1867-1887

Turn east on **Kennedy Road** for 0.2 miles.

Turn southeast onto **U.S. Highway 85** for 0.2 miles.

Turn north onto Yellowstone Road.

Present-day U.S. 85.

North on **Warren Avenue**, U.S. Highway 85-87 Business Route (now one-way northbound; Central Ave. is one-way southbound). Originally, Central Ave. north of Pershing Blvd. was Yellowstone Road.

Cheyenne Airport. Cheyenne was one of 14 cities on the first Transcontinental Air Mail Route. The first air mail service left Cheyenne airport, the highest on the route, September 18, 1920.

North on Yellowstone Road. This is old U.S. Highway 85-87.

Highway mileposts now reflect Yellowstone Road mileage.

Mile 0.0: **Yellowstone Road** (Wyoming Highway 219, 0.8 miles east of I-25 exit 12). This is old U.S. Highway 85-87. Old U.S. 87 will be followed north to I-25 exit 29.

> Breakfast at 5:30, Capitol Cafe. . . . we were off. Saw aeroplane start from the field at 6:45. Nothing ahead of us but sagebrush. Had an unexpected thrill in passing through the ranks of a U.S. Cavalry Co. on its way to Douglas fair. . . .   Blanche Johnston, 1926
> Had 3 punctures this P.M. going [southbound, on her return trip] into Cheyenne on the rim. As we passed the aero-field saw a plane ascending all lighted up. Rooms at the Windsor Hotel. Took Chiquita [name of her car] to Plains Garage.   Blanche Johnston, 1926

Mile 5.5: Intersect present-day U.S. 85. [Left 0.8 miles to Interstate 25 exit 17; right to Torrington and Lusk.] Here old U.S. 85 turned northeast. Cross U.S. 85 and continue north on old U.S. 87, now Laramie County Road 124.

Mile 10.7: Highway crosses **Lodgepole Creek**. Four miles upstream (west) was the Cheyenne-Deadwood Trail crossing of the creek. [This site can be accessed from I-25 exit 25; west 1.6 miles, then south 0.5 miles.] A 1958 marker here reads:

> **POLE CREEK RANCH** WAS THE FIRST REGULAR STOP ON THE CHEYENNE AND DEADWOOD STAGE. 18 MILES FROM CHEYENNE. A "HOTEL" WAS BUILT IN 1876.

Following Lodgepole Creek was the old **Lodgepole Trail**. This trail branched off the South Platte River Trail at Ovid, Colorado, and ran west along the creek to Cheyenne Pass, then over the Laramie Mountains. The trail intersected the Cherokee Trail (North Branch)-Overland Trail 15 miles west of Laramie.

The route up Lodgepole Creek was one of the finalists for the route of the Union Pacific transcontinental railroad. Surveyed as a possible railroad route in 1863, an 1866 Union Pacific report to Congress stated:

> The Cheyenne Pass over the Black Hills, in connection with the Lodge Pole Valley, its eastern approach, has long been a thoroughfare for travel, and was thus from the beginning brought prominently to the notice of those seeking a route for the Pacific Railroad.

Mile 12.8: The highway veers to the northwest. [West 2.0 miles to I-25 exit 25.]

Mile 16.1: **I-25 East Frontage Road**. (Old U.S. 87 continued northwest, passing the radio tower west of the interstate.) Continue north on the I-25 east frontage road.

Where is Wyoming's Old U.S. Highway 87?

Today, Wyoming's U.S. 87 is one and the same with Interstate 25 for the 160 miles from the Colorado-Wyoming border to exit 160, east of Glenrock. Through Glenrock and Evansville, U.S. 87 shares the route with U.S. 20 and 26. North of Casper, to Buffalo, U.S. 87 again is the same as I-25.

Before the interstate, U.S. Highway 87 was the route from Cheyenne to Casper. The route evolved from the earlier Yellowstone Highway.

What became of old U.S. Highway 87?

Some sections of the pre-interstate highway are still used as **Wyoming State Highways**:

Highway 223 (Terry Ranch Road) south of Cheyenne.
Highway 219 (Yellowstone Road) north of Cheyenne.
Highway 312 from Fergusons Corner to Wheatland.
Highway 320 (North Wheatland Road) from Wheatland to U.S. 26 near Dwyer.
Highway 319 from I-25 exit 94, through Glendo, to U.S. 18-20 east of Orin Jct.
Highway 91 and 96 west of Douglas.

Another section of old U.S. 87 remains as the **I-25 frontage road** from Orin Junction to Douglas.

I-25 Business Routes follow old U.S. 87 through Chugwater, Wheatland, and Douglas.

Some sections of the old highway are now **county roads**:
Laramie County Road 120 (True Road).
Albany Road 123 (Little Bear Road).
Platte County Road 117 (Pepper Road).
Converse County Road 36 (Sunflower Road).
Converse County Road 27 (east of Glenrock).

Some sections of the old highway are **short unnumbered public roads**, often leading to ranches.

Much of old U.S. Highway 87 is now on private property, not open to the public. Many of the now private sections are used by the owner as a **ranch road** or "**two track**." Other sections have virtually disappeared, now little more than a light scar on the land, often following utility poles across open fields.

Sections of old U.S. Highway 87 were **destroyed** by the newer Interstate 25.

On your journey north from the Colorado border to Casper, you will sample all of the above.

Where is Wyoming's Old U.S. Highway 87?
Above: Wyoming Highway 319, formerly U.S. 87, **south of Glendo**.
Interstate 25 passes the base of Sibley Peak.
Below: Interstate 25 frontage road southeast of Douglas. Former
U.S. 20-26-87 is now the frontage road between Orin Junction and Douglas.

Where is Wyoming's Old U.S. Highway 87?
Above: Albany County Road 123 (Little Bear Road). Note the even
older roadbed to the upper left, now a rancher's "two-track."
Below: The **ranch access road southeast of Interstate 25 exit 70** is a
still-paved section of old U.S. 87.

Where is Wyoming's Old U.S. Highway 87?

Above: Old U.S. 87, becoming overgrown with weeds, **3.5 miles south of Chugwater**.

Below: **A very locked gate** across the roadbed of old U.S. 20-26-87 west of Douglas.

Mile 17.8: Interstate 25 exit 29 (Whitaker Road exit).
Old U.S. 87 can be followed north from this exit. The old highway, now True Road, runs west of the interstate to I-25 exit 34. [To bypass the True Road route, continue north on I-25 for 5.0 miles to I-25 exit 34.]

Reset mile 0.0. West from I-25 exit 29 on **Whitaker Road** (Laramie County Rd. 228).
Mile 1.4: [To the south, old U.S. 87 is an unmarked, unimproved ranch road.]
North on **True Road** (Laramie County Road 120, **old U.S. 87**). The 5.2-mile road to I-25 exit 34 closely follows the **Cheyenne-Deadwood Trail**.
Mile 3.4 (approximate): The Cheyenne-Deadwood Trail crossed from the west side of the road to the east.
Mile 5.2: Cross Horse Creek. Here was the site of the **Cheyenne-Deadwood Trail's Horse Creek Ranch**, also known as **Fagan's Ranche**. A meal station, it was 28 miles from Cheyenne.
Mile 5.6 (approximate): The Cheyenne-Deadwood Trail crossed from the east side of the road to the west.
Mile 6.6: I-25 exit 34 (Nimmo Road exit).

Reset mile 0.0. Proceed north from I-25 exit 34 on the **I-25 East Frontage Road**.
Mile 1.4: Site of the **Little Bear Station** on the Cheyenne-Deadwood Trail.

Cheyenne-Deadwood Trail marker: Little Bear Station.
The marker is seen from the interstate, visited from the frontage road.

Little Bear Station marker text:

CHEYENNE, FT. LARAMIE, DEADWOOD TRAIL, 1867-1887, STARTED FROM CAMP CARLIN AND FORT D. A. RUSSELL ON THE WEST EDGE OF CHEYENNE. THIS ROAD FIRST RAN TO FT. LARAMIE AND IN 1876 WAS EXTENDED TO DEADWOOD, DAKOTA TERRITORY, AND THE BLACK HILLS GOLD FIELDS. IT ALSO JOINED THE BOZEMAN ROAD TO MONTANA. LITTLE BEAR STAGE STATION, 150 YARDS EAST, WAS OPENED AS A ROAD RANCH BY ISAAC BARD, MAY 4, 1875. IT BECAME A STAGE STATION IN 1877.

Mile 3.2: **Side trip**: 0.5 miles west on paved **Bristol Road** (Laramie County Road 237) to the **crossing of old U.S. 87**. Views only. A ranch "two-track" leads south. Excellent roadbed of the old highway leads north. Return to the I-25 frontage road.

Mile 5.8 (includes side trip above): I-25 exit 39 (Little Bear Community).

Reset mile 0.0. From I-25 exit 39, **Little Bear Road** (Albany County Road 123) runs east of the interstate, rejoining it at exit 47.

Mile 0.0: Proceed north on Little Bear Road.

Mile 0.7: The road turns northeast, leaving the interstate. Here old U.S. 87 merged from the southwest. The road now follows **old U.S. 87**.

Mile 1.4 (approximate): The Cheyenne-Deadwood Trail crossed the road from the south to the north.

Mile 4.1: Cross South Fork of Bear Creek. Older roadbed to the northwest.

Mile 6.4: North Bear Creek and the site of the **Bear Spring Stage Station**. Facilities included stables and a bar. Here the trail crosses to the east side of the highway. North of the creek crossing, an older roadbed can be seen to the northwest, part of the road now used as a rancher's "two track."

Mile 7.5: Little Bear Road turns to the west. Very broken asphalt of old U.S. 87 can be seen continuing due north.

Mile 7.7: The road passes beneath I-25. North on the **I-25 west frontage road**.

Mile 8.9: I-25 exit 47 (Bear Creek Road exit).

Reset mile 0.0. (At the I-25 West Frontage Road **South Chugwater Highway**). Continue north. The highway runs from I-25 exit 47 to exit 54 (Chugwater). The road enters Chugwater, then merges with the I-25 Business Loop from exit 54.

Mile 0.1: Old U.S. 87 to the west, running between two ranches.

Mile 2.0 (approximate): Cheyenne-Deadwood Trail crossed from east to west of road.

Mile 2.1: Old U.S. 87 visible to the west.

Mile 2.8: Old U.S. 87 runs between the highway and the bluff to the west.

> Took our first picture - a pretty but small cliff or butte just about 4 miles before reaching Chugwater, just passed this butte when we had our first trouble -- gas tank dropped at one end & we heard it hump -- humping along on the ground. Alighted to see what the trouble was and found a nice little gas-geyser all our own. Miss F. soon stopped that however by placing her thumb over it. A car of nice people stopped -- 3 men & 2 women -- the men unravelled the barbs from a barbed-wire fence & wired our tank up so that we went on to Wheatland.
>
> Blanche Johnston, 1926

83

Mile 3.9: Old U.S. 87 merges with the present-day road.
Mile 4.3: Old U.S. 87 veers to the left, along the fence line, then across the open field.

Mile 5.1: **Side trip**: 0.2 miles west on **Blue Rock Road** to views only of the crossing
of **old U.S. 87**.
South: unfenced; asphalt, overgrown with weeds.
North: old highway beyond the gated fence. Return to S. Chugwater Highway.

Mile 6.6 (includes side trip above): Cheyenne-Deadwood Trail crossed from the west
side of the road to the east (approximate location).
Mile 6.8: Old U.S. 87 merges from the southwest.
Mile 7.2: Cross Chugwater Creek.
Mile 7.5: Cross over the Burlington Railroad tracks into **Chugwater**.

Chugwater's still-standing Grant Hotel opened in 1917 and closed about 1970.
It replaced the earlier Banks Hotel which burned in 1916 (the hotel had a bank in it).
The Yellowstone Cafe was located a few lots north of the hotel.

All travelling becomes dull in exact proportion to its rapidity
John Ruskin
What good is speed if the brain has oozed out on the way?
Karl Krause, 1909

Mile 7.8: **Chugwater**. Chugwater was the headquarters of the **Swan Land and Cattle Company**, the largest in Wyoming in the 1880s. Ranch headquarters are 0.2 miles east of town on Wyoming Highway 313. Private property.

Buffalo were driven over the nearby cliffs and when they hit, they made a chug-like sound. Therefore the name - "water at the place where the buffalo chug."

1937 **Cheyenne-Deadwood Trail monument**, on the west side of 1st St.:

CHUGWATER   DIVISION STAGE STATION   CHEYENNE-BLACK HILLS TRAIL
ESTABLISHED MARCH 18, 1876   ABANDONED SEPTEMBER 1887
RUSSELL THORPE, OWNER

Hometown of the Chugwater Chili Corporation, established in 1986.

The town has an old soda fountain in a building that dates from 1918. The building has served as a drug store, then a grocery store. Since the 1940s it has been a soda fountain and community gathering place.

1916 *Yellowstone Highway* ad: "Chugwater Trading Company." [Opened in 1910 and burned in 1928.]

1924 *Park-to-Park Highway* ad: "filling station, only one between Wheatland and Cheyenne."

Continue north on the I-25 Business Loop 2.5 miles north to I-25 exit 57 (Chugwater-TY Basin exit). The highway parallels the Cheyenne-Deadwood Trail, the Burlington Railroad, and Chugwater Creek. All pass beneath Point of Rocks to the west.

Interstate 25: North from Exit 57 to Exit 73. Live with the interstate for 16 miles with several optional side trips.

I-25 milepost 58.3: **Chimney Rock** straight ahead.

I-25 milepost 60.9: Early Yellowstone Highway visible to the right approximating the Cheyenne-Deadwood Trail route.

I-25 milepost 61.0: **Laramie Peak** straight ahead. The peak was the first glimpse of the Rocky Mountains for the west-bound Oregon-California Trail traveler.

I-25 milepost 62.7: Old U.S. 87 veers to the northwest.

I-25 milepost 64.0: Richeau Creek. Old U.S. 87 visible to the west.

I-25 exit 65 (Slater Road exit): **Side trip**: Slater Road (Platte County Road 314) leads two miles east to the crossing of the **Cheyenne-Deadwood Trail** near Richeau Creek. Another 0.8 miles to the Burlington Railroad at **Slater**. To the southeast 1.5 miles is **Chimney Rock**, called "Castle Rock" on the 1916 *Yellowstone Highway* map.

I-25 milepost 65.9: Old highway crosses from the west side of the interstate to the east.

I-25 exit 66: Old U.S. 87 ran 0.1 mile east of the interchange. Just north of the interchange, the old highway crossed to the west side of the interstate.

I-25 milepost 69.8: Old road veers to the northeast.

I-25 exit 70 (Bordeaux Road exit): **Side trip**: 0.1 mile east of the interchange, **Old U.S. 87** can be followed south for 0.6 miles.

[Platte County Road 232, Bordeaux Road, runs six miles east to the **Bordeaux** area on the Cheyenne-Deadwood Trail and the Burlington Railroad. Here was the site of John Hunton's ranch and hotel, both on private property.]

[West of the I-25 exit 70 interchange, **Old U.S. 87** ran northwest to Fergusons Corner.]

I-25 exit 73 (Laramie exit): Old U.S. 87 followed west of I-25 from exit 73 to exit 78 (Wheatland exit). From I-25 exit 73, proceed west on **Wyoming Highway 34** for 1.7 miles to Fergusons Corner. Here was located a filling station and store.
> **Side trip**: South from Fergusons Corner is **old U.S. 87**. A gravel road runs for 0.6 miles, then it turns to a two-track.

[West from Fergusons Corner is Wyoming Highway 34. This is the "Wheatland Cutoff" and old Wyoming Highway 26 which traverses the Laramie Mountains to Bosler, on U.S. 30, the old Lincoln Highway.]

At Fergusons Corner, turn north on **Wyoming Highway 312**. This is **old U.S. 87**. In 6.2 miles the road turns east and enters Wheatland via South St., joining the I-25 Business Loop 0.3 miles north of I-25 exit 78 (Wheatland exit).

I-25 Business Loop runs east on South St. to 9th, then north on 9th to downtown Wheatland.

Wheatland. The region is the largest privately owned irrigation system in the nation. The 60,000-acre project began in 1885. The town was incorporated in 1905.

1915 postcard note mailed from Wheatland:
> Fair roads from Chugwater
> good weather
> 3 punctures
> towed up 1 sand hill.
> Hit Wheatland 2:30

1916 *Yellowstone Highway* guide: Commercial Hotel, "Where the tourists all stop. Headquarters for Automobile Parties." [Built in 1895, it was renamed the LaRamie Hotel.]
> McDougall Clothing Store: "Like a Good Road, a First-Class store is Always Appreciated by Touring Autoists."

1919 Wheatland yearbook: Globe Hotel. "The leading Hotel on the Yellowstone Highway."

1920 Park-to-Park Highway dedication tour: August 28, dinner at the Globe Hotel, public meeting at the Court House.

1924 *Park-to-Park Highway* guide: "Wheatland 'Grease Spot' service station: Watch our road bulletin for all road information. Have your mail addressed in our care when taking a trip over the Yellowstone Highway."

The Ramona Theater opened in the 1920s and was next door to the Park to Park Garage.

From 9th & Gilcrist, continue north 0.9 miles on the I-25 Business Loop to Wyoming Highway 320. Pass the old sugar beet factory which is now a marble plant.

Wheatland to Orin Junction

Miles

1916 map from the
*Yellowstone Highway in
Wyoming and Colorado*

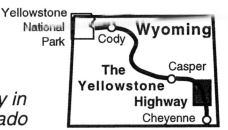

United States Geological Survey map
State of Wyoming, 1980

Present-day highways with
the drive guide route enhanced

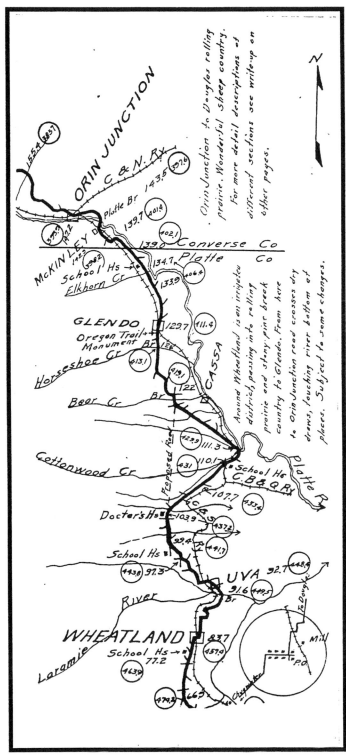

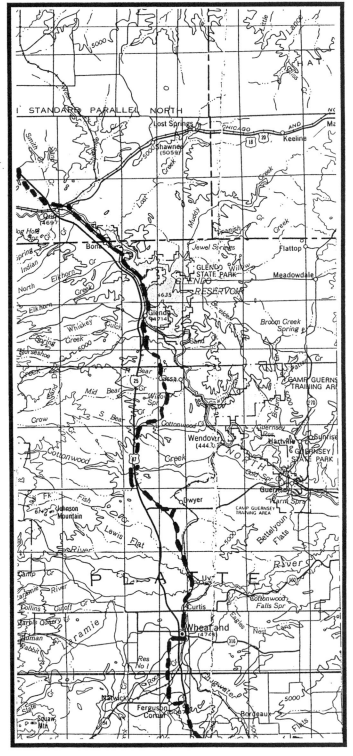

Highway mileposts now reflect Wyoming Highway 320 mileage.

Mile 0.0: **Wyoming Highway 320** (North Wheatland Road): This is **old U.S. 87** and runs north from Wheatland, intersecting U.S. 26, 3.0 miles east of I-25 exit 92.

Mile 3.9: Cross the **Laramie River**. The river runs east to pass Fort Laramie, then empties into the North Platte River. The headwaters of the Laramie River are in Colorado, near Cameron Pass, just north of Rocky Mountain National Park.

Mile 4.5: Jacques LaRamie 1941 marker on the west side of the highway. Marker text:

IN HONOR OF **JACQUES LaRAMEE** FREE TRAPPER WHO CAME TO THIS REGION ABOUT 1815 AND MET AN UNKNOWN FATE, PROBABLY AT THE HANDS OF INDIANS, ABOUT 1820, ON ONE OF THE RIVERS BEARING HIS NAME BETWEEN WHICH THIS MONUMENT STANDS. TRADITION SAYS HE WAS AN HONEST, JUST, AND COURAGEOUS LEADER AND TRADER. HIS NAME IS PERPETUATED BY THREE RIVERS, FT. LARAMIE, THE LARAMIE PLAINS, LARAMIE PEAK, LARAMIE CITY AND LARAMIE COUNTY.

Side trip: 1.0 mile east on Laramie River Road is the site (on private property) of **Uva** (Spanish for grape). The town had a railroad station, railroad section house, church, school, and store. Major shipping point for cattle in the 1890s. The town's importance declined with the growth of Wheatland. [The Yellowstone Highway crossed the Laramie River 0.7 miles to the east of Uva via a long iron bridge. The bridge was removed about 1952 because of many accidents caused by the steep approach from the south.]

1919 Wheatland yearbook: "The Oasis. Candies, ice cream, soft drinks, lunches, tobacco & lodging. We solicit tourist trade. Students - come down and visit us."

Town site of Uva on the old Cheyenne and Northern Railroad route. Foundation of the railroad employee housing building. Photograph taken in 2000.

Mile 5.0: Cross the **North Laramie River**. It empties into the main branch one mile to the southeast.

Mile 12.3: U.S. 26, end of Wyoming Highway 320. [I-25 exit 92 is 2.6 miles west.]

> **Side trip: Dwyer**. 0.7 miles east on U.S. 26 and 0.5 miles north brings one to Dwyer, on the Burlington Railroad. The depot closed in 1931. Area originally called Buckhorn. Developed as a "Homestead Town," Dwyer held local festivals in the 1920s, then was hard hit by the depression of the 1930s.
>
> The old school house, moved from across the railroad tracks, is now the Westgem Gallery.
>
> 1916 *Yellowstone Highway* guide: "Dwyer is a new community in the dry farming section and growing rapidly. A general store, coal and lumber yard, church and school have been established here. There is also a movement on foot for the establishment of a bank."
>
> The first route of the Yellowstone Highway passed through Dwyer, then continued northeast with the railroad to Wendover. The route was then changed to cross the Oregon-California Trail "hill road" near "Convict Hill," north of Dwyer.

An early branch of the Yellowstone Highway climbed "Convict Hill" north of Dwyer. A 1999 photograph shows a California-bound wagon train celebrating the 150th anniversary of that state's gold rush.

From U.S. 26, continue north on Pepper Road. The road is 1.1 miles west of Wyoming Highway 320 and 1.5 miles east of I-25 exit 92.

Dwyer (U.S. 26) to Casper

The Yellowstone Highway Route:

Waterways: The Yellowstone Highway now follows the great "transportation corridor," the North Platte River. U.S. Highway 87 crosses the river twice and crosses several creeks, the names of which are associated with the Oregon-California Trail and Pony Express: Cottonwood, Horseshoe, Elkhorn, La Prele, Box Elder, Deer, and Muddy.

Trails: Following the river was the Oregon-California Trail, early stage routes, the Pony Express, and the first transcontinental telegraph.

Railroads: The Chicago Burlington and Quincy follows the North Platte River. The now-abandoned Chicago & Northwestern joined the route at Orin Junction.

Auto Trails: Continuing north with the Yellowstone and National Park-to-Park Highways are the Buffalo Highway and Glacier to Gulf Highway. The Powder River Trail follows the route to Douglas, where it branches north to Buffalo. The Atlantic Yellowstone Pacific Hiway joins at Orin Junction; the Grant Highway at Douglas.

State Highways: Wyoming Highway 11 was the original number given to the Yellowstone Highway route.

U.S. Highways: U.S. Highway 87 is joined by U.S. 26 near Dwyer. This highway follows the North Platte River from Ogallalah, Nebraska. The highway follows the Oregon-California Trail, passing trail landmarks such as Scotts Bluff and Fort Laramie. U.S. 18-20 joins U.S. 26-87 at Orin Junction. The original U.S. Highway from Cheyenne to Orin Junction was given the number U.S. 185.

Today: Interstate 25 tracks northwest to Casper. U.S. 20-26-87 has its own identity from Glenrock west to Casper.

1915 *Automobile Blue Book*:

Douglas to Casper, Wyo. - 53.4 m.

Via Glenrock, following the general course of the Platte River all the way. The first part across Converse County good graded convict roads. Balance of the way fair to good graded roads.

1922 *Automobile Blue Book*:

Douglas to Casper, Wyo. - 53.8 m.

Via Glenrock and Parkerton. Dirt all the way, a few miles of which have been gravelled. This route follows the North Platte river practically all the way, and passes thru the Big Muddy oil field, in which Parkerton and Glenrock are located. This is a section of the Yellowstone highway.

 Red & white

Atlantic Yellowstone Pacific Hiway

BRISTLES SCRATCHED
HIS COOKIE'S MAP
THAT'S WHAT
MADE POOR
GINGER SNAP
Burma-Shave

 Yellow

Black

Yellow

Grant Highway

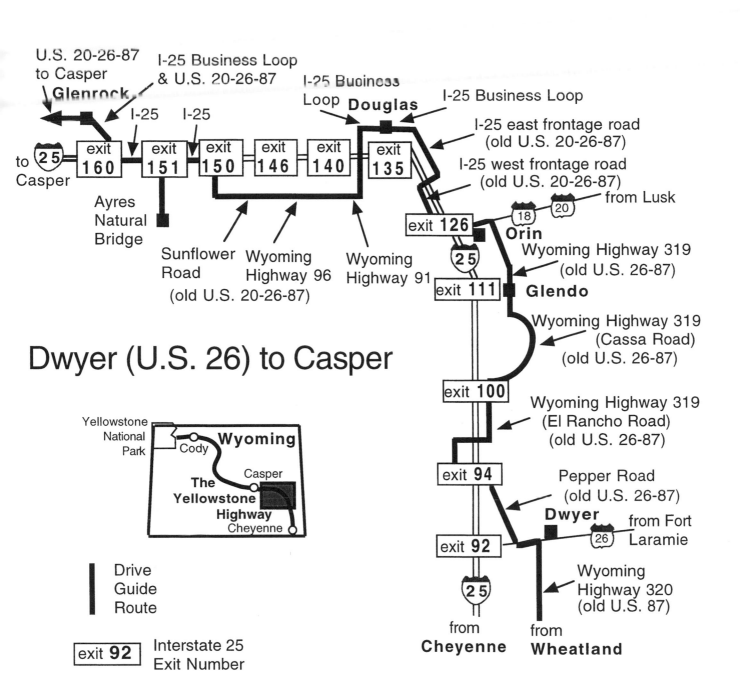

Dwyer (U.S. 26) to Casper

U.S. 20-26-87 to Casper
Glenrock

I-25 Business Loop & U.S. 20-26-87

I-25 Business Loop **Douglas**

I-25 Business Loop

I-25 east frontage road (old U.S. 20-26-87)

I-25 west frontage road (old U.S. 20-26-87)

I-25

I-25

to **25** to Casper

exit **160**

exit **151**

exit **150**

exit **146**

exit **140**

exit **135**

exit **126**

from Lusk

18 **20**

Orin

Wyoming Highway 319 (old U.S. 26-87)

25

exit **111**

Glendo

Ayres Natural Bridge

Sunflower Road (old U.S. 20-26-87)

Wyoming Highway 96

Wyoming Highway 91

Wyoming Highway 319 (Cassa Road) (old U.S. 26-87)

exit **100**

Wyoming Highway 319 (El Rancho Road) (old U.S. 26-87)

exit **94**

Pepper Road (old U.S. 26-87)

Dwyer

from Fort Laramie **26**

exit **92**

25

from **Cheyenne**

from **Wheatland**

Wyoming Highway 320 (old U.S. 87)

Yellowstone National Park

Wyoming

Cody

Casper

The Yellowstone Highway

Cheyenne

| Drive Guide Route

exit **92** Interstate 25 Exit Number

Friends
Don't Let
Friends
Drive the Interstate

Pepper Road (Platte County Road 117, **old U.S. 26-87**) runs northwest from present-day U.S. 26. The road starts 1.1 miles west of Wyoming Highway 320 from Wheatland and 1.5 miles east of I-25 exit 92. Pepperville, which had a service station and grocery store, operated here into the 1990s.

Proceed northwest on **Pepper Road** for 3.1 miles to I-25 exit 94. The road is now gravel, the asphalt having been recently removed.

From I-25 exit 94, Wyoming Highway 319 runs north to U.S. 18-20. This intersection is 1.8 miles east of I-25 exit 126 (Orin Junction exit).

Wyoming Highway 319 is old U.S. 26-87.

Highway mileposts begin at mile 3.1 [The distance from U.S. 26 via Pepper Road]:

Mile 3.2: I-25 exit 94. Follow **Wyoming Highway 319** (El Rancho Road) north along the west side of the interstate.

Mile 4.8: The road passes beneath Coleman Butte.

Mile 5.0: Pass under I-25. Wyoming Highway 319 now follows east of the interstate.

Mile 5.3: Cross Cottonwood Creek. The **Oregon-California Trail "hill road"** crossed the highway north of the creek. This was the early branch of the trail, used by the Mormons in 1847.

Mile 9.0: The old highway passes I-25 exit 100 (Cassa Road exit).

Wyoming Highway 319 highway mileposts change at I-25 exit 100.

Mile 100.1: I-25 (Cassa Road) interchange. North on Cassa Road. The highway, **old U.S. 87**, veers east, away from the interstate and beneath Pine Ridge to the south.

Mile 103.7: The highway descends from the plateau to the North Platte River valley.

Mile 105.2: The area was called "**Oasis,**" a popular campsite on the Yellowstone Highway. East 1.5 miles, the **Oregon-California Trail "river road"** descended to the North Platte River valley, following closely the power lines east of the highway. This branch was used by the stages, Pony Express, and telegraph.

Mile 111.0: Highway 319 approaches the interstate, at the base of **Sibley Peak**. The Peak was named for its shape which resembles a Sibley Tent of the Civil War era.

Mile 112.4: Marker for the **Horseshoe Pony Express Station** and the crossing of the **Oregon-California Trail "river road."** Site of the Bellwood stage station and a Pony Express station.

    1937 Marker Text: "530 yards southeast of this monument on the Oregon Trail was the site of Horseshoe Creek Pony Express and U.S. Military Telegraph and Stage Station built in 1860."

The Oregon-California Trail "river road" now veers northwest, away from the river. A branch of the **Bozeman Trail** continued north, crossing the North Platte River at Bridgers Ferry southeast of Orin Junction.

Mile 114.3: Cross the Burlington tracks. The road is now marked "South Yellowstone."

Mile 114 6· **Glondo**. 0.2 miles east of I-25 exit 111. "The most in a small town." The Glendo Museum is in the Town Hall building, on the west side of old U.S. 26-87. The Old West Saloon and Restaurant was opened in 1934. 1920 Park-to-Park Highway dedication tour: Lunch.

Right: "**Trail Hotel**" on Glendo's old U.S. 26-87, appropriately named North Yellowstone. The hotel was originally called the Glendo Hotel. A 2000 photograph.

At Glendo, the highway mileposts change again, starting at mile 211.9.

Mile 211.9: **Wyoming Highway 319** (old U.S. 26-87) continues north from Glendo, paralleling the Burlington Northern Railroad and Interstate 25, both to the west. Glendo Reservoir is to the east. In town, the highway is marked North Yellowstone.

Mile 215.3: The highway curves slightly to the left. Before completion of the **Glendo Reservoir** in 1958, the highway continued straight, now a gravel access road to a Glendo State Park picnic area.

Mile 217.9: Cross Elkhorn Creek. The **Elkhorn Pony Express Station** was located eight miles to the southwest.

Mile 218.8: The old "pre-Glendo Reservoir" highway merges from the right. The old highway is now a non-motorized path to the Glendo Reservoir.

Mile 223.6: McKinley railroad siding. The old McKinley Post Office was 0.5 miles to the northeast, across the North Platte River.

The 1915 *Blue Book* noted a long wooden bridge over the North Platte River. This bridge was built in 1914 to service the sheep operations in the area and was the early Yellowstone Highway crossing of the North Platte River.

Mile 225.3: Immediately south of the bridge over the North Platte River is the **Bridger Ferry** marker:

> "Jim Bridger's Ferry established in 1864, was located 1500 feet up the river from this monument   1937"

A Mrs. Carrington noted in 1866:

> Bridger's ferry boat ingeniously worked its own way to and fro by such an adjustment of cables, pulleys and such adaptations to the currents, that the round trip was made in about eleven minutes.

The ferry was established to cross Bozeman Trail travelers to the north side of the river and the Child's Cutoff branch of the Oregon-California Trail.

Mile 225.3: Cross the **North Platte River**.

Mile 226.1: **Wyoming Highway 319 ends** at the intersection with U.S. 18-20. Here, 1.8 miles east of I-25 exit 126 (Orin Junction exit), U.S. 18-20 from Lusk, Wyoming, merges with old U.S. 26-87. Also merging from the east is the old route of the Chicago & Northwestern Railroad and the Atlantic Yellowstone Pacific Hiway.

Highway mileposts now reflect U.S. 18-20 mileage.

Mile 1.8: End of Wyoming Highway 319 from Glendo. **West on U.S. 18-20**.

Mile 1.2: **Side trip**: 0.5 miles southwest on Converse County Road 1 (Irvine Road) to the settlement of **Orin**. The exit from U.S. 18-20 is just east of the highway overpass. Orin was a major railroad settlement.

1923-1924 *Harvey Tourist Auto Guide*:

> 'TOURISTS HOME' Just What the Name Implies
> Garage - Rooms - Lunches - Gas - Oil - Tobaccos - Cold Drinks - Candy - Baths   Free Auto Ground   Wood and Water

Mile 0.1: Rest area, southeast of I-25 exit 126. Across U.S. 18-20 and below the level of the present road are a bridge and roadbed of the old highway.

"Six Line Highway Jingles"

Burma-Shave signs appeared along highways from 1926-1963. The six 18-inch-high, 40 inch-wide signs advertised the early brushless shaving cream. The "mini billboards" were set approximately 50 yards apart, so that at 35 miles-per-hour, the signs were three seconds apart. The signs were red with white lettering and were made of white pine which absorbed gunfire.

SLOW DOWN PA	BEN	IF YOU
SAKES ALIVE	MET ANNA	DON'T KNOW
MA MISSED SIGNS	MADE A HIT	WHOSE SIGNS THESE ARE
FOUR	NEGLECTED BEARD	YOU CAN'T HAVE
AND FIVE	BEN-ANNA SPLIT	DRIVEN VERY FAR
Burma-Shave	*Burma-Shave*	*Burma-Shave*

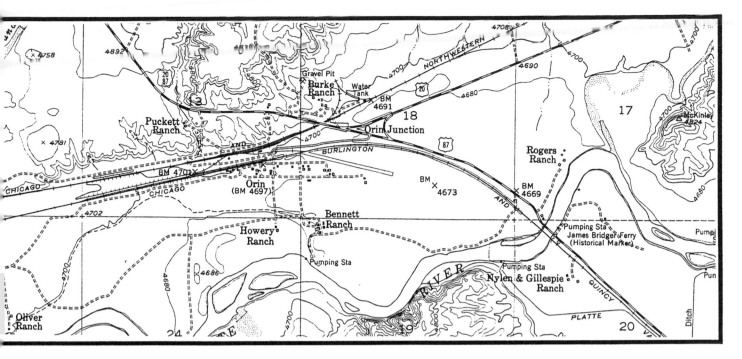

1950 United States Geological Survey **7.5 minute map, Orin Junction.**
Note the Bridger Ferry historical marker south of the North Platte River.

Orin was a major transportation junction, even before the coming of Interstate 25. The Chicago & Northwestern and the Chicago Burlington & Quincy railroads converge here. The Atlantic Yellowstone Pacific Hiway merges here, as does U.S. Highway 18-20 from Lusk. U.S. 18 ends at Orin Junction.

The 1941 Work Projects Administration (WPA) guide stated:

> The old Orin railroad crossing, an engineering freak that sent automobiles across two railroads on an incline and at an angle, became notorious as a danger point, and in 1936 an overpass was built and US 20-26-87 was rerouted past Orin.

I-25 **Frontage** **Road**. From I-25 exit 126, northwest to exit 135, the frontage road was **old U.S. 20-26-87**. It can be taken the entire nine miles, from Orin Junction to Douglas. The original Yellowstone Highway followed more closely the North Platte River to the southwest. This was the Child's Cutoff section of the Oregon-California Trail and the path taken by the railroads [now Converse County Road 1].

Highway mileposts now reflect miles from Orin Junction.

Mile 0.0: North on the Interstate 25 west frontage road. **Laramie Peak** dominates the skyline to the southwest. At an elevation of 10,272 feet, it was the first "real mountain" seen by the west-bound Oregon-California Trail traveler.

Mile 5.1: Pass under I-25, continue northwest on the I-25 east frontage road.

Mile 9.4: **Merge with the** **I-25** **Business** **Loop**. I-25 exit 135 is 0.2 miles to the southeast. Follow **old U.S. 20-26-87** (west on Richards St., north on 4th St., west on Center St.) for 2.8 miles to downtown **Douglas**.

95

Douglas. Established when the Fremont Elkhorn & Missouri Valley Railroad [later the Chicago & Northwestern] arrived in August 1886.

Douglas Railroad Interpretive Center is located between downtown and the fairgrounds, south of the highway. Here is the original Chicago & Northwestern Depot, built in 1886 and open continuously until the 1950s. Here are several railroad cars from various railroads and Burlington steam locomotive #5633. Douglas acquired the depot in 1990 and it houses the Chamber of Commerce.

Wyoming State Fairgrounds. The State Fair was first held here in 1905 on land donated by the Chicago & Northwestern Railroad.

The **Wyoming Pioneer Memorial Museum** is located on the state fairgrounds. The original log building was built in 1925, the modern facility opened in 1956.

The **College Inn Bar** opened in 1906 and has operated continuously since then. Originally it had nine sleeping rooms upstairs, with a tenth room used for gambling.

The **LaBonte Hotel**, opened in 1914, is still in operation.

The **Plains Motel and Restaurant** complex, on Richards St., has been added to over the years, including buildings brought in from other locations. Much of the woodwork in the restaurant, the kitchen equipment, and the motel registration desk are from the old Henning Hotel in Casper.

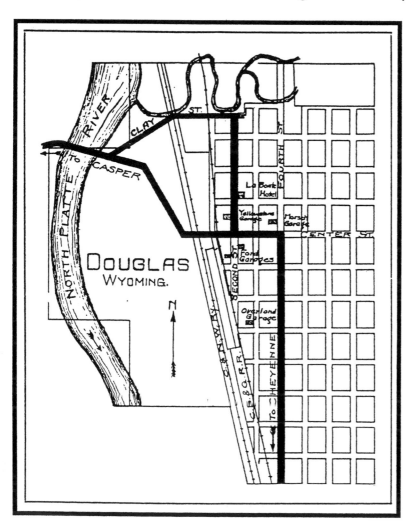

1915 *Blue Book* directions: "North on 2nd to Clay St., left, under 2 railroads, across long wood bridge over Platte River." [The Burlington overpass is still in use, and the Chicago & Northwestern grade is visible north and south of Clay St.]

The 1916 *Yellowstone Highway* guide called Douglas "The Good Roads Town." The Douglas Good Roads Club, predecessor of the Chamber of Commerce, was an advocate of good roads. The map shows the following garages: Overland, Morsch, Yellowstone, and Ford. It also noted the LaBonte Hotel.

Douglas Map from the 1916 *Yellowstone Highway in Wyoming and Colorado*.

1920 Park-to-Park Highway dedication tour: members presented programs at the Congregational Church and the Princess Theater. [Opened in 1916, the theater was renamed Mesa in 1937.] Dinner was at Esterbrook, south of Douglas.

1922 *Blue Book* ads:

"Yellowstone Garage, Tourist Headquarters." [In operation from about 1913 to 1928, it is now the Moose Lodge on Second St.]

"HOTEL LABONTE, On the Yellowstone Highway, one day's drive by motor from either Cheyenne or Lost Cabin."

1924 *Park-to-Park Highway* guide:

"FREE CAMP. Right in the State Fair Grounds Park. Splendid Shade, pure water, plenty fuel. Stop here a day."

Douglas is the official home of the Jackalope, a registered trademark of the Douglas Chamber of Commerce.

He sits prominently in Antelope Park, at Center and 3th St. From 1965 to 1984, a smaller version sat in the middle of Center St.

Jackalope.
sketch by Jane Whiteley

Some **Jackalope "facts"**:

Body of a jackrabbit, antlers like a deer, speed of an antelope.
Rarest animal in North America.
His scientific name is "pedigrus lepaisalopus ineptus."
His ancestors are the dynalopes and jackasaurs.
Can imitate the human voice.
Sings, in any key, only on dark nights, before thunderstorms.
When a full moon rises, gets confused, runs backwards.
As horns grow, they pull on his skull, causing him to become cross-eyed.
After drinking alcohol, attempts to catch bullets in his mouth.
Feeds on fur-bearing trout.
Hates fences, tries to destroy fence posts by chewing on them.
A group of Jackalopes is referred to as a "Committee."

Page from the **APY Hiway guidebook** used by Blanche Johnston in 1926.
Courtesy of the Carnegie Branch Library for Local History, Boulder, Colorado.

1926 Blanche Johnston diary: "At Douglas we first picked up our pretty APY signs which from then on [to Shoshoni] became our greatest guide and friend."

The Atlantic Yellowstone Pacific Hiway (APY) was established much later than the Yellowstone Highway. "APY" was often painted over the Black "H" on the Yellowstone Highway markers and rocks.

Leaving the Yellowstone Highway at Douglas, the Powder River Trail ran north through Buffalo, Wyoming, and Miles City, Montana. Joining the Yellowstone Highway at Douglas was the Grant Highway from Lusk, Wyoming.

<u>Side trip</u>: **Fort Fetterman State Historic Site**, eleven miles northwest of Douglas on Wyoming Highway 93. A supply post, it was established in 1867 to protect travelers on the Bozeman Trail. Abandoned in 1882. On the grounds are the restored officers quarters and an ordnance warehouse. Grounds open summers only.

Reset mile 0.0. **From downtown Douglas** (Center St. & 2nd), continue **west on the I-25 Business Loop**. **W. Center St. becomes West Yellowstone.**

Mile 0.5: Cross the North Platte River.

Mile 1.1: Interpretive sign on north side of highway: "Fort Fetterman."

Mile 1.2: Take **Wyoming Highway 91-94** (River Bend Drive) south. [This turn is 0.3 miles east of I-25 exit 140.]

Mile 1.5: Turn west to pass under I-25. Turn northwest on **Wyoming Highway 91** (Cold Springs Road). [Wyoming Highway 94 continues south to Esterbrook.]

Douglas through Casper

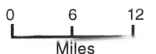

0 6 12
Miles

1916 map from the
*Yellowstone Highway in
Wyoming and Colorado*

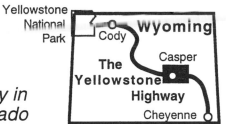

Yellowstone
National
Park

Cody **Wyoming**

**The
Yellowstone
Highway** Casper

Cheyenne

United States Geological Survey map
State of Wyoming, 1980

Present-day highways with
the drive guide route enhanced

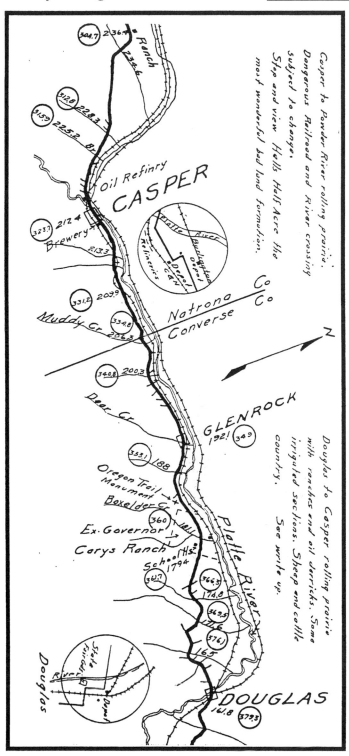

Casper to Powder River rolling prairie.
Dangerous Railroad and River crossing
subject to change.
Stop and view Hells Half Acre the
most wonderful bad land formation.

Douglas to Casper rolling prairie
with ranches and oil derricks. Some
irrigated sections. Sheep and cattle
country. See write up.

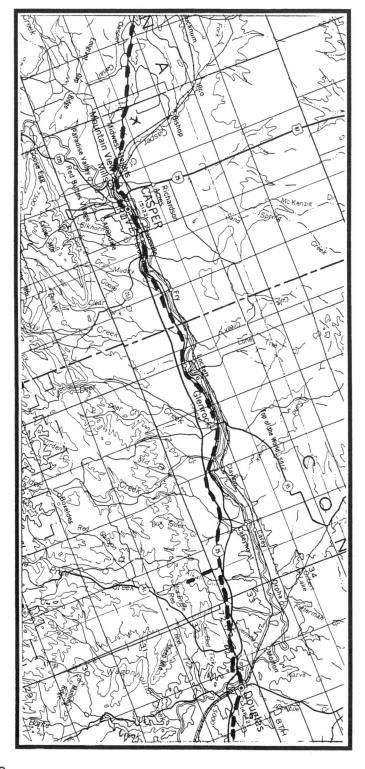

99

Highway mileposts now reflect Wyoming Highway 91 mileage.
Mile 0.0: Northwest on Wyoming Highway 91.
Mile 1.5: The highway (now old U.S. 20-26-87) turns due west, away from I-25.
Mile 3.0: Continue west on **Wyoming Highway 96**; Highway 91 turns south.
Highway mileposts now reflect Wyoming Highway 96 mileage.
Mile 0.0: West on Wyoming Highway 96.
Mile 0.9: **Two historic markers**, on the south side of the road.

Bill Hooker marker dates from 1931:

> COMMEMORATIVE OF **BILL HOOKER** BULLWACKER WHO BUILT AND LIVED IN A CABIN ON LABONTE CREEK TEN MILES FROM THIS POINT ON THE BOZEMAN TRAIL IN 1874

1913 Oregon Trail marker:

> **THE OREGON TRAIL**   1841
>   FOUR MILES SOUTH
> FT FETTERMAN 1867   SEVEN MILES NORTH
> HIGHWAY CROSSES FETTERMAN TRAIL
>   ROUTE HERE

Glenrock billboard at westbound I-25, exit 146. I-25 curves to the right while old U.S. 20-26-87 (Sunflower Road) continues west along the power poles.

Mile 3.1: I-25 exit 146 (La Prele exit).
Reset mile 0.0. Continue west, from I-25 exit 146, on **Sunflower Road** (Converse County Road 36, also marked Sunflower Trail at the east end). The 4.4-mile-long road is **old U.S. 20-26-87** and follows the power poles west to I-25, exit 150.
Mile 1.6: Cross La Prele Creek. The **La Prele Pony Express Station** was three miles upstream, to the southwest.
Mile 4.4: I-25 exit 150 (Inez exit). Note the field of farm machinery to the northeast.

West on **Interstate 25** one mile, from exit 150 to exit 151
I-25 exit 151 (Natural Bridge exit).

> **Side trip**: 5.0 miles south of the I-25 exit 151 interchange, on Converse County Road 13, is **Ayres Natural Bridge**. The bridge was noted by many Oregon-California Trail travelers. An interpretive sign is south of the interstate interchange. The **Oregon-California Trail** is crossed 2.4 miles south of the interstate. On the east side of the road is a 1913 **Oregon Trail marker**. The **La Prele Pony Express Station** was located a mile to the southeast.

Continue west on Interstate 25 from exits 151 to 160.

> [U.S. Highway 20-26-87 continued northwest from the I-25 exit 151 interchange on what was also called the "Old Douglas Road." The road is closed to the public.]

I-25 milepost 152.2: Parking area (westbound only). **Oregon Trail marker**:

> THREE MEN NAMED SHARP, FRANKLIN, AND TAYLOR, AND ONE UNKNOWN MAN WERE KILLED BY INDIANS JULY 12, 1864 WHERE THE OREGON TRAIL CROSSES LITTLE BOX ELDER CREEK 2 1/2 MILES S.W. OF HERE. THEY ARE BURIED 4 MILES S.W. BY THE GRAVE OF MARY KELLY WHO ALSO WAS KILLED JULY 13, 1864. ERECTED BY THE HISTORICAL LANDMARK COMMISSION OF WYOMING 1954.

I-25 milepost 155.9: Cross Box Elder Creek. The **Box Elder Pony Express Station** was a mile to the southwest. Here also was the Careyhurst Ranch. U.S. Senator Robert D. Carey was one of the largest ranchers in the area.

I-25 exit 160 (East Glenrock exit): Exit the interstate onto the **I-25 Business Loop** to Glenrock. This is **U.S. 20-26-87** which will be followed west to Casper.

Highway mileposts are a continuation of Interstate 25 mileage.

Mile 161.1: **Side trip**: 0.4 miles from I-25 exit 160, turn east for 0.4 miles on Converse County Road 27 to a 1913 **Oregon Trail marker**. The grave of trail traveler H. A. Unthank is south of the marker on private property. Unthank died July 2, 1850. The county road is **old U.S. 20-26-87**, also called "Old Douglas Road."

Mile 161.7: Chicago & Northwestern Railroad grade and bridge north of the highway.

Mile 165.6: **Glenrock**. Site of the Deer Creek Station, established in 1857 as a trading post and stage station. The site and interpretive sign is at 3rd & Center. The Chicago & Northwestern Railroad arrived in 1887.

> In town is the 1916 **Higgins Hotel**, now a bed & breakfast and its Paisley Shawl Restaurant. Billed in an early ad as the "Finest Hotel north of Denver."

> **F. V. Hayden marker** is located north of the Higgins Hotel in Kimball Park. Hayden wintered here in 1859, with the Raynolds expedition. Marker text:

> > To all Pioneers who passed this way and in memory of Pioneer Geologist **Ferdinand V. Hayden**   chief U. S. Geological Survey of the Territories 1867-78   Born at Westfield Mass. 1829   Erected by William Henry Jackson, a member of the Dr. F. V. Hayden expedition 1870-1878   1931

> 1916 *Yellowstone Highway* ad: "Hotel Kimball, Headquarters for Automobile Parties."

> 1920 Park-to-Park Highway dedication tour: members were entertained at lunch at the French Cafe by members of the Community Club.

1924 *Park-to-Park Highway* ad:

Glenrock - The place "Where the West Begins."   Free Tourist Camp
When One Travels One Must Eat!   Steam Heat, Good Rooms, Good Eats!
GLENROCK HOTEL

Mile 166.3: Interpretive sign: "Rock in the Glen."

Mile 168.4: North of the highway are the graves of J. P. Parker (died July 1, 1860) and M. Ringo. Marked by the Oregon-California Trails Association. Private property.

Mile 170.7: **Parkerton.**
　　Side trip: North on an unmarked road 0.1 mile to old U.S. 20-26-87.

　　　　West on the old highway 0.5 miles (passing an abandoned brick machine shop) to a **Pony Express marker**, a 1913 **Oregon Trail marker**, and the **Ada Magill grave**. She died in 1864. The grave is only 30 feet north of the old highway and 15 feet northeast of the Parkerton railroad siding.

　　　　Continue west 0.2 miles, then south 0.1 mile on Converse County Road 22 (Cole Creek Road) to rejoin U.S. 20-26-87 at milepost 171.6.

Mile 172.8: The old highway is visible following the power poles to the southwest.

Mile 180.3: The old road rejoins the present-day highway from the southeast.

Mile 182.6: Note old highway to the south.

Mile 186.9: **Evansville.** [South 0.2 miles to I-25 exit 185.]
　　Side trip: North on Curtis St. 1.0 mile to the site of **Reshaw's Bridge**. John Richard [Reshaw] operated a toll bridge here from 1851-1867.

　　Continue west on U.S. 20-26-87, the "Old Glenrock Highway."

Mile 187.9: Pass over I-25 near exit 186A. Continue west on U.S. 20-26-87 business route. This is **East Yellowstone Highway** following the tracks of the Chicago & Northwestern Railroad. In 1.6 miles, at Kimball St., jog west on **2nd St.** [An older route ran west on East "C" Street to McKinley St., then south to East Yellowstone Highway.] 0.3 miles west to 2nd St. and Center. **Downtown Casper.**

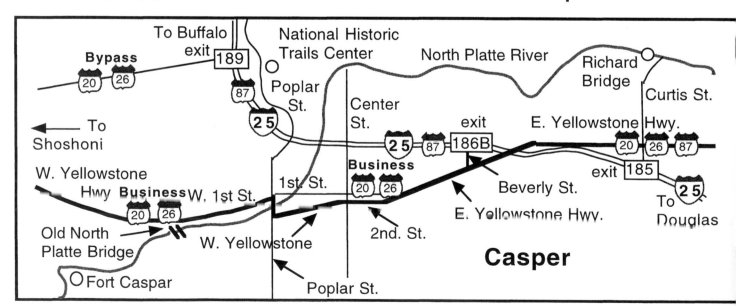

Casper. Louis Guinard built a bridge across the North Platte River here in 1858. This Platte Bridge Station was an army post from 1862-1867. The post was renamed Fort Caspar, in honor of Caspar Collins, who was killed here in 1865.

The town was established in 1888 when the Chicago & Northwestern Railroad arrived from Glenrock. Casper was end of track for 17 years. The tracks within the city are being converted into a hiking and biking trail.

Casper was known as the "Oil Capital of the Rockies." The first refinery was built here in 1895, but the big discoveries were made in 1915.

1136 Center Street, Looking South, Casper, Wyoming, Showing Hotels and Business District

Postcard of **Casper's Center Street**. Only an empty but structurally sound Hotel Townsend remains of the several large hotels along the street. Looking south to Casper Mountain in the background.

Fort Caspar was the site of Louis Guinard's bridge across the North Platte River. Abandoned as an army post in 1867, the fort buildings were reconstructed in 1936 as a WPA project. Modern museum.

The 1914 **Pioneer Memorial** is located at A Street and Center in front of the County Courthouse. The memorial was moved here in 1955 from Center and Midwest Ave. near the old Chicago & Northwestern depot. Marker text:
PIONEER MONUMENT   ERECTED ON THE SITE OF THE OLD OREGON TRAIL IN MEMORY OF THE PIONEERS WHO BLAZED THE WAY.   NATRONA COUNTY PIONEER ASSOCIATION.

National Historic Trails Center. Depicts the history of the Oregon-California, Pony Express, and Mormon Trails. 1501 N. Poplar St.

1920 Park-to-Park Highway dedication tour: members treated to dinner at the Henning Hotel, hosted by the Casper Auto Club and Chamber of Commerce.

1922 *Blue Book* ad: "'The Pride of Wyoming' Hotel Henning Wyoming's largest and Finest Hotel and on the Main Road to Yellowstone Park." [The hotel opened in 1917. When the hotel was razed, the hotel's kitchen equipment, registration desk, and some woodwork was moved to the Plains Motel complex in Douglas.]

1924 *Park-to-Park Highway* ad: "The Virginian Hotel - 50 Rooms - All Modern, The Family Hotel."

1926 Blanche Johnston diary:
"Lights twinkled on as we approached Casper. Paving about 2 miles out."

From downtown Casper, continue west on 2nd Street, old U.S. 20-26-87.
Reset mile 0.0. Downtown **Casper**, 2nd and Center. Proceed west on **2nd Street** which becomes **West Yellowstone Highway** west of David St.

Mile 0.1: At 230 W. Yellowstone is the 1918 Casper Auto Company building. It housed an auto dealership and garage until 1970.
1922 *Blue Book*: "On the way to the Park. . . . High Grade Motor Cars."

The Yellowstone Highway passed the Standard Oil Refinery west of Casper.
A pipeline is shown crossing the North Platte River.
Photograph courtesy of the Wyoming Division of Cultural Resources.

The now-closed Standard Oil Refinery was the largest in the world at one time. The refinery site is being converted to a public park.

Mile 0.6: Turn north on **Poplar Street** (Wyoming Highway 220) and cross the North Platte River. [West Yellowstone Highway (old U.S. 20-26-87) continued west, along the North Platte River and past the old Standard Oil Refinery.]
Mile 0.7: Turn west on **U.S. Business 20-26** (West 1st Street).

Highway mileposts now reflect U.S. Business 20-26 mileage. (Poplar St. is mile 2.5).
Mile 3.5 (one mile west of Poplar St.): The Yellowstone Highway and old U.S. 20-26-87 bridge across the North Platte River is to the south, opposite the bentonite plant. Here West 1st St. becomes **West Yellowstone Highway**. Here also, old U.S. 87 turned north to Buffalo and Sheridan.
1915 *Blue Book*: "oil tanks on left; bear right across long bridge over Platte River. Fork just beyond bridge (road straight ahead goes to Sheridan)."

The 1920 National Park-to-Park Highway dedication tour members
stop on the **highway bridge over the North Platte River** west of Casper.
Standard Oil Refinery and Casper Mountain across the river to the south.
A. G. Lucier photograph, courtesy of the Hinckley Library, Northwest College.

Mile 4.5: **Side trip**: One mile south to **Fort Caspar** via Wyoming Blvd.
Mile 4.9: Poison Spider Road branches west, closely following the Oregon-California Trail. The Yellowstone Highway now leaves the emigrant trail.
Mile 6.0: Merge with present-day **U.S. 20-26**. We will follow U.S. 20 all the way to Yellowstone National Park; but don't quit reading, we have side trips and more.

Casper to Shoshoni

The Yellowstone Highway Route:

Waterways: The highway leaves the North Platte River, crosses branches of Casper Creek and the South Fork of the Powder River, then follows down Poison Creek, a tributary of the Wind River. The early branch of the Yellowstone Highway through Lost Cabin ascended Bridger Creek, then descended Buffalo Creek to the Bighorn River, avoiding the Wind River Canyon south of Thermopolis.

Trails: The Bridger Trail is crossed approximately one mile west of the town of Waltman. The early branch of the Yellowstone Highway through and north of Lost Cabin followed closely the Bridger Trail.

Railroads: The highway follows closely the now-abandoned tracks of the Chicago & Northwestern Railroad from Natrona west to Shoshoni. The later Chicago Burlington & Quincy Railroad follows north of the same general path.

Auto Trails: The Buffalo Highway, Glacier to Gulf Highway, Grant Highway, and the Atlantic Yellowstone Pacific Hiway shared the route of the Yellowstone and National Park-to-Park Highways.

State Highways: Wyoming Highway 11 was the original state highway number for the Casper to Shoshoni road.

U.S. Highway: U.S. 20 was the original number assigned to the highway in 1926.

Today: U.S. Highway 20-26 runs an even 100 miles from Casper to Shoshoni.

1915 *Automobile Blue Book*:

Casper to Thermopolis, Wyo. - 138.7 m.

Via Lost Cabin. Fair to good natural dirt roads practically all the way.

1922 *Automobile Blue Book*:

Casper to Thermopolis, Wyo. - 133.7 m.

Via Powder River and Lost Cabin. Principally natural prairie roads with stretches of improved highway. During certain periods of the year it is best to use the Birdseye pass road via Shoshoni. Local inquiry should be made at Powder River. The road winds over hills and valleys thru a sparsely settled, barren sagebrush country.

Seeing America Swiftly has been made such a simple matter that a person really hasn't time to find out much about what one is really looking at. There isn't the incentive, for one thing.   Ned Frost, 1929

Red & white

Atlantic Yellowstone Pacific Hiway

THE CHICK
HE WED
LET OUT A WHOOP
FELT HIS CHIN AND
FLEW THE COOP
Burma-Shave

Yellow

Black

Yellow

Grant Highway

West of Casper through Lost Cabin

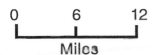
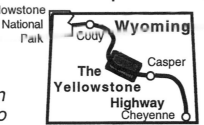

Yellowstone National Park

Cody

Wyoming

Casper

The Yellowstone Highway

Cheyenne

1916 map from the
*Yellowstone Highway in
Wyoming and Colorado*

United States Geological Survey map
State of Wyoming, 1980

Present-day highways with
the drive guide route enhanced

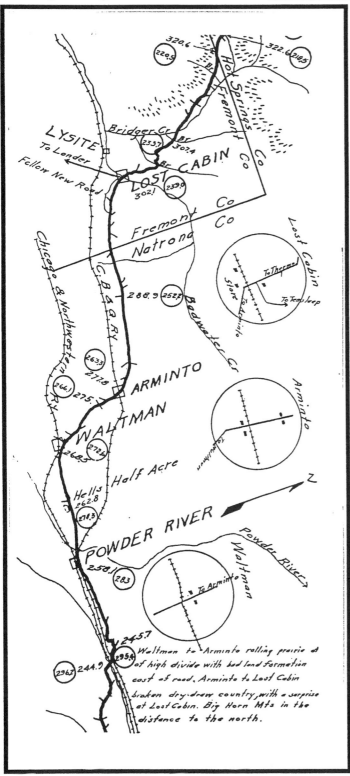

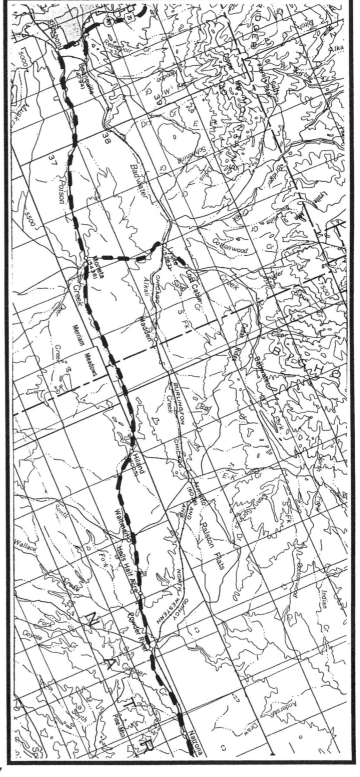

Highway mileposts now reflect U.S. 20-26 mileage from Casper.

Mile 6.0: **West on <u>U.S.</u> <u>20-26</u>** from the intersection of West Yellowstone Highway (U.S. <u>Business</u> 20-26) and U.S. 20-26.

Mile 18.4: Natrona County Road 125. [Access to the Bureau of Land Management's "South Big Horn / Red Wall Back Country Byway." This is a 101-mile loop that retraces the route of livestock pioneers who used it to trail cattle and sheep to the higher mountain pastures. Byway rejoins U.S. 20-26 at Waltman, 32 miles west.]

Mile 21.2: Stone ranch building north of the highway is an **old stage station**, in use from 1890-1906. Private property. The stage and freight road ran from the Chicago & Northwestern Railroad terminus at Casper to Thermopolis. The route closely followed the 1864 Bridger Trail. The stage line was discontinued in 1906 when the railroad extended its line to Shoshoni and Lander.

A 1999 photograph of the "**Stone Ranch**,"
a stage stop on the Casper to Thermopolis route, via Lost Cabin.

Mile 28.3: Highway rejoins the route of the Burlington Railroad and the now abandoned Chicago & Northwestern Railroad, both which took a more northerly course west of Casper.

Mile 30.4: **Natrona**. The present residence was moved from the north side of the railroad tracks and present-day highway. The early highway also ran north of the railroad tracks.

　　1915 *Blue Book*: "Pass Natrona station on left"

　　1924 *Park-to-Park Highway* ad: "Filling station, Garage and Store. Free water and Auto Camp. Lunches. Meals and Rooms if Desired. Plan your Drives so as to Stop a Night with Us."

Mile 32.3: **Sodium siding**. Shipping point for sodium from the lake beds to the north.

A 2000 photo of the **railroad siding at Sodium**. Here the old Yellowstone Highway crossed from the north side of the present-day highway to the south side.

Mile 39.5: **Powder River**. Here, the Burlington Railroad takes a more northerly route. Highway still follows the abandoned Chicago & Northwestern.

　　0.1 mile north of the highway to the old Chicago & Northwestern Railroad grade. Here was the railroad's Powder River Station, built in 1910. The station was used as the post office and telegraph station.

　　1922 *Blue Book* advisory: "Casper to Thermopolis via Powder River and Lost Cabin. . . . During certain periods of the year it is best to use the Birdseye pass road via Shoshoni. Local inquiry should be made at Powder River."

"**Nothing helps scenery like ham and eggs**."   Mark Twain.

Above: Old cafe in Powder River.

Below: Neon sign of the Tumble Inn in Powder River. The building was
moved here from the Ten Sleep, Wyoming, area in 1923.

Mile 41.2: Cross abandoned Chicago & Northwestern Railroad grade, just east of the highway bridge over the South Fork of the Powder River.

Mile 41.9: **Side trip**: East 1.5 miles on a public access road (limit travel to existing roads). This road is old U.S. 20-26 and leads to the old highway **bridge over the South Fork of the Powder River**. A good view of the river valley is obtained 1.1 miles along the old road. Note the huge Burlington Railroad fill to the north.

1915 *Blue Book* advisory: "Powder River Ford. Caution - if water is high make careful survey before attempting to ford the stream. Keep ahead, fording river, passing log house on other side."

Old U.S. 20-26 bridge over the South Fork of the Powder River.
A 2000 photograph.

Mile 42.0: Old highway crosses the present-day highway from north to south, following the power poles west to Hell's Half Acre.

Mile 45.1: **Hell's Half Acre**. 320 acres of highly eroded rock. Footpaths wind through the rock formations. The formations were also known as the "Devil's Kitchen." [Not to be confused with the Devil's Kitchen east of Greybull.]

The old highway can be seen descending the hill east of the campground. The old road kept south of the present-day highway and entered old Waltman from the southeast.

The Chicago & Northwestern Railroad ran south of Hell's Half Acre.
1922 *Blue Book*: "It is worth while to stop and view this remarkable phenomenon caused by erosion."

Mile 50.7: **Waltman**. [West end of the Bureau of Land Management "South Big Horn / Red Wall National Back Country Byway."]

The old settlement of Waltman, originally called Makoma, is 0.5 miles south of the present-day highway. Some of the former buildings were moved here from the old town of Wolton, six miles to the northwest. Old Chicago & Northwestern Railroad grade on the south edge of town.

1915 *Blue Book*: "station on left. Turn right between general store and log saloon."
The railroad station was torn down in 1970.

[The earliest branch of the Yellowstone Highway turned north at Waltman to follow the general route of the Bridger Trail to the Bighorn River. The highway passed through the towns of Arminto and Lost Cabin.]

Arminto. Second incorporated town in Natrona County.

1915 *Blue Book*: "station on right."

Mile 51.5 (approximate): **Cross the Bridger Trail**. The trail crossed the South Fork of the Powder River approximately four miles to the southeast.

Mile 53.2: Rest area. Interpretive sign: "Bridger Road - Waltman Crossing." Also a sign on "Mama Sage" describing the antelope and sagebrush of the region. Abandoned Chicago & Northwestern Railroad grade across the highway.

Mile 59.5: **Hiland**. Originally called Wolton. The "Bright Spot" general store opened in the mid 1920s and was famous for its "Sagebrush" ham sandwiches.

[Two miles east of Hiland are the ruins of Wolton, an early road house on the stage and freight line from Casper to Lost Cabin and the Big Horn Basin. When the Chicago & Northwestern Railroad was extended to Lander in 1906, the town of Wolton moved west and later the name changed to Hiland.]

Mile 67.0: **Abandoned Chicago & Northwestern Railroad grade** visible 50 yards south of the present-day highway for the next ten miles. The railroad was abandoned in 1943 and the steel rails salvaged for the war effort.

Mile 70.0: Fifty yards south on the unmarked Deer Creek Road are in-place railroad ties of the Chicago & Northwestern Railroad.

Mile 79.3: **Moneta**. Established in 1906 when the Chicago & Northwestern Railroad arrived from Casper. The freight line to Lost Cabin then left Moneta.

Side trip: Lysite and Lost Cabin.

Reset mile 0.0. Turn north on the Lysite-Moneta Road.

Mile 8.0: **Lysite**. General store and post office. On the route of the Burlington Railroad.

Mile 8.2: Turn right on Badwater Road.

Mile 11.3: **Lost Cabin**.

Lost Cabin. Founded in 1884 by John B. Okie, the town was headquarters for his Bighorn Sheep Company.

1915 *Blue Book*: "Tourists coming in from Arminto or Moneta can have reservations phoned from the stores at either place free of charge." [Okie owned both stores, as well as stores in Lysite, Kaycee, and Shoshoni. Okie also bought six Piggly Wiggly stores in Mexico.]

1916 *Yellowstone Highway* guide: "This village, though small, is strictly up to date -- has gravity water system, electric light, concrete sidewalks, local and long distance telephone, daily mail and automobile stage to the railroad three miles distance [Lysite]. There is a comfortable hotel, garage, store and blacksmith shop."

The 1916 *Yellowstone Highway* guide book noted a saloon just out of town, across the bridge, towards Arminto. The guide also noted: "At Lost Cabin, the Yellowstone Highway is joined by the road from Salt Lake, Rock Springs, Lander and Shoshoni."

Okie built his still-standing 16-room mansion in 1901. It was called the "Big Tepee." Here Okie had a large aviary, with a fine collection of rare birds.

Lost Cabin ad from the 1916 *Yellowstone Highway in Wyoming and Colorado*.

The Oasis Hotel, Lost Cabin, Wyoming

The Oasis

Lost Cabin, Wyoming

The Only Strictly Modern Hotel Between Casper and Thermopolis - -

Telegraph, Local and Long Distance Telephone

Hot and Cold Water
Steam Heat In Every Room
Electric Lights

Rooms $1.00   Meals 75c

The Gateway to J. B. Okie's Home, Lost Cabin

113

[From Lost Cabin, an early auto road ascended Bridger Creek, then descended Kirby Creek to the Bighorn River. This route followed closely the Bridger Trail. When the Chicago & Northwestern Railroad reached Casper, this route was used by freight wagons and stages to Thermopolis and the Big Horn Basin. In 1915 the route was changed to descend Buffalo Creek, reaching the Bighorn River four miles south of Thermopolis. This Bridger Creek-Buffalo Creek route was used by the Yellowstone Highway.]

1918 *Goodrich Tour* guide:

Lost Cabin to Thermopolis, Wyo. via Buffalo Creek. First thirty-three miles very rough, unimproved roads with many cross washes and high centers. Next ten miles good graded road, thence on to Thermopolis, extremely rough trail . . . 15.3 [miles from Lost Cabin]. Take left fork. Right fork is the old road to Thermopolis via Kirby Creek, now abandoned because of all bridges and culverts being washed out. Follow road over rolling country going up Owl Creek Mountains.

The Goodrich guide noted that the road from Lost Cabin to Thermopolis required negotiating 20 road junctions or turns, six gates to open, and grades up to 20%.

Bighorn Sheep Company Commissary, Lost Cabin, Wyoming.
Written on the unmailed, undated postcard:
"This is a dandy store inside. Have a $50,000.00 stock.
We have electric and gas plants here in the cabin also."

Mile 100.0: **Shoshoni**. Established in 1905 when the Shoshone Reservation opened for settlement. Chicago & Northwestern Railroad arrived in July 1906.

Today, the old Chicago & Northwestern Railroad grade is the **Wyoming Heritage Trail**. This **"Rails to Trails" hiking trail** extends 22 miles to Riverton. From the trailhead at the southwest edge of town, it is a one-half mile hike to the old trestle over Poison Creek.

A railroad spur line still runs to Shoshoni from the Burlington tracks at Bonneville, three miles to the northeast.

The Shawver Hotel, built in 1909, also housed a drugstore until the 1940s.

The **Yellowstone Drug Store** is now located in the C. H. King Building, which formerly housed a grocery store, then the National Bank of Shoshoni. King was the grandfather of former U.S. President Gerald Ford. The Yellowstone Drug Store is noted for its malts and milk shakes. The tradition for many Casper to Yellowstone tourists was to get "Sagebrush" ham sandwiches in Hiland and a malt or shake at Shoshoni.

Postcard of Shoshoni, looking east along U.S. 20-26.
C. H. King building, extreme right, now houses the Yellowstone Drug Store.
Across the street from the King building is the former Shawver Hotel.

At Shoshoni, present-day U.S. 26 turns southwest to Riverton and Lander. This was the route of the Grant Highway and the Atlantic Yellowstone Pacific Hiway.

North on U.S. Highway 20 to follow the Yellowstone Highway through the Wind River Canyon to Thermopolis.

Shoshoni: A choice of routes to Yellowstone.
Above: Present-day billboard enticing the tourist north through Thermopolis, Cody, and Yellowstone's east entrance, **the old Yellowstone Highway**.
Below: A second billboard promotes U.S. 26 through Riverton and Dubois.

The Grease Spot Says:

Only the highest grade of gasoline and oil dispensed at our stations.

Kelly-Springfield and Firestone Tires

Free road maps.—Ladies' rest room

Let our road signs be your guide

Service Filling Station Company
Wheatland, Wyoming

A. O. HEYER

GROCERIES, MEATS, DRY GOODS, LADIES' AND GENTS' FURNISHINGS

——

Shoshoni, Wyo.

Motto: "HEYER HAS IT"

MODERN IN EVERY RESPECT

GLOBE HOTEL WHEATLAND WYO. On the Yellowstone Highway

EXCELLENT CAFE in Connection

HOTEL TOWNSEND
CASPER, WYOMING

Casper's Finest Home of Hospitality
EXCELLENT CAFE AND LUNCH ROOM
HECTOR MARTI, Mgr.

PAT ROYCE FILLING STATION

Wholesale and Retail
GASOLINE AND OILS
448 West Yellowstone

Casper   Wyoming

CASPER, WYOMING, On the Main Automobile Road to Yellowstone Park

HOTEL HENNING
"Wyoming's Largest"

Excellent Dining and Lunch Room in Connection

W. F. HENNING, Owner

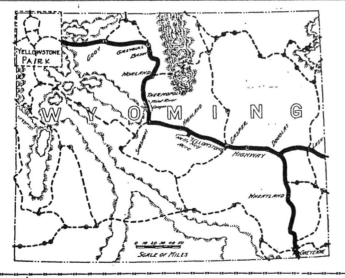

The Yellow Dot Service Station

Ladies' and Gents' Rest Rooms

EVERYTHING FOR THE AUTOMOBILE
SERVICE WITH A SMILE

Douglas, Wyo.

LeBar Service Station

REPAIRS, MACHINE WORK
BATTERY SERVICE
ACCESSORIES

Authorized Ford Agents

Douglas, Wyo.

LUSK MOTOR COMPANY
Ford Sales and Service
GENERAL REPAIR WORK

——

HOTEL-IN CONNECTION
Lusk, Wyo.

The Brightest Spot on

The Yellowstone

SMITH'S GARAGE
Highland, Wyoming

Advertisement page from *Wyoming Roads*, July 1926.
Lusk was on the Grant Highway and the Atlantic Yellowstone Pacific Hiway.
The town of Highland is now spelled Hiland.

Shoshoni to Greybull

The Yellowstone Highway Route:

Waterways: The Yellowstone Highway follows the Wind River through Wind River Canyon. At the north end of the canyon, the name of the river officially changes to Bighorn. The Bighorn River is followed to Greybull.

Trails: The Bridger Trail ran well east of Wind River Canyon, striking the Bighorn River at present-day Lucerne. The trail then followed the river north to a point opposite present-day Manderson, where it veered northwest, away from the river.

Railroads: The Chicago Burlington and Quincy built its line up the Bighorn River to Kirby in 1907. Tracks were extended south through the Wind River Canyon in 1913.

Auto Trails: Coinciding with the Yellowstone and National Park-to-Park Highways were the Buffalo Highway and Glacier to Gulf Highway. The first route of the Yellowstone Highway ran through Lost Cabin, then descended Buffalo Creek to the Bighorn River south of Thermopolis. A pre-1924 branch of the Yellowstone Highway traversed Birdseye Pass between Shoshoni and Thermopolis, the route being several miles east of the current highway through the Wind River Canyon. At Worland the Yellowstone Highway was joined by the Black and Yellow Trail, the George Washington National Highway, and the Short-Cut West Highway.

State Highways: Wyoming Highway 11 was the original number given to the route, first over Birdseye Pass, then, in 1924, through the Wind River Canyon.

U.S. Highways: U.S. Highway 20 was the original federal number given to the Wind River Canyon route of the Yellowstone Highway. U.S. Highway 16 joins at Worland.

Today: U.S. Highway 20 runs from Shoshoni north to Greybull. The Shoshoni to Thermopolis section is a AAA Designated Scenic Byway.

1915 *Automobile Blue Book*:   **Thermopolis to Basin, Wyo.** - 69.5 m.

      Via Worland and Manderson, following the general course of the Big Horn River all the way. Fair to good natural roads the entire distance.

1922 *Automobile Blue Book*:   **Thermopolis to Basin, Wyo.** - 70.7 m.

      Via Worland and Manderson. Most of the route follows newly constructed dirt roads, which provide good going when weather conditions are favorable. The ungraded stretches are fair and improvements are constantly in progress. The route follows the Big Horn river basin thru prosperous irrigated districts separated in places by low rolling hills and unimproved prairie country. This is a section of the Yellowstone highway.

Yollow

Black H

Gray

Yellowstone Highway

SANTA'S
WHISKERS
NEED NO TRIMMIN'
HE KISSED KIDS
NOT THE WIMMIN
Burma-Shave

GLACIER
TO
GULF

Black

White, black letters

Black

Glacier to Gulf Highway

Mile 100.0: **Shoshoni. North on U.S. 20**.

Mile 102.7: Cross Badwater Creek. In 1923, Badwater flooding washed out several miles of railroad track to the east. Burlington Railroad tracks north of the creek.

Mile 103.3: **Side trip**: 3.0 miles east on Badwater Road to the old railroad town of Bonneville.

    Reset mile 0.0.

    Mile 2.5: Abandoned Bonneville Cafe, near the BTI Plant. Left to Bonneville.

    Mile 3.0: **Bonneville**. The town was heavily damaged in the 1923 Badwater Creek flood.

Former cafe west of Bonneville.
The Yellowstone Highway passed through the railroad town.

We take for granted our paved, well drained, properly marked highways that are equipped with an elastic chain link life net - forgetting entirely the ruts, the mud, the heavy dusts, or the dangerous wooden guard rails of yesterday. Catching up with the string of cars ahead of us we fret and fume at the truck that leads the procession and which temporarily slows our thirty-six mile speed to a more leisurely twenty-seven mile gait; forgetting the while that twenty-seven miles an hour is fully four times as fast as it was possible to travel a few short years ago. *Colorado Highways*, July 1928

Mile 109.1: [Birdseye Road, closed to through traffic. The road to the northeast leads to **Birdseye Pass**, the route of a freight and stage line to Thermopolis from the Chicago and Northwestern Railroad at Shoshoni. This was also one of the branches of the Yellowstone Highway before the completion of the road through the Wind River Canyon in 1924. Birdseye stage station, 0.5 miles south of the pass, had a false-front log station and out-buildings. Established in 1907, the station burned in the 1950s.]

Birdseye stage station, 0.5 miles south of Birdseye Pass.
Photograph courtesy of the Hot Springs County Museum and Cultural Center.

Devil's Slide, on the north side of Birdseye Pass, was an especially steep and narrow section of road:

> . . . we went from Shoshoni to Thermopolis twice, when once came very near being too many, the Devil's Slide giving the Studebaker more than it could do without me at the back and pushing my daylights out.
> Calvin W. Williams, describing his 1909 trip

> Another objection I have to that road [Birdseye Pass] is the Devil's Slide. I requested the County Commissioners of Hot Springs County to make at least one or more turn-outs on the road, but this is not done, and until it is, that particular part of the road is really unsafe for the general run of travel.
> L. L. Newton letter to the Wyoming Highway Department, 1920

Stagecoach descending Devil's Slide north of Birdseye Pass.
The driver: John Burge.
The horses: Charley, Eagle, Snoball, Buttons, Old Spook, and Renegade.
Photograph courtesy of the Hot Springs County Museum and Cultural Center.

Mile 112.5: Enter **Boysen State Park** and **Wind River Canyon**, a great cleft in the Owl Creek Mountains. The road through the canyon was completed in 1924 and was realigned slightly after the completion of the new Boysen Dam in 1951. The Burlington Railroad, completed through the canyon in 1913, and the Wind River share the canyon with the highway.

[Wind River Canyon Road] . . . the highway will be a boulevard second to no canyon road in the known world . . . at no spot is there danger of collision or danger of jumping off into the boiling stream below. Women drivers can spin through this canyon on high in perfect safety.   *The Casper Tribune*, 1924

Mile 113.7: **Boysen Dam** overlook and interpretive sign.
Mile 114.0: **Side trip**: Boysen Dam, power plant and **old U.S. 20**. *Reset mile 0.0*.
   Mile 0.2: Just before the dam, turn north, down to the pre-dam railroad grade.
   Mile 0.4: The present-day railroad grade and tunnel were opened in 1948. Road now follows the old railroad grade. Present-day railroad tunnel to the southeast.
   Mile 0.7: Pass under the railroad trestle. Note the old railroad tunnel and bridge supports of the old railroad crossing of the Wind River. Continue along old U.S. 20 for 0.5 miles to the Upper Wind River Canyon Campgrounds.
   Mile 1.6: Access back to U.S. 20 at milepost 115.5.

Mile 116.0: Interpretive sign, "Site of Original Boysen Dam." The old Boysen Dam, completed in 1909, was located just north of the north end of the Lower Wind River campground. The dam flooded portions of the railroad and, after a long court battle, the water level was lowered. The dam was totally dismantled in 1948.

Train carrying members of the 1920 National Park-to-Park
dedication tour at the **site of the old Boysen Dam**.
A. G. Lucier photograph, courtesy of the Hinckley Library, Northwest College.

A newspaper account said of the dedication tour:
    Arrangements have been made to send most of the members of the party through Wind River canyon from Bonneville by train to Thermopolis, only the drivers of the cars going over Birdseye pass. This, because the officers of the Yellowstone Highway association feel that it is imperative that a road be constructed through the canyon on the opposite bank of the river from the railroad, doing away with the necessity of crossing the mountains to reach Thermopolis.
    Casper Daily Tribune, August 31, 1920

Prior to 1924, Casper to Thermopolis was the "weak link" of the Yellowstone Highway route. In 1917, the newly formed Wyoming Highway Department decided that a road must ultimately be built through the Wind River Canyon.

South of Thermopolis there was a range of mountains to cross and no one seemed to know just where the Yellowstone Highway crossed the mountains. It seemed that every trail leading south from Thermopolis was marked with yellow painted stones and the traveler making three or four inquiries for the best road out, would generally receive as many different recommendations of route to follow. Invariably the stranger was at a loss which way to go and would always wish that he had taken a different route, for in his opinion it could not have been worse than the one he followed. . . . Seldom did the local residents who knew the nature of these mountains venture out of the Basin to the south in their own cars and most of this travel was made by rail.

Wyoming Roads, September, 1924

Mile 116.1: First of **three tunnels**, enlarged since the road opened in 1924.

Postcard showing the third of three tunnels below the old Boysen Dam.
Note the railroad grade across the Wind River.

Mile 119.8: Location of a Texaco filling station which burned in the 1960s.
Mile 120.3: 1941 WPA Guide: "Bob White's Place . . . a little terraced homestead on the mountainside, has buildings of local stone, with thatched roofs."

Mile 123.5: Pullout on left for views of **Leaning Rock and Chimney Rock** on the east side of the road.

Mile 124.1: **Memorial** to Reverend William Pugh (1889-1950), killed here in a traffic accident. USGS map erroneously marks the site "Grave."

Mile 127.5: "**Wedding of the Waters**" pullout on the west side of the highway. Here the Wind River officially becomes the Bighorn River. An historical marker at the site has been removed.

> Much to the consternation of the uninitiated geography student, the Indians had two names for the stream: Big Horn for the lower portion and Wind for the headwaters. . . . The dividing point in the stream is at the north end of the Wind River Canyon where "The Wedding of the Waters" takes place. It is akin to a bride entering a church under one name and leaving it with another. This adds a bit of romance to the two names that have continued to designate the one stream down through the years.
>
> David J. Wasden, 1973

Mile 127.6: **<u>Side</u> trip**: Leave present-day U.S. 20 and follow Wyoming Highway 173 (Hot Springs County Road 31, South Yellowstone Road) branching off to the east. **This is an older section of U.S. 20**.

Reset mile 0.0.

Mile 1.4: Buffalo Creek Road to the east. Here the first Yellowstone Highway route through Lost Cabin and the later road from Shoshoni and Birdseye Pass both reached the Bighorn River. Both routes were used prior to the opening of the Wind River Canyon highway in 1924.

Gus Holm's of the Yellowstone Highway Association stated in 1920:

> I have placed at the junction of the road on Buffalo Creek where the Shoshoni road turns off the Lost Cabin Road, a sign which reads: "Casper via Shoshoni, follow markings." This gives the public the opportunity to go either way they choose. But between you and me, I have not the nerve to send anyone over Birdseye Pass.

Mile 1.6: "**Fourmile Bridge**" spans the Bighorn River.

Mile 2.2: Cross the Burlington Railroad tracks.

Mile 3.0: Rejoin U.S. 20 at milepost 129.9. **Continue north to Thermopolis**.

> You people who have seen Wyoming only from the train, and think it is a desert, a wilderness of sage brush and cactus, should have been with us on a recent trip along the Yellowstone Highway from Casper to Lost Cabin, Shoshoni and Thermopolis. It truly was the most enjoyable trip I have ever made. . . . I thought I had seen splendid colors, but I've never seen anything like those of Wyoming - mountains of purple and bronze and green and even bright red! Even the dirt in the road is not satisfied to be just plain ordinary dirt, but must needs be green or yellow or red dirt. The road is a real trail - it wanders hither and yon, dipping and curving just, it seems, to give one a continuous change of picture, a wonderful view at every turn.
>
> *Wyoming Roads*, December 1924

West of Lost Cabin through Worland

1916 map from the
*Yellowstone Highway in
Wyoming and Colorado*

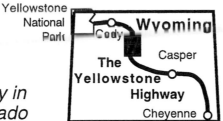

United States Geological Survey map
State of Wyoming, 1980

Present-day highways with
the drive guide route enhanced

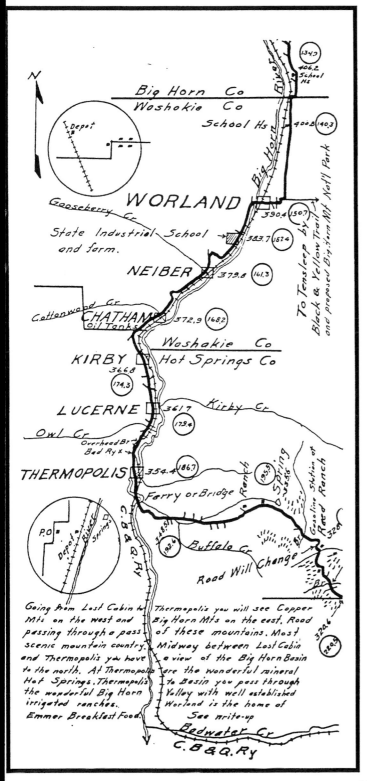

Going from Lost Cabin to
Thermopolis you will see Copper
Mts on the west and
Big Horn Mts on the east. Road
passing through a pass
of these mountains. Most
scenic mountain country.
Midway between Lost Cabin
and Thermopolis you have
a view of the Big Horn Basin
to the north. At Thermopolis
are the wonderful mineral
Hot Springs. Thermopolis
to Basin you pass through
the wonderful Big Horn
Valley with well established
irrigated ranches.
Worland is the home of
Emmer Breakfast Food.
See write-up

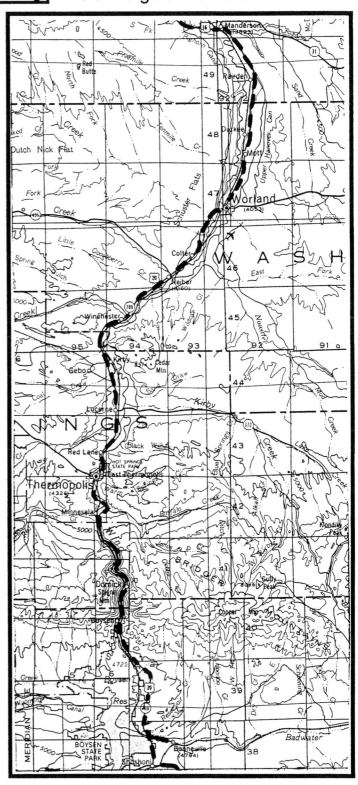

125

Mile 132.5: **Thermopolis**. Present town established in 1897 when settlement was opened around the site of the hot springs. Town named for *thermal* (Latin: hot baths or spring) and *polis* (Greek: city). The flagpole, at 5th and Broadway, was noted in early guidebooks. The Treasurer's office in the Washakie County Courthouse has a display of old license plates. The Burlington Railroad depot still stands near 3rd and Broadway.

1916 *Yellowstone Highway* ads:
Washakie Hotel and Bath House
Emery Hotel   [Built in 1906]   "The Home of the Tourist"
Keystone Hotel   [Built in 1899]
Peters Garage, 6th & Broadway
The Wigwams (rooms)
1920 National Park-to-Park Highway dedication tour: the party was treated to lunch at the Washakie Hotel.
1922 *Blue Book*: "Thermopolis Hot Springs - On the Road to Yellowstone Park. A delightful break in the trip to or from Nature's Wonderland."

The old Emery Hotel in Thermopolis.
It was located at the northwest corner of 6th and Broadway.
Photograph courtesy of the Hot Springs County Museum and Cultural Center.

Mile 133.1: Entrance to **Hot Springs State Park**. Here is the Star Plunge, TePee Spa, and the free State Bath House.

126

Postcard (mailed in 1917) of the **Star Plunge** in the Hot Springs State Park.

1916 *Yellowstone Highway* guide: "Take a bath at the Star Plunge. Water supply from the Big Horn River. Radium Hot Springs flows 18,600,000 gallons hot water every 24 hours. Cures Rheumatism, Paralysis, Blood and Skin Diseases, Stomach Trouble, etc."

Mile 133.6: Inspiration Point to the east, overview of the Hot Springs State Park area. Interpretive sign: "Hot Springs State Park."

> . . . About 2 miles out [from Thermopolis] we had our first puncture. . . . Delayed almost an hr. Speed along for an hour or so   pop - another flat. So out we got & began our toil. Help almost at once however & were delayed only about 1/2 an hour. On to Greybull where we had both patched while we hunted up the camp-grounds . . .
>
> Blanche Johnston, 1926

Mile 138.4: Owl Creek. Site of the pre-1897 town of Thermopolis.
Mile 139.8: **Lucerne**. After descending Kirby Creek, the old **Bridger Trail crossed the Bighorn River** approximately two miles to the northeast. The trail parallels the Yellowstone Highway to the Manderson area before leaving the River to pass west of Bridger Butte, west of Emblem. Also following the route of the Bridger Trail to the Bighorn River was the Casper to Thermopolis stage line which ran from the Chicago & Northwestern Railroad in Casper.

Mile 142.7: Interpretive sign: "Bridger Trail: Bighorn River Crossing." Near here the Bridger Trail descended Kirby Creek to reach and cross the Bighorn River.

Mile 143.3: Old U.S. 20 veered east to Kirby; present-day highway bypasses the town.

Mile 144.6: **Kirby**. 0.4 miles east of the highway. The Burlington Railroad arrived in 1907 and was the southern terminus of the line for two years. Shipping point for the Gebo mining district to the west. Old U.S. 20 ran west of the railroad tracks, along Bryan St.:
>South Bryan: 0.6 miles of broken asphalt road to a gate.
>North Bryan: 0.3 miles thru old railroad yards to the present tracks.
>[West from Kirby on Hot Springs County Roads 18 and 30 for two miles to the old Gebo mining district, abandoned in the 1950s.]

Mile 145.6: Old U.S. 20 from Kirby merges with the present highway.

Mile 148.6: **Side trip**: To travel an older section of the highway through **Winchester**, leave U.S. 20 and take Washakie County Road 86 (**pre-1953 U.S. 20**) which branches off to the east of the highway (a rather hidden intersection).
Reset mile 0.0.
Mile 0.4: East of the road is the site of The Willows stage stop, under the hill.

The old store at Winchester. This was also the filling station.
The railroad station here was known as Chatham.

Mile 1.5: **Winchester**. The town was called Chatham by the Burlington Railroad because Postmaster R. S. Winchester did not want his name plastered on the side of the train station. The town had a school, store, filling station, and post office. Town boomed in 1917, supplying material to the Grass Creek Oil Fields.
1918 *Goodrich Tour* guide: "Pass Chatham. (R. R. station and store only.)"
Mile 1.8: Cross Cottonwood Creek on an old iron bridge.
Mile 2.3: Rejoin present-day U.S. 20 at milepost 150.8. Continue north.

Mile 151.2: The 1941 *Wyoming Work Projects Administration* guide noted:
At Tie-down Hill, on the east bank of the Big Horn River, lived "Tie-Down" Brown, so named for his agility in tying down and branding other rancher's calves . . . for himself.
Mile 156.7: **Neiber**. 1915 *Blue Book*: "P. O. [post office] on left."
Mile 159.9: Wyoming Boys School.
1916 *Yellowstone Highway* map: State Industrial School and farm.
1918 *Goodrich* guide: "Pass Colter R. R. siding. (State Reform School over to left.)"
Mile 164.4: Interpretive sign, north of the highway: "Original Worland Town Site."
Mile 164.7: Turn east, off present-day U.S. 20, to cross the Bighorn River on the old Culbertson St. Bridge. To the south is the Holly Sugar plant, established in 1917. North on 5th Street, just east of the railroad tracks, for two blocks to rejoin U.S. Highway 20, Big Horn Avenue. East on U.S. 20.

Mile 165.4: **Worland**. When the Burlington Railroad arrived in 1906, buildings on the west side of the river were skidded across the ice to the railroad side.
1916 *Yellowstone Highway* guide: "Heart of the Big Horn Basin. . . . [home of] Professor Buffums Emmer Breakfast Food factory."
Emmer is a type of wheat from the Middle East. Burt Buffum, often called the "Luther Burbank of Wyoming," improved the grain and began producing breakfast food. His original mill was near Loveland, Colorado.
1920 National Park-to-Park dedication tour: members were treated to a banquet at the Dorman Hotel by the members of the Alfalfa Club. (The Dorman Hotel was later renamed the Washakie Hotel.)
Auto trails merging with the Yellowstone Highway at Worland were the Black and Yellow Trail, the George Washington National Highway, and the Short-Cut West Highway. They all passed through Gillette, Buffalo, and Ten Sleep, Wyoming.
Mile 165.7: U.S. Highway 20 merges with U.S. Highway 16 from Buffalo and Ten Sleep. **North on 10th St., U.S. 16-20**.
Mile 179.8: Big Horn County Road 34 to the west is a section of old U.S. 16-20. It can be followed for 1.8 miles, rejoining the present-day highway at milepost 181.6.
Mile 184.3: Road north to **Manderson**, originally called Alamo. The Town Hall and Library occupies the old filling station and garage. Early businesses included the Commercial Hotel, the Manderson Hotel, and the Manderson Livery.
1916 *Yellowstone Highway* guide: "in a direct line from the village of Manderson is a proposed Big Horn National Park. This park consists mainly of the lakes and scenic mountains of Cloud's Peak."
Cross the railroad tracks and rejoin U.S. 16-20 at milepost 185.0.

The Manderson Livery.
Facilities such as this serviced both the wagon and automobile traveler.
Photograph courtesy of the Manderson Town Hall and Library.

Below and opposite page: Panoramic view of downtown Greybull.
Looking north along N. 6th St., U.S. 14-16-20, the Yellowstone Highway.
Present-day U.S. 14 from Sheridan (right) merges with the Yellowstone Highway here.
Road (left) leads to the Burlington Railroad tracks.
March 1920 photograph. Courtesy of the Greybull Museum.

Mile 185.1: Cross the Bighorn River. Here the Bridger Trail loft the river and veered northwest, passing just south of the town of Otto.

Mile 187.8: Turn north on **Orchard Bench Road** (Big Horn County Road 229). This is **the pre-1960s highway**. The 6.7-mile-long highway passes several old homesteads and modern farm and ranch operations.
Rejoin **U.S. 16-20** at milepost 195.1. **Continue north to Basin.**
Mile 195.2: Wyoming Retirement Center to the west, on the grounds of the former State Tuberculosis Sanitarium, founded in 1921.

Mile 196.4: **Basin**. Originally called Basin City. County seat of Big Horn County. Town known as the "Lilac City" since a planting drive began in 1936. The railroad depot has been moved to Deaver, Wyoming.
1916 *Yellowstone Highway* guide: Markham Hotel. Antlers Hotel, "the place to get a good bed and a good meal."
1920 Park-to-Park Highway dedication tour: members were entertained by the Basin band at the new dance platform.
1924 *Park-to-Park Highway* guide: "Yellowstone Garage."

To follow a pre-1960s section of U.S. 16-20 north of Basin, turn west on **"C" Street** for 0.3 miles, then north on **Wyoming Highway 36** (Golf Course Road) for 2.7 miles, rejoining **U.S. 16-20** at milepost 199.2. Continue north.

Mile 204.0: **Greybull**. Founded in 1906, the town was named for the legend of the albino buffalo bull that roamed the region. Greybull was a division point for the Burlington Railroad with a maintenance center including a 20-stall roundhouse. Passenger service to the Big Horn Basin was discontinued in 1967.
1924 *Park-to Park Highway* ads: "The Griffin Inn, Yellowstone Garage."
Merging with U.S. 16-20 at Greybull is U.S. 14 from Gillette and Sheridan.

Continue north, then west, on U.S. 14-16-20, to Cody and Yellowstone.

131

Early Yellowstone Highway via Otto and Burlington

An early branch of the Yellowstone Highway ran west from Basin, through Otto and Burlington. The route rejoined present-day U.S. 14-16-20 west of Emblem. This route was also used by the Short-Cut West Highway and an early branch of the Black and Yellow Trail. This approximate route can be followed by taking Wyoming Highway 30 west from Basin for 12 miles to Otto, 10 more miles to Burlington, then four miles north to U.S. Highway 14-16-20 at milepost 85.7.

1915 *Automobile Blue Book*: **Basin to Cody, Wyo.** - 57.9 m.
 Via Otto and Burlington. Mostly good graded roads to Burlington; from there on fair, natural prairie road. Be sure to get full supply of water at Burlington, as there is no more until Cody is reached. This is a section of the Black and Yellow Trail.

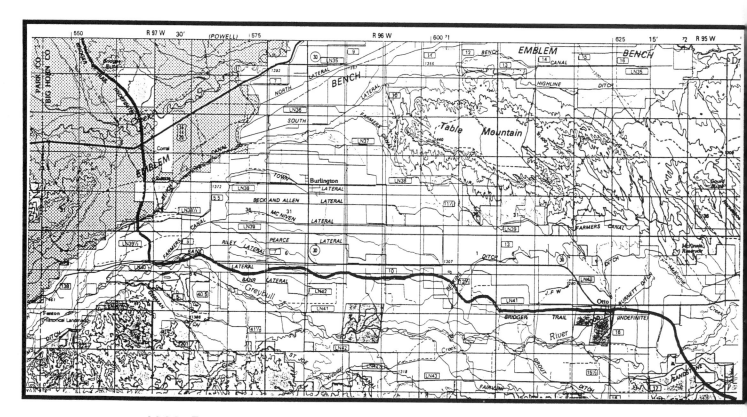

1992 Bureau of Land Management map, Basin, Wyoming
showing the Bridger Trail in the Otto and Bridger Butte area.

The Bridger Trail followed down the west side of the Bighorn River from present-day Kirby to the Manderson area. The trail then left the river and veered northwest. It crossed the Greybull River approximately two miles southeast of present-day Otto. It ran south of present-day Wyoming Highway 30, then turned north to cross present-day U.S. 14-16-20 near milepost 80.0. **The trail then passed west of Bridger Butte and continued northwest to Virginia City, Montana.**

132

Manderson to Cody

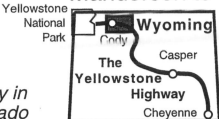

Yellowstone National Park

Wyoming

Cody

Casper

The Yellowstone Highway

Cheyenne

United States Geological Survey map
State of Wyoming, 1980

1916 map from the
*Yellowstone Highway in
Wyoming and Colorado*

Present-day highways with
the drive guide route enhanced

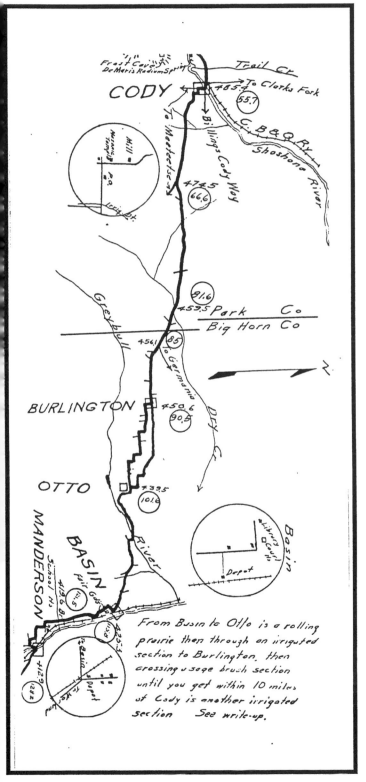

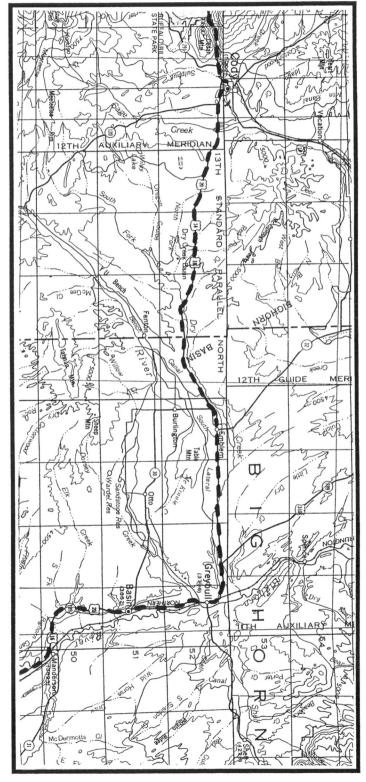

From Basin to Otto is a rolling
prairie then through an irrigated
section to Burlington, then
crossing a sage brush section
until you get within 10 miles
of Cody is another irrigated
section. See write-up.

Greybull to Yellowstone National Park

"Like the soldier of fortune seeking new fields to conquer, the motorist is ever on the alert to try his skill and his car in the more mountainous sections of the country; and as a result the pathways leading toward the snow-capped Rockies are fairly alive with motor-parties."

Charles J. Belden, 1918

The Yellowstone Highway Route:

Waterways: The highway leaves the Bighorn River and follows up the Dry Creek drainage, then crosses to the Shoshone River at Cody. The highway ascends the Shoshone River then, above the Buffalo Bill Dam, ascends the North Fork of the Shoshone. Within Yellowstone Park, the road ascends Middle Creek to within a mile of Sylvan Pass, the summit of the Absaroka Range.

Trails: The Bridger Trail is crossed eight miles west of the town of Emblem.

Railroads: No railroads run along the route. The Burlington Railroad reached Cody from the north.

Auto Trails: Running from Greybull west to the Park: the Yellowstone Highway, National Park-to-Park Highway, George Washington National Highway, and the Black and Yellow Trail. The Buffalo Highway ran west to Cody, then turned north to Billings, Montana.

State Highways: Wyoming Highway 26 was the original number given the road.

U.S. Highways: U.S. 20 was the original number assigned to the highway in 1926.

Today: U.S. Highway 14-16-20 runs from Greybull to the Park. West from Greybull is a AAA designated Scenic Byway. The highway through the Shoshone National Forest west of Cody is designated the Buffalo Bill Scenic Byway.

1922 *Automobile Blue Book*:

Basin to Cody, Wyo. - 65.4 m.

Via Greybull and Emblem. Gravel highway to Greybull; graded dirt and gravelly sand roads to Emblem, a small settlement located in a fertile farming community. Natural prairie roads then predominate thru barren, uninhabited country to within 7 miles of Cody, from which a gravel highway is followed thru an irrigated district balance of way. This is a section of the Yellowstone highway.

Yellow

Black H

Gray

Yellowstone Highway

YOU KNOW
YOUR ONIONS
LETTUCE SUPPOSE
THIS BEETS 'EM ALL
DON'T TURNIP YOUR NOSE
Burma-Shave

Black

Yellow

Black

Black & Yellow Trail

Mile 204.0: **Greybull. West on U.S. 14-16-20.**

Mile 205.5. Cross the Burlington Railroad tracks for the last time on our tour.

Mile 206.6: South Big Horn County Airport. Home of Hawkins and Powers Aviation and the Museum of Flight and Aerial Fire Fighting. Collection of WW II airplanes.

Mile 209.0: U.S. 310 from Billings, Montana, and Lovell, Wyoming, from the north.

Highway mileposts west of the U.S. 310 junction reflect U.S. 14-16-20 mileage from Yellowstone's east entrance. Mile markers are on the south side of the highway.

Mile 100.7: U.S. 310, from Billings. Continue west.

Mile 90.5: Wood box structures in the alfalfa fields are for beehives.

Mile 87.8: **Emblem**. This community was originally called Germania for the many German settlers in the area. The name was changed during World War I. Sugar beets are a major crop in the area. Note the old white stone school.

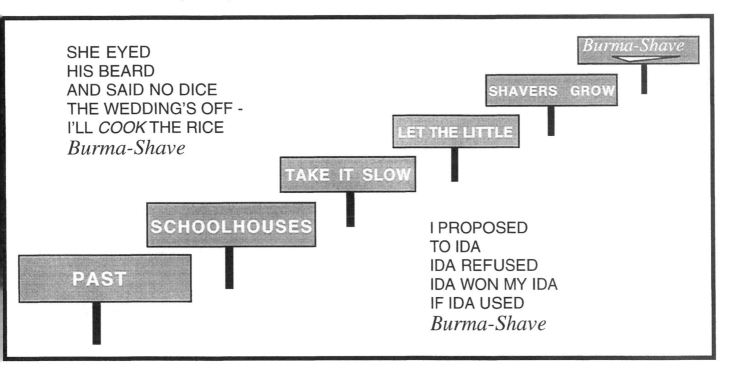

Mile 85.7: Wyoming Highway 30 from Burlington merges from the south. From Basin, the early branch of the Yellowstone Highway passed through Otto and Burlington.

Mile 80.0: **Bridger Butte** to the north. The **Bridger Trail** crossed the road here, then passed west of the butte. Interpretive signs on the Bridger Trail and on Wild Horses are located to the south of the highway.

Mile 75.6: Traces of the old road run due west as the present-day road curves slightly to the northwest. The old section rejoins the present-day road at milepost 74.4.

Mile 70.0: Good views of the **Absaroka Mountains to the west.**

Mile 64.7: **Eagle Pass**. Interpretive sign 0.1 mile south of the highway: "Irrigation system by Solon Wiley." Good view of the Absaroka Mountains to the west.

Mile 62.0: Heart Mountain to the northwest. East of the mountain was the World War II Heart Mountain Relocation Center.

Mile 58.0: Shoshone Canyon visible directly ahead. Cedar Mountain to the south of the canyon; Rattlesnake Mountain to the north.

Mile 52.0: **Cody**. Named for William "Buffalo Bill" Cody who helped found the town in 1896. The town is located at the terminus of the Chicago Burlington & Quincy Railroad's 131-mile-long "Frannie Branch" which arrived in 1901.

1685. THE IRMA HOTEL. CODY. WYO.

Souvenir card of **William Cody's Irma Hotel**.
The town of Cody had only 89 residents when the hotel opened in 1902.
Named for one of his daughters, the hotel is still in full operation.

The Cody Club established the Buffalo Bill Memorial Association in 1922 to preserve the memory of William Cody. The Chamber of Commerce is located in the 1927 original Buffalo Bill Museum log building.

The **Park County Historical Archives** and reference center is located in the Park County Courthouse, opened in 1912.

The railroad's Burlington Hotel opened in 1924 and was torn down in 1980.

The **Buffalo Bill Historical Center** consists of five museums: the Buffalo Bill Museum, the Cody Firearms Museum, the Plains Indian Museum, the Whitney Gallery of Western Art, and the Draper Museum of Natural History. Here also is the McCracken Research Library. Located on the grounds is William Cody's boyhood home, moved here from Le Claire, Iowa. The Cody Statue, northwest of the museum buildings, was dedicated in 1924.

Old Trail Town is a collection of over 20 historically documented buildings of the late 1800s. All were moved to this location, which is near the original site of Cody. Many of the buildings contain exhibits.

The 1920 Park-to-Park Highway dedication tour: September 2. A reception at the Irma Hotel, a banquet at the Methodist Church, and a "picture program" at the Temple Theater.

1922 *Blue Book* ads: "Hotel Chamberlin. I have a few rooms with bath which I can reserve for tourists who make reservations in advance."

"The IRMA, The Late Col. W. F. Cody, Founder. Rates $2.00 and up. 50 miles from Eastern entrance to Yellowstone Park. Daily automobile service from Hotel to Park line, through the wonderful Shoshone Canyon. Home of Buffalo Bill Curios."

1924 *Park-to-Park Highway* ads: "The Master Scenic Highway of America enters the park from the east through Cody and the Shoshone Canyon, which is considered the most scenic 70 miles of highway in the world."

"Irma Hotel. If you have children, use them as an excuse to visit the forests and parks, they will thank you for it."

1926 Blanche Johnston diary:

Cody 10:30 P.M. Scouted about & finally got rooms in a rustic hotel called the Irma Hotel, rooms in annex - musty, clean . . . man upstairs used typewriter all night, clickety, click, click.

Kozy-Korner in early-day Cody.
The corner building, which later housed a bank, is now Peter's Cafe Bakery.
Note the "Park Garage   Auto Livery" sign on the building to the left (west).
Courtesy of the Buffalo Bill Historical Center, Cody, WY. Photo P.5.1464.

Two auto trails ran to Cody from the Yellowstone <u>Trail</u> in Montana. The Billings-Cody Way ran from Laurel, Montana, to Cody via Powell, Wyoming. The Black & White Trail ran from Columbus, Montana, to Cody via Red Lodge and Belfry, Montana.

Buffalo Bill Museum at Cody, Wyoming, in the heart of a frontier region where the famous plainsman wrote his glowing passages into the history of the West. A pleasant interlude for Burlington travelers entering or leaving Yellowstone Park via the Cody gateway.

Postcard of the original Buffalo Bill Museum.
The building now houses the Chamber of Commerce.

Ads from the *Park County Enterprise*, July 20, **1910**. **Cody has always been a tourist town.** Even before automobiles were allowed into Yellowstone, the railroad and stagecoach business was booming as was automobile service to the east entrance.

Cody's Celebration of the Opening of Yellowstone National Park to Automobiles.

Right: From *The Northern Wyoming Herald* (Cody), **July 23, 1915.**

Below: From the same newspaper, **July 30, 1915.**

Entrance Day Today

All is in readiness for the greatest event in Cody's history—the marking of the passing of a little town located somewhere out west and the emerging of a thiving western city known world wide as CODY, WYOMING, the Scenic Entrance to Yellowstone Park.

Cody welcomes her guests with the true western spirit. Make yourselves at home.

Few cars entered the park during the celebration because of rainy weather over much of Wyoming.

Only 193 automobiles entered Yellowstone via the East Entrance during the 1915 season.

ENTRANCE DAY PROGRAM

The Cody Club has invited the Automobilists of the Nation to come to Cody, the scenic Entrance to Yellowstone National Park and celebrate the Opening of the Park to Rubber Tires and the committee has prepared a program in which it is desired that Wyoming people shall participate and extend the warm hand of welcome to our guests

July 29 to August 3

July 29 8:00 p. m. Organization Wyoming State Automobile Association

July 30 10 a. m. Historical parade showing various methods of travel

1 p. m. Wild West show

7 p. m. Dinner to County Commissioners of Wyoming, Montana and Idaho and organization.

July 31 Procession of cars led by Buffalo Bill to Yellowstone Park---Entertainment and dance at Pahaska and Holm lodge.

August 1 Entrance to Yellowstone Park

August 3 Grand Jubilee at Canyon hotel

Afternoon Program of Thrilling Events, July 30

Grand Parade at the Arena 1:00 o'clock

Cowboy Race, stock saddle, chaps, race horses barred	$15	$10	$5
Bucking Steers, Steers furnished ride with rigging, First half		10	5
Tournament Riding, Horses to be Ridden at full gallop	$5 in trade by J M Frost		$2.50 Pair of Gloves by Dave Jones
Bucking Horse Contest, Horses to be drawn for, First half	McAlennan medal	Shelly $15 Bridle	
	$5 will be paid each rider who rides his mount		
Stage Coach Holdup	Thirty Cowboys and Indians		
Relay Race, three horses ridden	$20	$5	Wool Shirt Henry Haid
Bucking Steers, 2nd half			
Stake Race	Stetson Hat Newton Company		Saddle Rope Brundage Hardware
Cow Girl Race	Rider to furnish horse, and stock saddle	$10	Hat Madame Volckmer $5
Bulldogging Steer, usual rules	$20	$10	$5
Grab Race, get ready for the big laugh	$5	$2.50 in trade Cody Trading Company	
Bucking Horse Contest, 2nd half			
Potatoe Race, spears furnished	$5	$2.50 in trade Cody Trading Company	
Wild Horse Race	Horses furnished by Fred Morris. Entries ride against time once around the track	$20 $15	5
Best Bucking Horse, used in above events	Ten Dollars, by Joe Jones		

A special invitation is extended to the Old Timers of the West to participate in this program given in honor of the coming of the automobile and for the entertainment of our eastern visitors who will come from all over the United States for this event and to enter Yellowstone Park.

All Entries must be made before 12 o'clock on the 30th
ENTRIES FREE

Cody to Yellowstone's Grand Loop Road

1916 map from the
*Yellowstone Highway in
Wyoming and Colorado*

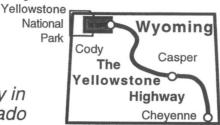

United States Geological Survey map
State of Wyoming, 1980

Present-day highways with
the drive guide route enhanced

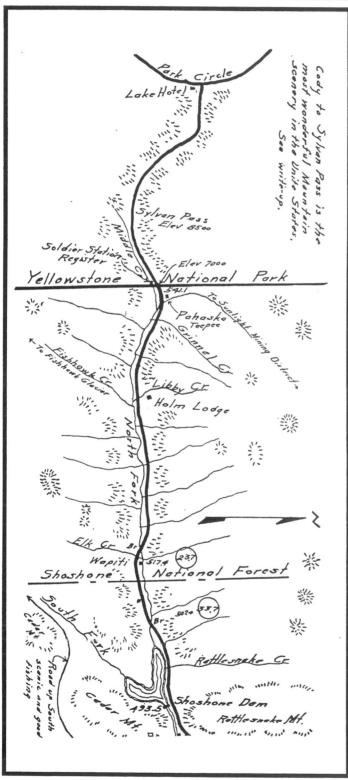

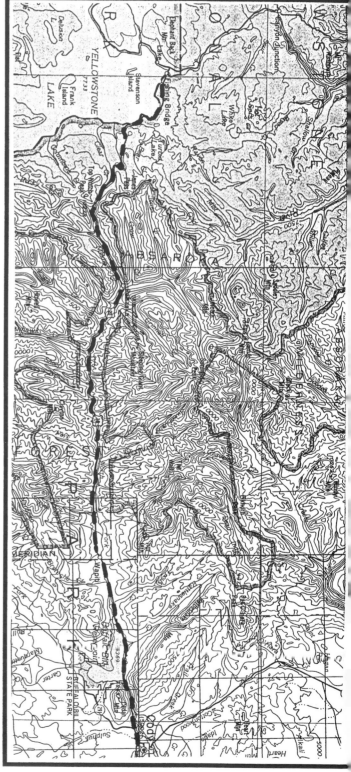

140

The "Cody Road"

"To visit Yellowstone without seeing the Cody Road is comparable to going all the way to New York and then coming away without seeing Broadway or Fifth Avenue. It is the 'show road' to or from the Park."
Northern Pacific Railroad ad, 1935

1915 *Automobile Blue Book*:
Cody to Yellowstone National Park, Wyo. - 54.4 m.

Via Shoshone Canyon, Holm Lodge and Pahaska Tepee. Good government stone road practically all the way. This is a section of the Black and Yellow Trail, and is one of the most scenic trips in the country, being well worth the tour across the continent. . . .

It is still too early in the season to determine whether or not it will be possible to permit the joint use of automobile and animal-drawn vehicles on the roads in the Yellowstone National Park. Considerable work in widening and improving the surface of the roads in the park will have to be done before it will be expedient to admit motor-propelled vehicles.

1922 *Automobile Blue Book*:
Cody to Yellowstone National Park (Lake Sta.), Wyo. - 83.8 m.

Via Shoshone Dam and Sylvan Pass. General conditions on this mountain road are fair to good and under normal conditions no difficulties should be encountered. Some steep grades and narrow stretches of roadway require careful driving and good brakes.

Today **Shoshone Canyon**, west of Cody, is traversed with ease. U.S. 14-16-20 passes through two short tunnels, then one long tunnel, whisking one from Shoshone River level to Buffalo Bill Reservoir level. This has not always been the case.

The arrival of the Burlington Railroad in Cody spurred the construction of the east entrance road to Yellowstone. An early, undated, Burlington Railroad ad stated:

The Cody Road is a pioneer's trail blazed through a region primeval, and in all the distance from Cody to the Lake Hotel there is no suggestion of anything else. No stores, no shops, no furnace smoke, no "social etiquette" - nothing but the great rugged West, crude, heroic and cordial. The invader finds no sign-boards warning him off the grass or forbidding him to enter private grounds.

Prior to 1910, Yellowstone-bound traffic avoided Shoshone Canyon altogether. The road west of Cody passed south of the canyon, south of Cedar Mountain.

The Buffalo Bill Dam, originally called Shoshone Dam, was built in the canyon between 1905 and 1910. A construction road was built from Cody, up the canyon, on the north side of the Shoshone River to a point one mile west of the dam site.

After completion of the dam, the "construction road" through the canyon was extended west along the north shore of the new reservoir, connecting with the old south road. **Tourist travelers preferred the narrow, steep canyon road over the south road. It was ten miles shorter and much more scenic.**

Because of its popularity, the canyon road was included in the Federal-aid and the Wyoming forest highway systems.

From Cody, the canyon road ran north of the Shoshone River. From the Irma Hotel, the road ran north on 2nd St. (present-day 12th St.), crossed the Shoshone River, then continued west along the north side of the river.

In 1923, the road west of Cody was changed. The Shoshone River was crossed west of town at the Hayden Arch Bridge.

The modern bridge across the river and the present-day highway alignment, with the two short and one long tunnels, was completed in 1961. The old canyon road, from river level to reservoir level, through the old tunnel, can be <u>walked</u> today.

West of the Buffalo Bill Reservoir, **the Cody Road ascends the valley of the North Fork of the Shoshone River to Pahaska Tepee** within two miles of the east entrance to Yellowstone National Park. In 1899, the U.S. Government improved the road through the forest reserve. In 1910, William Cody purchased Palace White Steamers to carry passengers from Cody to Pahaska Tepee. **This was end of road for automobiles until 1915.**

West of Cody, going to Yellowstone Park, we found the best roads in the state . . . it gave us something to talk about in an un-profane way.
Calvin W. Williams, describing his 1909 trip

The Cody, or Eastern entrance as it is sometimes called, has the endorsement of the Secretary of the Interior's Office as the most beautiful and most attractive entrance to any National Park in the United States.
Yellowstone Highway in Wyoming and Colorado, 1916

The distance from Cody to the Park line is 55 1/2 miles. Cody is reached either by C. B. & Q. Railroad, or via automobile road -- a new transportation company, known as Cody-Sylvan Pass Motor Company, is now operating transportation cars as far as Lake Hotel in the Park, where it is then necessary to take regular transportation around the Park, leaving Cody in the morning, stopping for lunch half way and reaching Lake Hotel for dinner.

The Eastern entrance invites everyone, and to once go over this road means to come back again or send a friend, with assured satisfaction and fast friendship to this -- the most magnificent country of dreams.
Yellowstone Highway in Wyoming and Colorado, 1916

"Bridge & Wagon at Holy City," 1903
Joseph Stimson traveled to Yellowstone on the newly opened east entrance road.
He was hired to produce photographs to be displayed at the
Louisiana Purchase Exposition in St. Louis.
Photo by Joseph Stimson, courtesy of the Wyoming Division of Cultural Resources.

From Cody, continue west on <u>U.S.</u> 14-16-20 (Yellowstone Avenue).

Mile 48.8: Interpretive signs near the **DeMaris Springs**, thermal water springs visited
by John Colter in 1807. Thereafter the region was known as "Colter's Hell." The
springs were also known commercially as "Needle Plunge."

Mile 48.3: Interpretive sign: "Shoshone Canyon."

To the west is the entrance to Shoshone Canyon. South of the River is Cedar
Mountain, named by Capt. William Jones in 1873. Cedar Mountain is the
location of **Shoshone Caverns**, a National Monument established in 1909,
but the designation was abolished in 1939. It was opened as Spirit Mountain
Caverns from 1957-1966. The caves were also known as Frost's Cave, for its
discoverer, Ned Frost, Sr. North of the river is Rattlesnake Mountain.

Mile 48.1: Interpretive sign: "**Shoshone River Siphon.**" William Cody helped
establish the region's irrigation system.

The old road is visible north of the river.

143

Shoshone Canyon

Left: **Road in Shoshone Canyon** below Shoshone (now Buffalo Bill) Dam. Looking downstream (east). Photo by A. G. Lucier. Author's collection.

Right: **Road ascending "dam hill"** from river level to reservoir level. Looking upstream (west). Photo by F. J. Hiscock. Author's collection.

Suddenly, with no warning but the conventional "Slow-down-to-six-miles-per-hour-blow-your-horn" sign, the road plunges down along the almost vertical walls of Shoshone Canyon to the very brink of a foaming torrent below. . . . The road picks its way gingerly along ledges and over bridges, sometimes forcing its way through tunnels in the solid rock, for when this mountain was cleaved asunder to allow passage of a river, no surplus room was left, and a more forbidding place for a road has rarely confronted man in his untiring energy to penetrate nature in her wildest haunts.

Charles J. Belden, 1918

1688. EXIT FROM TUNNEL NO.2 IN THE SHOSHONE CANYON, CODY, WYO.

Souvenir card of the second tunnel in Shoshone Canyon.
After leaving the tunnel, the west-bound motorist began the ascent
of "dam hill," the steep climb from river level to reservoir level.

The Shoshone Canyon road, opened to the public in 1910, was built in 1905 as a construction road for the Buffalo Bill Dam. Canyon tunnel number one was removed during later construction. The 22% grade of "dam hill" was the steepest of any U.S. numbered highway. The current highway, opened in 1961, passes high above the old road.

Mile 47.3: **Side trip**: Hayden Arch Road to the north. **Access to a hiking trail through Shoshone Canyon along the old Yellowstone Highway. The old roadbed passes through tunnel two, then climbs "dam hill" to Buffalo Bill Dam.** (The road is used by the U.S. Bureau of Reclamation.)
Reset mile 0.0.
Mile 0.1: Cross the Shoshone River via the 1923 **Hayden Arch Bridge**.
(Park here on weekends and evenings.)
Mile 0.6: Pass beneath the present-day bridge over the Shoshone River.
Mile 1.0: Parking for canyon hikers (7:45 A.M. to 4:30 P.M. Monday-Friday only).
Mile 1.7: Site of the first of two tunnels in the lower, or river level, of the canyon.
Mile 1.9: Kaiser's Face rock formation, just above the road.
Mile 2.0: Tunnel at lower end of "dam hill." The road then climbs to reservoir level.
Mile 2.2: Road dead-ends just below the Buffalo Bill Dam Visitor Center with no access to the center.

Mile 46.7: Cross the Shoshone River on the bridge opened in 1961.
Mile 46.2: Large pullout south of the highway. Views of Shoshone River below and the present-day tunnels ahead.

> Shoshone Canyon is no place for an inexperienced or inebriated driver. It will not do to pilot a car through it without looking at the road. But it offers no difficulties for any careful motorist whose steering-gear is trustworthy.
> Melville Ferguson, 1925

Mile 46.1: Enter the first of two short tunnels.
Mile 46.0: Enter main tunnel.

Mile 45.4: Exit main tunnel. Parking lot to the Buffalo Bill Dam Visitor Center ahead on the left.

1090. OBSERVATORY SUMMIT ON SHOSHONE DAM. ON THE CODY ROAD TO YELLOWSTONE PARK.

Souvenir card of Buffalo Bill Dam, originally called Shoshone Dam.
The name was officially changed in 1946.

Mile 45.3. **Buffalo Bill Dam**. Built between 1905-1910, it was the highest in the world when completed, 325 feet. It was the first concrete-arch dam and one of the first projects of the U.S. Bureau of Reclamation. The dam was raised 25 feet in 1993. The **visitor center**, **open summers**, has historical displays and views of the old highway below the dam.

146

"A steep ascent terminated by a long tunnel through the rock brings the motorist to the level of a wonderful, placid body of water stretching away toward the mountains and held prisoner by a mass of concrete cleverly placed at the mouth of this gorge, little more than two hundred feet across."
Charles J. Belden, 1918

Mile 44.0: Leave Shoshone Canyon.
Mile 43.2: Interpretive sign: "Buffalo Bill Reservoir."
Mile 42.0: Main entrance to **Buffalo Bill State Park**.
Mile 37.2: Short section (0.2 miles) of the older highway to the north.
Mile 35.0: Morris Ranch site, south of the highway. Location of the Morris Post Office from 1913-1923.
  1920s Cody Lions Club guide: "Oldest 'dude' ranch in the Buffalo Bill country. Auto Camp. Yellowstone Park trips. Store on Road. Meals and lodging."
Mile 34.5: Stovepipe rock formation to the south.
Mile 32.0: Cross the **North Fork of the Shoshone River**. The river was originally named "Stinking Water River." The name was changed in 1901.

Buffalo Bill Dam and Reservoir.
Photo by A. G. Lucier.
Author's Collection.

Aubrey Haines, in *The Yellowstone Story*, quotes Hiram Chittenden:
    This stream has heretofore been known as the Stinking Water River. It was so named in 1807 by its discoverer, John Colter, who came upon it where there is a large tar spring near the junction of the two forks . . . The name was wholly inappropriate as the stream is one of the finest in the mountains . . . As the valley of the river will soon be followed by a tourist route from upwards of 50 miles, it was considered important that an appropriate name be adopted.

Mile 31.9: **Wapiti**. Rural settlement with a post office, fire station, restaurant, and an elementary school, opened in 1911.
Mile 30.7: Interpretive sign: "Absaroka Volcanic Field." Chinese Wall rock formation to the north. These dikes were feeders for lava flows.

147

Mile 30.3: **Chinese Wall** to the north, leading directly toward the highway.
Site of the Green Lantern camp site.

1920s Cody Lions Club guide: "Camp, lunches, cold drinks and ice cream. Special - Fried Chicken."

Mile 29.5: Frost and Richard Ranch site, south of the highway.

1920s Cody Lions Club guide: "Typical stock ranch. Comfortable rooms. Home style cooking. Daily horseback trail trips. Also horseback camp trips thru Yellowstone Park."

Mile 29.1: "Pagoda House" to the south: unusual architecture, never occupied.

Mile 28.5: To the west, **Flag Peak** (south of the highway) and **Signal Peak** (north of the highway) mark the entrance to Shoshone National Forest.

Mile 27.8: **Mountain View Campground**.

1920s Cody Lions Club guide: "Groceries, gas and oil. Lunches, hot cakes and waffles, ice cream, cold drinks. Cabin camp, and saddle horses for hire."

Mile 27.5: The **Trail Shop** opened in 1923. The original shop was housed in one of the existing cabins. The old road ran north of the Trail Shop.

1920s Cody Lions Club guide: "Lunch room, hot waffles and honey our specialty. Home made ice cream and cold drinks. Fresh milk, home baking. You are never too late or too early. Gas and oil. 'Cabin camp.'"

"Yellowstone Tourists at the Trail Shop on the Cody Road."
Photograph courtesy of the Park County Historical Archives.

Mile 27.5: Enter **Shoshone National Forest**, the oldest timber reserve in the nation. The "Yellowstone Timber Reserve" was established in 1891 and in 1908 renamed Shoshone National Forest. The highway in the forest is designated the Buffalo Bill Scenic Byway.

The **Capt. William Jones expedition of 1873 was one of the first recorded ascents of the North Fork of the Shoshone River**. He noted local landmarks and the many rock formations along the river:

> Marched 18.8 miles to the North Fork of the Stinking Water River [Shoshone], crossing the South Fork. . . . About twenty miles northeast from this point is a small, isolated cluster, which is probably the Heart Mountain of the early trappers and guides. . . . A few miles lower down, below the cañon, a mass of sulphur springs [DeMaris Springs area west of present-day Cody] occur which still give good cause for the river's name.

> . . . up the North Fork of the Stinking Water . . . The conglomerate weathers into the most fantastic pinnacles, needles, and grotesque forms. . . . Compared with any mountain scenery that I have seen, the effect is quite peculiar, and even magnificent. . . .

> The grotesque forms of the conglomerate previously alluded to afforded great amusement to the party.

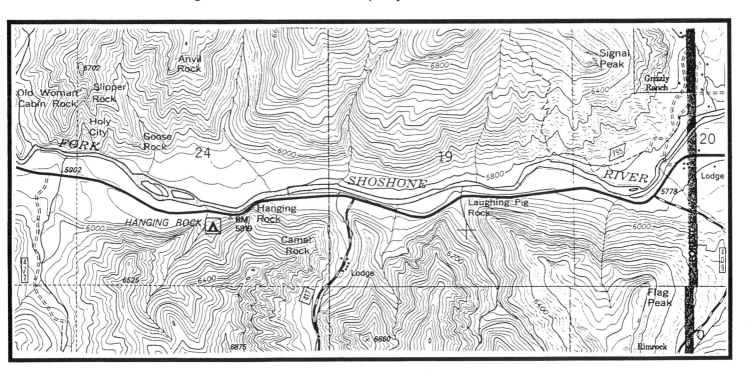

United States Geological Survey Map, Flag Peak 7.5', 1991.
Signal Peak, north of U.S. 14-16-20, and Flag Peak, south of the highway, mark the entrance to Shoshone National Forest. The peaks were called "The Sentinels" by Capt. William Jones in 1873. Because of the many unusual rock formations, early tourists called this road up the North Fork of the Shoshone River the "Zoo Park Road."

The Cody Road through the Shoshone National Forest
The "Zoo Park Road"

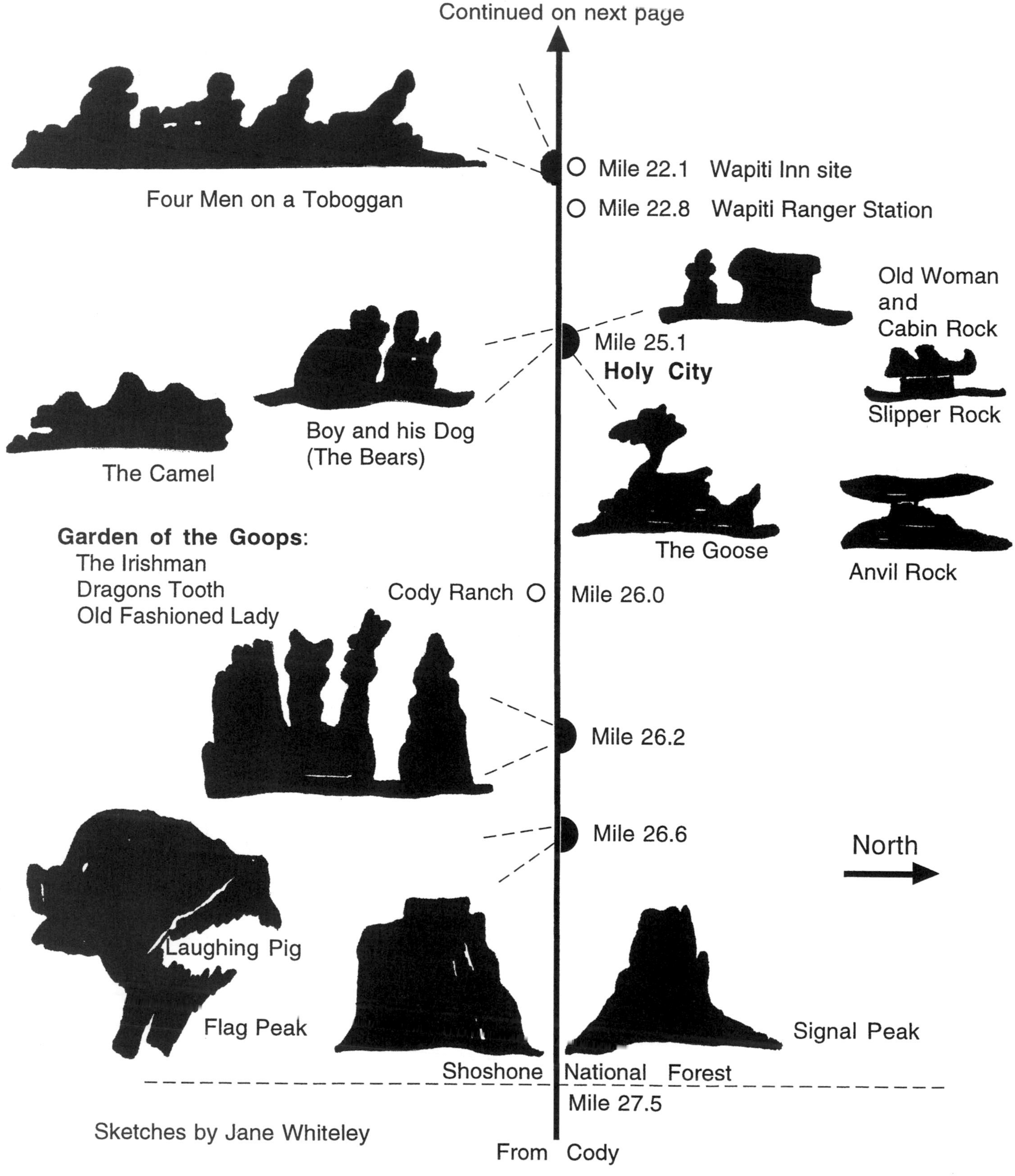

Continued on next page

Four Men on a Toboggan

O Mile 22.1   Wapiti Inn site

O Mile 22.8   Wapiti Ranger Station

The Camel

Boy and his Dog
(The Bears)

Mile 25.1
Holy City

Old Woman
and
Cabin Rock

Slipper Rock

The Goose

Anvil Rock

Garden of the Goops:
The Irishman
Dragons Tooth
Old Fashioned Lady

Cody Ranch O   Mile 26.0

Mile 26.2

Mile 26.6

North

Laughing Pig

Flag Peak

Signal Peak

Shoshone National Forest

Mile 27.5

Sketches by Jane Whiteley

From Cody

150

To Sylvan Pass, Fishing Bridge,
and the Grand Loop Road

Yellowstone National Park

East Entrance Station

Cody Peak

Interpretive Sign

Shoshone National Forest

O Mile 2.1   Pahaska Tepee

Mile 3.1

O Mile 3.6   Shoshone Lodge

O Mile 7.9   Wayfarers Chapel

O Mile 8.3   Crossed Sabres Lodge (Holm Lodge)

O Mile 10.0   Goff Creek Lodge

Mile 11.3

Chimney Rock
(Needle Rock)

Elephant
Head Rock

O Mile 11.7
Elephant Head Lodge

O Mile 12.3   Absaroka Lodge

Mutilated Hand
(Mitten Rock)

Henry Ford
and his Flivver

Mile 12.7

Mile 13.4

Cameo Rock
(Window Rock)

The Palisades
(Cathedal Rocks)

Triple Point
(Trinity)

Mile 14.2

Blackwater
Firefighters Monument O   Mile 15.1

Blackwater Creek Resort O   Mile 15.2

O Mile 15.9   Mummy Cave

UXU Ranch O   Mile 17.0

O Mile 19.8   Clearwater CCC Camp site

From top of previous page

151

Mile 26.6: **Laughing Pig Rock** immediately next to the highway, on the south side. Pullout, north side of highway, just west of the rock.

Mile 26.2: Pullout on right. **Garden of the Goops** rock formations to the south.

Mile 26.0: Cody's Ranch Resort. Originally called Lazy Bar H, it was built in 1925.

Mile 25.1: **Holy City** interpretive signs. Holy City volcanic rock formations north of the river including **Old Woman and Cabin Rock**, **Slipper Rock**, the **Goose,** and **Anvil Rock**. To the southeast, south of the highway, is **Camel Rock**. South of the Camel are The Bears (sitting on their haunches), also called **Boy and his Dog**.

Mile 22.8: **Wapiti Ranger Station**. The station was the first in the U.S., opened in 1903. Interpretive sign on the station and early Forest Rangers.

Mile 22.1: Near the Wapiti Campgrounds is the site of the **Wapiti Inn**, opened by William Cody in 1905. During the horse and carriage days, the Cody to Pahaska Lodge drive was too long for a day's ride. The Wapiti Inn served as the intermediate rest stop. The inn closed in 1913 when motorized vehicles reduced the need for the stop. Some of the salvageable material was used in the cabins at Pahaska Tepee. The inn was located on the east side of Elk Fork, north of the highway.

William Cody's Wapiti Inn on Elk Fork.
Four Men on a Toboggan rock formation on the horizon.
Photograph courtesy of the Park County Historical Archives.

Mile 20.3: Cross the North Fork of the Shoshone River. **Four men on a Toboggan** rock formation on the skyline to the southwest.

Mile 19.0: Clearwater Creek. Site of the Civilian Conservation Corp (CCC) camp, established in 1934. The CCC built trails, campgrounds, and bridges in the region. The buildings were removed in 1942 and moved to the Heart Mountain Relocation Center northeast of Cody.

Mile 17.0: **UXU Ranch**, opened in 1929.

Mile 15.9: **Mummy Cave** is a large alcove carved in the cliff by the waters of the river. A mummified prehistoric man and numerous artifacts were unearthed here in 1963. Much of the cave's overhang has been removed for safety reasons.

Mile 15.2: **Blackwater Creek Resort**. Hunting lodge with cabins dating from 1929.

Mile 15.1: **Blackwater Memorial**. A monument to the 15 firefighters who died in a 1937 forest fire. Twelve of the victims were enrolled in the CCC program. The Rex Hale campground is named for the Forest Service employee who died in the fire. The memorial was built in 1939 by CCC members. A five mile trail leads from the monument up Blackwater Creek to the site of the disaster.

Mile 14.2: **Triple Point** (Trinity) rock formation to the west.

Mile 14.0: East end of **The Palisades**, north of the highway.

Mile 13.4: Pull-out, south side of highway, for views of **Henry Ford and His Flivver** rock formation to the south. The Palisades to the east.

Looking east to the Palisades, also known as Cathedral Rocks.

Mile 12.7: **Cameo Rock** [Window Rock] to the northwest.

Mile 12.3: **Absaroka Lodge**. Built as a home in 1910, it opened as a lodge in 1917.

Mile 11.7: **Elephant Head Lodge** and rock formation to the north. The lodge was opened by a niece of William Cody. A travel brochure stated that the lodge "is a small place - accommodations limited to the requirements of eighteen or twenty guests - and should not be confused with a hotel or a tourist resort."

1920s Cody Lions Club guide: "A convenient overnight stop going in or coming out of the park. Home cooking, comfortable beds, saddle horses."

Northeast of **Elephant Head Rock** is **Mutilated Hand**, also called Mitten Rock.

Mile 11.3: **Chimney Rock**, north of the highway.

Mile 10.0: **Goff Creek Lodge**. Opened in 1906, cabins were added in 1924.

Mile 8.3: **Crossed Sabres Ranch** to the north. Originally called **Holm Lodge**, the original lodge was built in 1907 and had wall tents with wooden flooring for tourist accommodations. Built by Tex Holm (brother of Good Roads advocate Gus Holm's), he ran a transportation company using Stanley Steamers to transport visitors from Cody to the lodge, then to Yellowstone.

1924 *Park-to-Park Highway* ad: "Amidst God's Grandest Masterpieces
and Beyond Man's Fondest Hopes.
The Beginning of Sublime Rest and Contentment."

1920s Cody Lions Club guide: "Crossed Sabres Ranch. One of the attractions of the Cody Road. Warm rooms, good meals, saddle horses. You are invited to drive in."

Holm Lodge (Crossed Sabres Ranch). This original lodge was built in 1907. Photograph courtesy of Buck Norris.

Mile 7.9: **Wayfarers Chapel**, a pleasant 225-yard walk through the forest.

Mile 3.6: **Shoshono Lodge.** Opened in 1924 as the Red Star Campground and Store. The name was changed to Shoshone in the early 1940s.

> 1920s Cody Lions Club guide: "Meals and lunches. Good camp, shower baths, excellent water. No dampness, no mosquitoes, and where you get service. Star Mercantile, Milling and Lumber Company."

Mile 3.1: **Interpretive sign on Grizzly Bears**. View of Cody Peak to the west. The peak was named for William Cody by the Cody Club in 1931.

Mile 2.1: **Pahaska Tepee** was built as a hunting lodge for William Cody in 1904. "Pahaska" loosely translates to "long hair's lodge" in the Crow Indian language. The three cabins adjacent to the original lodge were built in 1909. The lodge was "end of the road" for automobiles until August 1, 1915, when they were allowed in Yellowstone. The west wing of the original lodge was removed after being damaged in the 1957 earthquake.

> 1924 *Park-to-Park Highway* ad: "The place you are looking for . . . Stop for a meal or a month."

> 1920s Cody Lions Club guide: "The famous hunting lodge of Buffalo Bill. Saddle horse parties, camper's supplies and lunches. Stop for a meal or for a month. Garage and filling station."

Souvenir card of automobiles at Pahaska Tepee.

Mile 0.0: **East entrance to Yellowstone National Park.**

Yellowstone Highway
Yellowstone National Park's East Entrance Road

> "Few places in the world are more dangerous than home; fear not, therefore, to try the mountain passes."
>
> John Muir, quoted by Charles J. Belden, 1918

Yellowstone's east entrance road ascends Middle Creek, crosses Sylvan Pass, then descends to Yellowstone Lake. The road joins Yellowstone's Grand Loop Road at Fishing Bridge Junction, 1.5 miles north of the Lake Hotel. Maps in the 1916 Yellowstone Highway Association's guide book end at the Lake Hotel.

The east entrance road is also known as the "Cody Road."

Capt Hiram Chittenden, chief highway engineer, noted in an 1899 report to the Secretary of the Interior:

> It is probable that before many years it may be necessary to make an approach from Big Horn Basin via Jones's Pass to the outlet of the Yellowstone Lake. The necessity for such a road, however, will be contingent upon the advent of a railroad in the Basin.

The Burlington Railroad arrived in Cody in 1901. Construction of the east entrance road began that very same year, but the road ran over Sylvan Pass, not Jones Pass. Philetus Norris, second superintendent of Yellowstone, discovered Sylvan Pass in 1881 while following an Indian trail. Sylvan Pass is six miles south-southeast of Jones Pass, discovered by Capt. William Jones in 1873.

Chittenden noted that Sylvan Pass was chosen instead of Jones Pass because:

> The pass [Sylvan] is one of great scenic beauty and will be an important addition to the attractions of the Park. . . . [the pass] is unique among mountain passes in that it is almost entirely loosened from the cliffs on either side by the action of frost.

Although **the east entrance road opened to the public in July of 1903**, only about 300 visitors entered by this entrance that year, out of a total visitor count of over 13,000. **The east side of Sylvan Pass was so steep that it was almost impassable until 1905 when bridges, including the famous "corkscrew bridge," were completed**. At the "corkscrew" the road crossed over itself in the narrow, steep valley below Sylvan Pass. In 1919 this wooden bridge structure was replaced by a more substantial 60-foot-long rock-fill bridge.

In 1927 construction was started on relocating the road across Sylvan Pass. The new road ran higher on the mountain, above Middle Creek. Completed in 1931, it offered better grades and much better views. A new road was also completed around the west end of Lake Butte. This route, along the shore of Yellowstone Lake and away from Turbid Lake, added to the scenic value of the road.

East entrance of Yellowstone National Park. Courtesy of the
Buffalo Bill Historical Center, Cody, WY. Jack Richard Collection, photo P.89.2755.

Front and back of a **Yellowstone windshield sticker**, often called a "paster."
It indicated that the vehicle entrance fee had been paid.
Used from 1919-1941, they were originally 5" across, later reduced to 2 1/2".
Courtesy of the National Park Service, Yellowstone National Park.

157

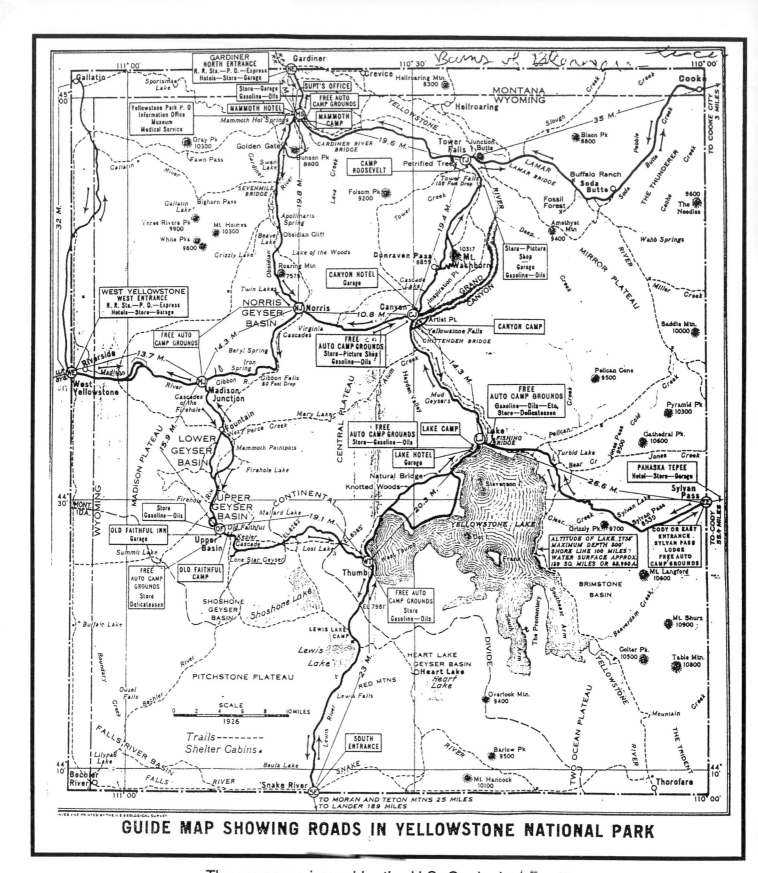

GUIDE MAP SHOWING ROADS IN YELLOWSTONE NATIONAL PARK

The map was issued by the U.S. Geological Survey.
The park rules and regulations (opposite page) were also given to
tourists at the entrance stations. **Both map and regulations
were pasted in Blanche Johnston's 1926 trip diary.**
Courtesy of the Carnegie Branch Library for Local History, Boulder, Colorado.

You should consult your guidebook for the complete rules and regulations of the Park. The following is an abstract of the motor vehicle rules:

1. The park gateways are open from 6 a. m. to 9:30 p. m. only.

2. Where a car is rented for the park trip, or is a jitney, it cannot be admitted unless the owner has a Government franchise to operate in the Park.

3. Motorcycles are admitted to the Park.

4. Motor trucks are subject to special restrictions and special permit fees.

5. At the Park gateway, a permit, good for the entire season must be procured, and must be kept for identification in the Park.

6. Fees for permits are $3.00 for automobiles and $1.00 for motorcycles.

7. (Quoted in full) Direction.—Automobiles shall pass around the road system forming the "loop" in the direction opposite to that of the hands of a clock, as indicated by the arrows printed in red on the automobile guide map. The reverse direction may be taken as follows:

Norris Junction (N. J.) to Mammoth Hot Springs (M. S.) any time, day or night.

Madison Junction (M. J.) to Norris Junction (N. J.) any time of day or night except the periods 9 a. m. to 11:30 a. m., and 2 p. m. to 4:30 p. m.

Upper Geyser Basin (Old Faithful—O. F.) to western entrance (W. E.) any time, day or night.

Canyon Junction (C. J.) to Lake Junction (L. J.) any time, day or night.

Mammoth Hot Springs (M. S.) to Tower Falls, early enough to reach Tower Falls by 1 p. m. Distance 19.6 miles.

Canyon Junction (C. J.) to Norris Junction (N. J.) direct, any time, day or night.

Lake Junction (L. J.) to West Thumb (W. T.) and south entrance (S. E.) (but not Old Faithful—O. F.) any time, day or night.

Summit of Mt. Washburn (Mt. W.), down north side to junction of Dunraven Pass road, thence to Canyon Junction (C. J.) after 3 p. m.

The Superintendent has authority to change routing of cars if necessary.

8. On park roads, automobiles must be 50 yards apart, except when passing; gears must be enmeshed except when shifting; tires and brakes must be in good condition; cars must carry one extra tire.

9. Speed limits are 12 miles on grades and curves; not exceeding 25 miles per hour on straight stretches.

10. Horns shall be sounded when approaching curves, and before passing other vehicles or pedestrians.

11. Automobiles must be equipped with head and tail lights. Dim headlights when meeting other vehicles.

12. Muffler cut-outs must be closed while passing hotels, camps, and horses.

13. Relates to passing teams. Teams have the right of way.

14. Relates to overtaking vehicles.

15. Relates to accidents and stopovers.

16. Violation of the automobile rules and regulations is a misdemeanor and is punishable by a fine of not more than $500, or imprisonment of not exceeding 6 months or both, plus costs of proceedings, or the automobile permit may be cancelled, and the offender ejected from the Park or any combination of these penalties may be imposed.

1926 Yellowstone "Automobile and Motorcycle Regulations."

159

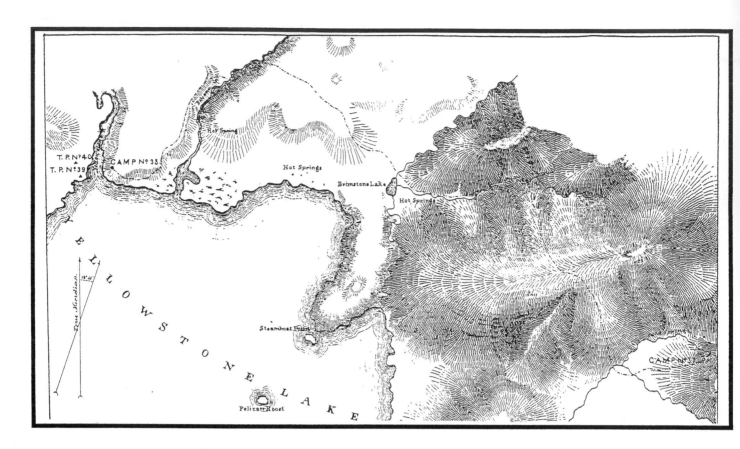

East Entrance Trails and Highways

Above: Capt. **William Jones map, 1873**. He crossed Jones Pass, six miles north-northwest of Sylvan Pass. He descended Bear Creek and passed Brimstone Lake (now Turbid Lake) to the outlet of Yellowstone Lake (present-day Fishing Bridge).

Below: An **1896 map** shows the Lake Hotel and the Grand Loop Road. There was only a trail along the northeast shore of Yellowstone Lake. A trail ran past Turbid Lake to Jones Pass. United States Geological Survey (USGS) map, Canyon 30', 1896.

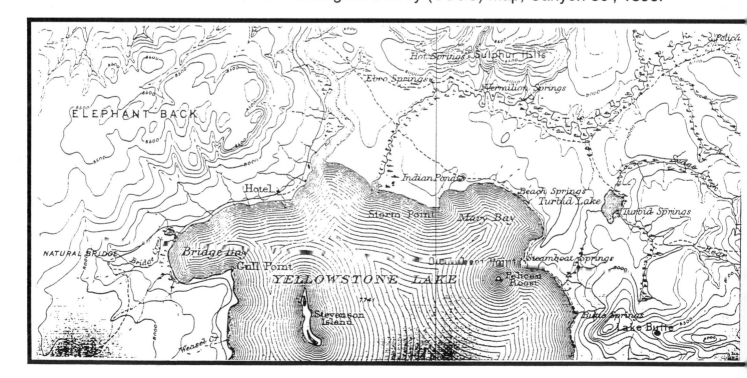

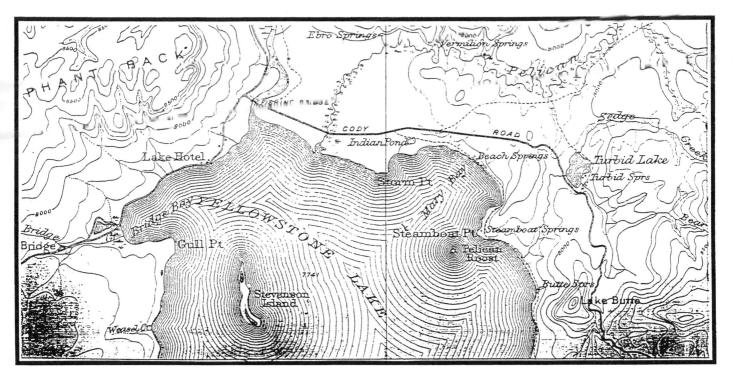

Above: A **1918 map** shows the East Entrance Road, labeled Cody Road. The road from Sylvan Pass passed east of Lake Butte and along the southwest shore of Turbid Lake. USGS map, Canyon 30', 1918.

Below: A **1961 map** shows the present-day alignment of the East Entrance Road. It passes south and west of Lake Butte and along the shore of Yellowstone Lake. The Grand Loop Road is shown running between the Lake Hotel-Lake Lodge complex and the lake. Note the former campgrounds at Fishing Bridge, Pelican Creek, and Squaw Lake. The name of Squaw Lake has since reverted back to its original name, Indian Pond. USGS map, Yellowstone National Park 1:250,000, 1961.

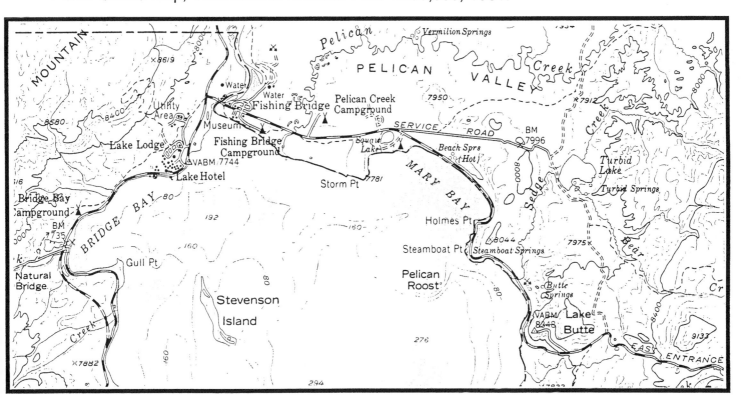

East Entrance Road

*Reset mile 0.0 at the East Entrance (**No mileposts in the park**).*
Mile 0.0: **East entrance to Yellowstone National Park**. Site of the **Sylvan Pass Soldier Station**, a frame station built in 1904.

> We pass the boundary line of the Forest Reserve and enter the Park proper. There is a new two-story and wing house and ice house and barn here where the eastern gate caretaker resides.
>
> Charles A. Heath, 1905

> Soldier Station on left. . . . It will be necessary for tourists to stop and register at this station, paying the entrance fee; be sure to secure a book of rules showing the schedule on which one must travel throughout the park. Be sure to have two good extra casings on your car or you will not be allowed to enter. *Goodrich Tour* guide, 1918

> . . . east entrance to the park. The fee for entering was $3.50 only. We had to give our license no. & assure them that we did not have fire arms or fishing tackle (both of which they would have confiscated & then sent on to entrance you were coming out) and tell them how long we expected to stay & which entrance we were going out.
>
> Blanche Johnston, 1926

Sylvan Pass Ranger Station.
The sign over the porch reads: "STOP   REGISTER HERE"
Photograph courtesy of the National Park Service, Yellowstone National Park.

1924 postcard of the Sylvan Pass Lodge.
Photograph by Jack E. Haynes.
The Haynes family operated the photo shops in the park.

The east entrance was the site of the **Sylvan Pass Lodge**, a rustic lodge opened in 1924. It was used as a lunch stop by Burlington Railroad bus passengers from Cody to the Lake Hotel. Also available were several tents for overnight accommodations. The lodge was torn down in 1940.

1924 *Park-to-Park Highway* guide:

"When Touring the Yellowstone you will find it very convenient to stop for lodging or meals at any or all of the six PERMANENT CAMPS. Conducted by the Yellowstone Park Camps Co. Camps are located at: Mammoth Hot Springs, Upper Geyser Basin, Grand Canyon, Tower Falls, and Eastern Entrance."

Mile 1.7: **Middle Creek** access road to the south. The pre-1931 road followed closely the creek. It can be hiked, both upstream and downstream.

The Middle Fork has a more rapid current than even the rapid North Fork of the Shoshone . . . Our road follows the banks closely all the way and has been so carefully constructed and built by the government that it is a veritable boulevard of the forest; any automobile could easily pass along it, except at Bear Creek, which has not been bridged.

Charles A. Heath, 1905

Mile 2.0: The present-day highway begins its climb out of the bottom of the valley of Middle Creek. From Pahaska Tepee to within a mile of Sylvan Pass, the old road closely followed Middle Creek.

Above: Souvenir card of the original "**Corkscrew Bridge**."
Completed in 1905, it made the east ascent to Sylvan Pass easier.
Below: In 1919, the "Corkscrew" was upgraded with this rock and dirt fill structure.
The bridge remains, well below the level of the present-day highway.
Photograph courtesy of the Park County Historical Archives.

Mile 6.5 (0.45 miles east of Sylvan Pass summit): Small pullout on the right. Walk (watch for cars) 150 yards east for a view of the **"corkscrew bridge"** in the valley. The original loop was built of timber in 1905 and replaced with a dirt fill structure in 1919.

Charles Van Tassell, an early park employee, said of the corkscrew bridge design: "you pass one place three times before you get by it, and then meet yourself on the road coming back."

Mile 6.6: Pullout on left. To **hike to the corkscrew bridge** walk west, towards the Sylvan Pass summit, for 200 yards. Here the old road merges with the present-day highway. Follow the old road east (downhill) for 0.3 miles. The old road makes a double "S" curve, then passes through a grove of trees before arriving at the corkscrew bridge.

Mile 6.9: **Sylvan Pass**, elevation 8557'. This is the summit of the Absaroka Mountain Range. To the south is Top Notch Peak; to the north Hoyt Peak, named for John Hoyt, Wyoming Territorial Governor and first president of the University of Wyoming.

The greatest work of the frost and ice yet seen is now on our right, and for nearly 1,500 feet is a precipitous incline called the "Devil's Slide," running from the highest point of Sylvan Pass to our very wagon road, which zigzags through this field of fine rock for the balance of the way to the top of the Pass.   Charles A. Heath, 1905

20. On the Snow at Sylvan Pass, July 25th. Elevation 9035 feet, Cody Route.

Postcard of the **rock fields at the summit of Sylvan Pass.**

Mile 7.5: Lake Eleanor. Named for Hiram Chittenden's daughter.
Mile 8.6: **Sylvan Lake**.
    Eleanor and Sylvan Lakes are skirted in turn; the latter a dainty body
of water set in the depth of an alpine forest and guarded by a grim peak
at its head [Top Notch Peak].   Charles J. Belden, 1918

1916 Haynes postcard of "**Automobile Stages at Sylvan Lake**."
Operated by photographer Frank J. Haynes, the Cody-Sylvan Pass Motor Company
ran, in the summer of 1916, the park's first line on motor stages.
The automobiles are eastbound, heading for Sylvan Pass and the East Entrance.

Mile 14.8: Pullout to the left. **View of Yellowstone Lake** to the west and the Teton
    Mountains, 60 miles to the southwest.

Mile 16.2: **Side trip**: Road leads 0.8 miles to the northwest to the **Lake Butte** view
    point of Yellowstone Lake.
        [Yellowstone Lake] It is a scene of transcendent beauty which has
    been viewed by few white men, and we felt glad to have looked upon it
    before its primeval solitude be broken by the pleasure seekers which at
    no distant day will throng its shores.   David Folsom, 1869

    An interpretive sign at Lake Butte overlook: "Water Wilderness. You are looking
    south across thirty miles of water into an area farther from a road than any place
    in the lower 48 states. . . ."

The original route of the Yellowstone Highway ran past **Turbid Lake**, passing to the east and north of Lake Butte. The old road rejoined the present-day highway at Indian Pond. The 1873 Jones map notes Turbid Lake as "Brimstone Lake."

Turbid Springs and Turbid Lake. The ground everywhere in and about the place is emitting steam, vapors and odors, and is hot beneath the feet; many of us feel that hell is nearer than we expected to see it.

Charles A. Heath, 1905

[Turbid Lake] . . . a big basin of water, from which steam issued from a myriad of vents. . . . found it in a slow turmoil, the mud rising from the bottom in little fountains of turbidity, the whole effect being that which might be expected if some mud-eating giant were watching his evening porridge, expecting it momentarily to boil.   Herbert Quick, 1911

Mile 18.6 (includes the 1.6 mile round trip to Lake Butte view point): Arrive at the shores of **Yellowstone Lake**. The lake is North America's largest high altitude (greater than 7,000 feet) lake.

Mile 20.8: Steamboat Point and **Steamboat Springs**. Interpretive sign: "Hot Lake Bed."

The Hayden survey party camped near here August 19, 1871. A. C. Peale, expedition member noted:

Our camp was situated on a high bluff on the edge of the lake. Near us there were two vents, from which the steam, in escaping, made a noise exactly like a large steamboat letting off steam. . . . Every night while at this place we experienced earthquake-shocks, each lasting from five to twenty seconds. We named it Earthquake Camp.

The geology report of the Capt. Jones expedition of 1873 reported:

The groups of hot and cold springs at Steam Point and in the neighborhood are rather numerous . . . Among these none is more interesting than the Steamboat, the noise of which so closely resembles the puffing of a small lake-steamer that one involuntarily casts a longing eye over the surface of the water in the hope that such is really there.

Mile 24.1: **Indian Pond**. A "hydrothermal explosion crater." Here the old road past Turbid Lake merged with the present-day highway. The Nez Perce camped here on August 26, 1877. The name was changed to Squaw Lake for a time, but has officially changed back to Indian Pond.

Mile 25.7: Cross **Pelican Creek**. A campground was once located east of the creek, north of the highway. After camping at Indian Pond, the Nez Perce ascended Pelican Creek, then crossed over to the Lamar River, on their attempted trek to Canada.

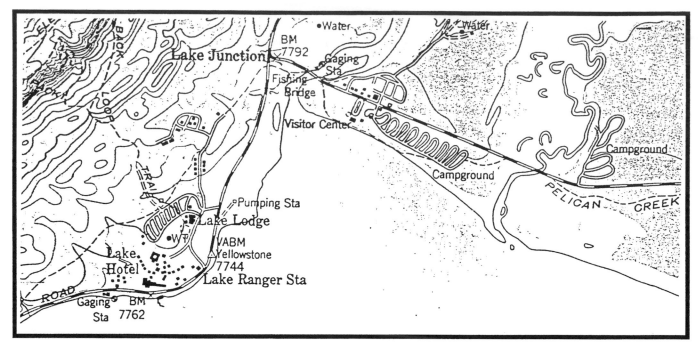

United States Geological Survey map, Canyon Village 15', **1959**.
Note the former campgrounds at Pelican Creek and Fishing Bridge.
The old Grand Loop Road passed between Yellowstone Lake and the Lake Hotel.
The 1959 Lake Junction is now known as Fishing Bridge Junction;
Lake Junction is located where the road to the Lake Hotel-Lake Lodge complex
branches off the new Grand Loop Road.

Mile 26.5: East end of the "**Fishing Bridge Historic Strip**."

> The 1928 *Haynes New Guide* noted the following, all located just east of the Fishing Bridge: Public automobile camp, Hamilton Store, Cafeteria, Haynes Picture Shop and Photo Finishing Plant, and housekeeping cabins.

> Much is gone, much remains of one of the first examples of "strip development" in Wyoming.

The current structures, from east to west, along the strip:

The Fishing Bridge Recreational Vehicle Park (north of highway) is for hard-sided camping units only, this because of the Grizzly Bear activity in the area. The old, very large campground south of the highway and east of the visitor center was closed in 1989.

Hamilton Stores men's dormitory (north of highway).

The present-day warming hut (south of highway) was the original ranger station.

The Hamilton Store (north of highway).

Filling station (north of highway).

Fishing Bridge Visitor Center and Museum (south of highway). One of the four "Trailside Museums" opened in the park in 1931. The museum houses the original bird and wildlife exhibit. The amphitheater also opened In 1931.

Auto and R. V. service center (north of highway).

Five cabins (north of highway) remain of the many cabins that comprised the Fishing Bridge tourist cabin camp.

Mile 27.0: **Fishing Bridge**. The present-day bridge is the third structure across the Yellowstone River at the outlet of Yellowstone Lake. The first bridge was built in 1903 and was named "Fishing Bridge" in 1914. The first bridge, 360 feet long, angled more to the southeast than the present-day bridge. A sharp right angle turn was needed at the east approach to the bridge and there was a slight jog to the left at the west end of the bridge. The bridge was rebuilt in 1919 and the current bridge built in 1936-37. Fishing Bridge was closed to fishing at the end of the 1973 season. The marina was also closed the same year.

963 FISHING BRIDGE, NEAR LAKE JUNCTION, YELLOWSTONE NATIONAL PARK

OVER YELLOWSTONE RIVER AT YELLOWSTONE LAKE   2A-H698

Postcard of the first Fishing Bridge.
A sharp right angle turn was needed at the east approach to the bridge.

Mile 27.3: The pre-1970 Grand Loop Road crossed the present-day highway. This is 100 yards east of Fishing Bridge Junction. Access to the old road is via the stairs at the southwest corner of Fishing Bridge. The trail, using in part the old road, leads south to the Lake Hotel-Lake Lodge complex. **The trail is closed until mid-June because of bear activity.** Check at the Fishing Bridge Visitor Center.

Mile 27.4: **Fishing Bridge Junction** and the Yellowstone **Grand Loop Road**. Left to Lake Junction and the Lake Hotel-Lake Lodge complex. [**Before 1970, "Fishing Bridge Junction" was known as "Lake Junction."** The new Lake Junction is located 1.6 miles south, where the Lake Hotel-Lake Lodge complex road branches off the new Grand Loop Road.]
Left (south) at Fishing Bridge Junction.

Mile 29.0: **Lake Junction. Left to the Lake Hotel-Lake Lodge complex**. The original Yellowstone Highway-Grand Loop Road followed more closely the shoreline from Fishing Bridge Junction.

Lake Lodge. Construction began in 1921, with major additions made in 1926. It was the last of the Yellowstone lodges. They gave the automobile tourists a choice other than tent camps and higher-priced hotels. The "Pioneer" cabins began appearing in the mid 1920s, replacing the tent camps.

Loading passengers at **Lake Lodge**.
Picture taken before the major lodge expansion of 1926.
Photograph courtesy of the National Park Service, Yellowstone National Park.

Lake Ranger Station was completed in 1923. The old highway passed in front of the Ranger Station. A hiking trail leads north of the ranger station, following in part the old road, to Fishing Bridge Junction. **The trail is closed until mid-June because of bear activity.** Check at the ranger station.

The **Lake Hamilton Store** was opened in 1922. The store and the now vacant filling station are located between the ranger station and the Lake Hotel. The first Hamilton Store at Lake was opened in 1917, near the hotel, in the former Yellowstone Park Boat Company store. Charles Hamilton built and operated stores and filling stations throughout the park. He opened a small store at the auto camp at Fishing Bridge in 1924. His company bought the Haynes Photo Shops and all park stores are now managed by Hamilton Stores, Inc.

Lake Hotel. Construction of the hotel was started in 1889 and opened in 1891 with 80 rooms. The Ionic columns and 80 rooms were added in 1903, with an additional 50 rooms added in 1904. The sun room was added in 1928. The hotel was extensively renovated in 1988 and now has 296 rooms.

1925 postcard of the **Lake Hotel**. The Ionic columns were added in 1903.

. . . come to the Lake Hotel on the northwest corner of Yellowstone Lake; new and spacious three-story structure, finely built with southern exposure overlooking the lake, broad steps and entrance through imposing, pure white corinthian columns 50 feet in height; and the building itself painted a soft yellow; it extends a welcome that is in keeping with the generous atmosphere of the Park.

Charles A. Heath, 1905

The old Grand Loop Highway continued southwest to Bridge Bay following closely the shoreline of Yellowstone Lake. It is now a hiking trail. The boathouse, southwest of Lake Hotel, was part of the old fish hatchery.

The Yellowstone Highway ended at the Lake Hotel-Lake Lodge complex. The National Park-to-Park Highway continued north on Yellowstone's Grand Loop Road.

Yellowstone's Grand Loop Road

"Gravel and bridges and engineering skill alone do not make a great road. The footprints and the hoofmarks, and, if you will, the tire prints of countless travelers are required. And, too, the road must lead somewhere . . . Slowly but as certainly as mathematics The Grand Loop Road of Yellowstone Park is becoming a great national highway. It is a road entwined in the lives and the dreams of an ever-growing number of people, the path of pilgrims seeking the God of the Open Air."   Harry W. Frantz, 1923

Yellowstone's 140-mile-long interior "Belt Line" or "Circuit Road" was also called the "Park Circle" by the 1916 *Yellowstone Highway in Wyoming and Colorado*. The name **"The Grand Loop Road of Yellowstone Park" was suggested by Harry W. Frantz in 1923. The road connects all the major attractions of the park**. Yellowstone's East Entrance Road joins the park's Grand Loop Road at Fishing Bridge Junction.

Richard Bartlett in his *Yellowstone: A Wilderness Besieged* noted that Park Company President Charles Gibson, in 1888, called for completion of the Loop Road. Gibson pointed out that Yellowstone Lake, Mt. Washburn, and Tower Falls were "still approachable only to hardy mountaineers." Visitors from Mammoth could travel to Old Faithful and back, but had to travel from Norris to the Yellowstone Canyon then backtrack to Norris. Gibson said "When he is being jostled over the stumps, gullies, and rocks of the trail in the park his spread-eagle Americanism droops in shame . . ."

The last section of the Grand Loop Road, completed in 1905, was the Canyon Junction to Tower Junction road over Dunraven Pass. That same year, the road to the top of Mount Washburn was completed.

In 1909, the Loop Road was adequate for horse-drawn conveyances, and beginning in 1913, road improvements were geared toward their use by automobiles.

When automobiles were permitted in Yellowstone on August 1, 1915, the Grand Loop was primarily a one way, counterclockwise road. Autos left designated points one-half hour before horse-drawn stages.

By the 1920s, the direction of travel around the Grand Loop Road was still primarily counterclockwise. While some sections were now full-time two way roads, others were open for clockwise travel at certain times of the day. Oiling of the Grand Loop Road began in 1925 and asphalting began in 1927.

The Old Faithful-to-Craig Pass section was not paved until after World War II.

As with emigrant trails, the Yellowstone Highway (and National Park-to-Park Highway) was a two-way road, taking travelers from Yellowstone to points south, including Rocky Mountain National Park.

From the park's Grand Loop Road, the Yellowstone Highway (Cody Road) runs east from Fishing Bridge Junction:

> the Cody Road beckoned them eastward, as a side road always beckons to the true wanderer. . . . What does it run to?   Wyoming . . . its nothing but scenery and curiosity.
> Herbert Quick, 1911

From Fishing Bridge Junction, the National Park-to-Park Highway continued north on the Grand Loop Road to Mammoth, via Canyon Junction and Tower Junction. At Mammoth the "auto trail" leaves the park via the north entrance at Gardiner, Montana.

North from Fishing Bridge Junction on Yellowstone's <u>Grand Loop Road</u>.

Reset mile 0.0 (No highway mileposts in the park).
Mile 0.0: Fishing Bridge Junction.
Mile 0.2: The old loop road runs through the meadow to the east. Many of the trees are actually in the old roadbed.

Old section of the Grand Loop Road,
1/2 mile northwest of Fishing Bridge. A 2000 photograph.

Mile 5.0: **<u>Side trip</u>**: 0.3 miles east to the **Buffalo Ford picnic area**. The Nez Perce crossed the Yellowstone River here, on August 25, 1877, and nooned on the east side. They had entered the park via the Madison River, then crossed the Central Plateau to the Yellowstone River. The ford was also called Chief Joseph's Crossing and is now officially called **Nez Perce Ford**.

Mile 7.0: Enter **Hayden Valley**. It is named for Ferdinand V. Hayden, leader of the first U.S. expedition to Yellowstone in 1871.

Mile 11.1: **Alum Creek**.

Alum is an astringent. It causes things to shrink. . . . we are now on the road between the [Canyon] hotel and the lake - Yellowstone Lake. It is one of the loveliest roads in the park. But in summer, it's apt to be dusty. In the old stagecoach days, with the hosses, it was even more so. And so one day the colonel gave orders to water the road each morning with water from Alum Crick. . . . Well, these savages [stagecoach drivers] began to notice that they were making awful good time between the lake and the hotel. And they kept on making better and better time. They'd get the doods [dudes] up to the hotel long before the cooks were ready with the grub. . . . The mystery solved . . . I'm goin' to take a surveyor and his chains over that piece of road to-morrow, and when we've got its length, we'll compare it with the original figures of the engineer who built the road. . . . sure enough, the figgers proved that piece of road had already shrunk up one-quarter its original length. After that, in due course, orders come to stop sprinkling the road with water from Alum Crick.

Elizabeth Frazer, 1920

Mile 13.2: **Otter Creek**. Here was the largest and the last of the public bear feeding sites. Seating was behind a chain link fence overlooking a concrete platform. Bears, including Grizzly Bears, would appear each summer night to forage on hotel garbage. The feeding area and a now closed campground is 0.5 miles upstream from the present-day Loop Road.

A score or more bears lumber out of the forest and seek their nightly feast at "the salad bowl," where quantities of surplus food from the hotel and camp are dumped for the bruins. . . . "Ranger," asks one of the visitors, "why do you rangers carry rifles at bear pits - is that so you can shoot bears if they bother the people?" "Naw," says the ranger. "That's so we can shoot the people if they bother the bears."

Frank J. Taylor, 1930

Bear feeding "shows" began in the 1890s when kitchen garbage from the Fountain Hotel was given to bears.

In the early 1930s, the Otter Creek feeding grounds near Canyon opened. Bear feeding shows were discontinued in 1941 when tourist visitation declined because of World War II.

In the 1960s, the popular act of feeding bears along roads and in campgrounds was stopped.

Left: Ad from an undated "Canyon Attractions" brochure.

Bears in Yellowstone

Prior to the admittance of horseless carriages to the Park, it was argued that the smell and the unnatural noise of the motors would drive the animal life away from the roads . . . when at night the bears, having feasted on "beefsteaks that have proved too tough for the tourists," make bold actually to clamber into the motor-cars and despoil seat cushions in search of sweets unwittingly left in the side pockets, it will be appreciated that the contentions that the motor-car would frighten these animals was quite without foundation.   Charles J. Belden, 1918

Sketch from *Scribner's Magazine*, June 1918.

"'Come on, Mr. Bear, have some candy. That's right. Stand over there, will you, so we can take a picture. Here's another piece. Attaboy, stand up. That's a good old thing. No, not so close. You're outa focus. Hey, stay over there in the sun! No, go on away. That's all the candy I have. G'wan back. That's all there is, I tell you. Beat it!'

The Yellowstone bears have heard that line of chatter so often they know it by heart. Our bears must know not only the American language, but they must be up on the latest slang as well."

Horace M. Albright, in
"Why Bears behave like Human Beings," *Collier's*, June 29, 1929

Mile 13.7: Junction with the **Artist Point Road** and the **Chittenden Bridge** over the Yellowstone River. Dead-end road to the Upper Falls and Artist's Point.

The Canyon Hotel, opened in 1911, replaced the original hotel.
The hotel closed in 1959 and burned in 1960.

Mile 16.0: **Canyon Junction. Continue north on the <u>Grand</u> <u>Loop</u> <u>Road</u>** (after visiting the **Grand Canyon of the Yellowstone**).

Mile 21.0: **Dunraven Pass**. This is the highest point reached on the Grand Loop Road. Here the old road split. The road to the east climbed to the top of **Mount Washburn**. It is now a 3.2-mile hiking trail to the summit. This old road continued north, leading to present-day Chittenden Road. The Mt. Washburn Road was closed to automobiles because of a lack of parking at the summit.

At Dunraven Pass the road forks, the left branch around the summit for those of faint heart; the right branch for those who have confidence in their motor and in themselves. . . . In the four miles from Dunraven Pass to the summit of Washburn, the motorist climbs steadily upward over a well graded, though steep and sometimes narrow, road that winds back and forth across the rocky face of the mountain . . Crossing at last a narrow, rocky "hog's back" from which cliffs plunge sharply down on either side, the road sweeps around the very tip of the peak in a graceful, eagle-like spiral, and presently the motorist finds nothing above him but blue sky and racing clouds.
Charles J. Belden, 1918

Hiking trail (and former road) to the summit of Mount Washburn.
Note the patches of asphalt of the old road in front of the hiker.
The shelter house is at the summit, elevation 10,243'. Photograph taken in 2000.

The drive from the Canyon to the summit of Mount Washburn is not surpassed anywhere in the world for its magnificent grandeur of view, and the sensation of the up, up, up, all the time is fascinating. . . . We leave Dunraven Pass to the left, our road turning abruptly to the right and at once striking steeper grades, and the zigzag crooks and turns . . . There is another automobile that left Canyon some minutes after we did; we can hear their voices and yet there's a mile of road between us.
Campbell's Complete Guide, 1923

August **1928 postcard**, mailed to Wisconsin:
Say, Fred has been up in the air ever since we entered the Park.
Why shouldn't he be?
No place less than 6000 feet up in the air.
Good times we are having.
Old Faithful some geyser.
Mt. Washburn some up too.

Mile 35.0: **Tower Junction**. Here the northeast entrance road to Cooke City, Montana, branches off the Grand Loop Road. Here also is the **Roosevelt Lodge**, opened in 1906 to commemorate Theodore Roosevelt's visit to the area in 1903.

Continue west on the <u>Grand Loop Road</u> to Mammoth.

Mile 53.0: **Mammoth Junction**. Site of old **Fort Yellowstone**. The U.S. Army patrolled Yellowstone from 1886 to 1918, when National Park Service Rangers assumed the duties.

**Former Fort Yellowstone's Bachelor Officer's Quarters.
It is now the Albright Visitor Center at Mammoth Hot Springs**.
Sign at left end of porch: POST OFFICE   YELLOWSTONE PARK WYO
Center sign: INFORMATION OFFICE   PARKS PUBLICATIONS MUSEUM
Sign at right: MEDICAL SERVICE   DR. J. M. WOLFE PARK PHYSICIAN
Photograph courtesy of the National Park Service, Yellowstone National Park.

The National Park-to-Park Highway route coincided with the Yellowstone Highway from Cheyenne to Fishing Bridge Junction in Yellowstone. The highway then followed the park's Grand Loop Road counterclockwise to Mammoth. Here the National Park-to-Park Highway left Yellowstone via the five-mile-long north entrance road to Gardiner, Montana. The original Mammoth to Gardiner road is now a one-way north-bound gravel road, open in dry weather conditions only. The road starts behind the Mammoth Hot Springs Hotel.

At the north entrance is the **Roosevelt Arch**, dedicated in April of 1903 by Theodore Roosevelt.

> After two delightful weeks, with no event more untoward than a single blow-out, we brought up at the stone arch which marks the north entrance of the Yellowstone. At a ranger tent we were halted a moment to check out. As there had been no complaints telephoned against the number of our permit, this formality proved no more intricate than having the seals officially broken on our "hardware," [a rifle and a revolver] and reporting the fishing luck we had enjoyed.
>
> Ethel and James Dorrance, 1920

North of Yellowstone National Park

From Gardiner, the National Park-to-Park Highway ran north to Livingston, Montana, sharing the route with the Glacier to Gulf Highway and the Yellowstone-Glacier Bee Line (present-day U.S. Highway 89). Through Livingston ran the east-west Yellowstone <u>Trail</u> and National Parks Highway. Both had a branch running south to Yellowstone, also following the National Park-to-Park Highway route.

North of Livingston, the National Park-to-Park Highway followed closely present-day U.S. Highway 89 to Glacier National Park passing through White Sulphur Springs, Belt, Great Falls, Choteau, and Browning.

From Glacier, the National Park-to-Park Highway turned west to continue the tour of the National Parks of the West:

> **Mt. Rainier** in Washington
> **Crater Lake** in Oregon
> **Lassen Volcanic, Yosemite, General Grant** (now incorporated into Kings Canyon), and **Sequoia** in California
> **Zion** in Utah
> **Grand Canyon** in Arizona
> **Mesa Verde** in Colorado . . . . **then back to Denver**.

The 1920 National Park-to-Park Highway dedication tour at Roosevelt Arch at the north entrance to Yellowstone.
A. G. Lucier photograph, courtesy of the Hinckley Library, Northwest College.

Pages from the Blanche Johnston diary,
summarizing her nine-day trip to Yellowstone in 1926.
Courtesy of the Carnegie Branch Library for Local History, Boulder, Colorado.

No. of miles btw. towns.

Boulder	to Longmont	20.0
	Loveland	.38.0
	Ft. Collins	54.0
Cheyenne	Cheyenne	97.4
	Chugwater	48.7
	Wheatland	80.6
	Douglas	151.0
	Glenrock & Parkerton	180.2
Boulder	Casper	204.8
Casper	"	302.2
	Shoshoni	101.9
	Thermopolis	137.1
	Greybull	214.8
Boulder	Cody	271.9
Cody	"	574.1
	Shoshoni Dam	8.0
	Yellowstone Park	55.4
	Sylvan Pass	63.0
	" Lake	65.2
	Lake St.	82.0
	Canyon St.	143.1

cont. over next page

Gasoline Bill.

Town	No. of Gal.	Price Gal.	Totals
Boulder	5	.22	$ 1.10
Cheyenne	3	.29	.87
Wheatland	4	.29	1.16
Douglas	5	.22	1.10
Casper	4	.29	1.16
Shoshoni	4	.34	1.36
Greybull	8	.34	2.72
Cody	4	.32	1.28
Lake St.	6	.35	2.10
Canyon St.	3	.35	1.05
Old Faithful	5	.35	1.75
Moran	7	.40	2.80
Riverton	7½	.24	1.80
Casper	6	.29	1.74
Douglas	3	.26	.78
Guernsey	8	.26	2.08
Cheyenne	4½	.29	1.31
			$ 26.16

Mileage

Boulder	15299
Cheyenne	15406
Casper	15620
Old Faithful	16118
Moran	16226
Dubois	16300
Riverton	16388
Casper	16536
Guernsey	16683

Room Rent

Cheyenne	$ 4.00
Casper	1.50
Cody	4.50
Canyon St.	4.50
Old Faithful	7.50
Moran	9.00
Dubois	5.50
Casper	4.50
Cheyenne	3.50
	$ 44.50

Boulder	to Guernsey	1221.2
Guernsey	Cheyenne	100.6
Cheyenne	Boulder	97.4
Boulder or Total"		} 1419.2

Total Expenditure
(except for meals, etc.)

Garage Bills	$ 2.50
Repairs, Oil + Grease	16.15
Gasoline	26.16
Room Rent	44.50
	$ 89.31

Each one of us took $50.00
Making a total of $150.00
— $ 89.31

Meals + Sundries Total		$ 60.69
" " "	Each 3)	60.69
		$ 20.23

Souvenir Postcards from Yellowstone National Park.
Above: 1928 view of **Old Faithful Inn and Geyser**.
Note the stagecoach on display at right.
Below: **Lower Falls of the Yellowstone River**.
The early stagecoach road took visitors to the very brink of the Canyon.

Great Falls and Grand Canon, Yellowstone National Park. 88-2

4321. Crater of Mud Volcano, Yellowstone National Park

Souvenir Postcards from Yellowstone National Park.
Above: Crater of **Mud Volcano** on the Grand Loop Road
north of Fishing Bridge Junction.
Below: The lookout at the **summit of Mount Washburn**.
The old road to the summit is now a hiking trail. A 1923 postcard.

23475 THE LOOKOUT, SUMMIT OF MT. WASHBURN, 10,346 FT. YELLOWSTONE PARK HAYNES

Souvenir Postcards from Yellowstone National Park.
Above: Tourists enjoying the **bears at one of the public feeding grounds.**
The practice was stopped in 1941.
Below: "**The Campfire Entertainment**" was originated for the
"sagebrushers" who camped out instead of staying at park hotels. A 1923 postcard.

III. References and Resources

Museums and Libraries
Along the Yellowstone (and National Park-to-Park) Highway

Colorado

Denver Public Library. Large collection of western history books, maps, manuscripts, photographs, and newspapers in the Western History Department. 10 West 14th Ave. Pkwy., 80204. (303) 640-6291.

Colorado Historical Society and Museum. Denver. Permanent and changing exhibits on the history of Colorado. Special events. Western history books, manuscripts, and photographs. 1300 Broadway, 80203. (303) 866-3682.

Forney Transportation Museum. Denver. Carriages, automobiles, trains, etc. 4303 Brighton Blvd., 80216. (303) 297-1113.

Adams County Museum. Brighton. History and cultures of Adams County. 9601 Henderson Road, 80601. (303) 659-7103.

Fort Lupton Museum. History of southern Weld County. 453 First Street, 80621. (303) 857-1634.

Fort Vasquez Museum. Platteville. Reconstructed fort. Visitor center and museum on the history of the fur trade. 13412 U.S. Highway 85, 80651. (970) 785-2832.

Platteville Prairie Museum. Platteville. Local and Fort St. Vrain history.

City of Greeley Museum. Cultural history of the high plains. Historic buildings have been relocated to Centennial Village. 919 7th St., 80631. (970) 350-9220.

Bowles House Museum. Westminster. Local history. 3924 W. 72nd Ave., 80030. (303) 426-1858.

Lafayette Miners Museum. Local history, coal mining history. 108 E. Simpson St., 80026. (303) 665-7030.

Carnegie Library for Local History. Boulder. Books, photographs. 1125 Pine St., 80302. (303) 441-3110.

Lyons Redstone Museum. Local and county historical displays in the 1881 school building. 340 High St., 80540. (303) 823-6692.

Enos Mills Cabin Museum and Gallery. South of Estes Park. Mills homestead. 6760 Colorado Highway 7, Estes Park, 80517. (970) 586-4706.

Estes Park Area Historical Museum. Regional History. Stanley Steamer Automobile. 200 Fourth St., 80517. (970) 586-6256.

Rocky Mountain National Park Archives. Park history. Check at the Beaver Meadows Visitor Center, U.S. Highway 36. (970) 586-1362.

Loveland Museum and Gallery. History of Loveland and the Big Thompson Valley. Sugar beet display. 530 N. Lincoln, 80537. (970) 962-2410.

Fort Collins Museum. History of Fort Collins and Laramie County. Large collection of Folsom points. 200 Mathews St., 80524. (970) 221-6738.

Fort Collins Public Library. Local history collection. 201 Peterson St., 80524. (970) 221-6688.

Wyoming

Wyoming Transportation Museum. Cheyenne. Emigrant trail, railroad, and highway history. Union Pacific Depot. 121 W. 15th St., 82003. (307) 637-DEPO.

Wyoming State Archives. Cheyenne. Official state repository for public records. Microfilmed and original records from 1867. 2301 Central Ave., 82002. (307) 777-7826.

Wyoming State Museum. Cheyenne. Wyoming's human and natural history. 2301 Central Ave., 82002. (307) 777-7022.

Cheyenne Frontier Days Old West Museum. Western art, cowboy life, large collection of carriages. 4610 N. Carey Ave., 82001. (307) 778-7290.

Chugwater Museum. Local history. 315 1st St., 82210. (307) 422-3440.

Laramie Peak Museum. Wheatland. Local and Platte County history. 1601 16th St., 82201. (307) 332-2052.

Glendo Museum. Local history, rock and mineral collection. 204 So. Yellowstone, 82213. (307) 735-4242.

Douglas Railroad Interpretive Center. Located in the Chicago & Northwestern Depot. Displays in the several rail cars. Brownfield Road & Yellowstone Highway, 82633. (307) 358-2950.

Wyoming Pioneer Memorial Museum. Douglas. Historical material related to western expansion and Wyoming Pioneers. State Fairgrounds. (307) 358-9288.

National Historic Trails Center. Casper. History of the Oregon-California, Mormon, and Pony Express Trails. 1501 N. Poplar St., 82601. (307) 265-8030.

Fort Caspar Museum. Casper. Fort history, social and natural history of central Wyoming. 4001 Fort Caspar Road, 82601. (307) 235-8462.

Hot Springs Historical Museum. Thermopolis. Old West, Indian, and petroleum history. Frontier town. 700 Broadway, 82443. (307) 864-5183.

Washakie County Museum. Worland. Local and archaeological history. 1115 Obie Sue, 82401. (307) 347-4102.

Greybull Museum. Local history, geology, and earth sciences. 325 Greybull Ave., 82426. (307) 765-2444.

Park County Historical Archives. Cody. Books and photographs. 1002 Sheridan Ave., 82414. (307) 527-8530.

Buffalo Bill Historical Center. Cody. Buffalo Bill Museum, Whitney Gallery of Western Art, Plains Indian Museum, Cody Firearms Museum, and the Draper Museum of Natural History. McCracken Research Library. 720 Sheridan Ave., 82414. (307) 587-4771.

Old Trail Town. Cody. Historic buildings, collection of Wyoming frontier and Indian artifacts. Horse drawn vehicles. 1831 DeMaris Drive, 82414. (307) 587-5302.

Buffalo Bill Dam Visitor Center. West of Cody. Historical exhibits. (307) 527-6076.

Fishing Bridge Museum. Yellowstone National Park. Bird exhibits. (307) 242-2450.

Yellowstone National Park Archives. Mammoth Hot Springs. Yellowstone history. P.O. Box 168, Yellowstone National Park, 82190. (307) 344-2267.

185

Bibliography: Primary Sources

Albright, Horace M. "Why Bears Behave Like Human Beings." *Collier's Magazine*. June 29, 1929.

Automobile Blue Book. The Automobile Blue Books, Inc., New York & Chicago, 1915.

Automobile Blue Book. The Automobile Blue Books, Inc., New York & Chicago, 1922.

Belden, Charles J. "The Motor in Yellowstone." *Scribner's Magazine*. Vol. 63(June, 1918).

Campbell's Complete Guide and Descriptive Book of the Yellowstone Park. Saint Paul: J. E. Haynes, 1923.

Dorrance, Ethel & James. "Motoring in the Yellowstone." *Munsey's Magazine*. Vol. 70(July, 1920).

Faris, John. *Roaming American Highways*. New York: Farrer & Rinehart, 1931.

Ferguson, Melville. *Motor Camping on Western Trails*. New York: The Century Co., 1925.

Folsom, David. Quoted in *The Spirit of Yellowstone*, by Judith L. Meyer. Lanham, MD: Rowman and Littlefield, 1996.

Frantz, Harry W. Quoted in *Haynes Guide - Yellowstone National Park*. Bozeman, MT: Haynes Studios, Inc., 1949

Frazer, Elizabeth. "The Land of the Whopper." *The Saturday Evening Post*. May 1, 1920.

Frost, Ned. "Going Through the Park?." *The Saturday Evening Post*. Vol. 201, No. 39(March 30, 1929).

Goodrich Tour No. 2255. Denver to Yellowstone National Park. The B. F. Goodrich Rubber Co., 1918.

Harveys Tourist Auto Guide. No place. 1923.

Heath, Charles A. *A Trial of a Trail, From Cody to the Yellowstone*. Chicago: The Franklin Press, 1905.

Johnston, Blanche, diary, 1926. Carnegie Branch Library for Local History, Boulder, Colorado.

Jones, William A. "Report Upon the Reconnaissance of Northern Wyoming, Made in the Summer of 1873." U.S. House of Rep., 43rd Cong. 1st sess., Serial Set 1615, 1874.

Lincoln Highway Association. *A Complete Official Road Guide of the Lincoln Highway*. Fifth Edition. Tucson: The Patrice Press, reprint, 1993.

Midland Trail Guide. Reprint. Glorieta, New Mexico: The Rio Grande Press, Inc., 1969.

The National Park-to-Park Highway. Wyoming Edition. Casper: The Commercial Printing Company, 1924.

Peale, A. C. "United States Geological Survey of Wyoming and portions of Contiguous Territories." 42nd Cong. 2nd Sess., Ex. documents, Serial Set 1520, 1872.

Quick, Herbert. *Yellowstone Nights*. Indianapolis: The Bobbs Merrill Company, 1915.

Smith, F. Dumont. *Summit of the World, Trip Through Yellowstone Park*. Chicago: Rand NcNally & Company, 1909.

Taylor, Frank. "Speaking of Vacations." *Sunset Magazine*. April, 1930.

Van de Water, Frederic. *Family Flivvers to Frisco*. New York: D. Appleton and Company, 1927.

Williams, Calvin. "Seeing Wyoming From A Studebaker E. M. J. in 1909." *Annals of Wyoming*. Vol. 51, No. 1(Spring, 1979). Cheyenne: Wyoming State Historical Society.

Yellowstone Highway in Colorado and Wyoming. ed. Gus Holm's. 1916.

Secondary Sources

Barnhart, Bill. *The Northfork Trail*. Cody: Rustler Printing and Publishing, 1982.

Bartlett, Richard A. *Yellowstone: A Wilderness Besieged*. Tucson: The University of Arizona Press, 1985.

Buchholtz, C.W. *Rocky Mountain National Park: A History*. Boulder: Colorado Associated University Press, 1983.

Culpin, Mary Shivers. *The History of the Construction of the Road System in Yellowstone National Park 1872-1960*. Rocky Mountain Region, National Park Service, No. 5, 1994.

Doyle, Susan Badger. "The Bozeman Trail, 1863-1868." *Annals of Wyoming*. Vol. 70, No. 2(Spring, 1998). Cheyenne: Wyoming State Historical Society.

Franzwa, Gregory M. *The Lincoln Highway, Wyoming*. Tuscon: The Patrice Press, 1999.

Haines, Aubrey L. *Historic Sites along the Oregon Trail*. St. Louis: The Patrice Press, 1981.

----------, *The Yellowstone Story: A History of our First National Park*. Volume Two. Niwot: University of Colorado Press, 1996.

Lincoln Highway Association. *A Complete Official Guide of the Lincoln Highway*. Tucson: The Patrice Press, reprint, 1993.

Lowe, James A. *The Bridger Trail*. Spokane: The Arthur H. Clark Company, 1999.

Morison, Jack L. "Early Colorado Auto Trails." *The Denver Westerners Roundup*, Vol. 47, No. 1(January-February, 1991). Denver: The Denver Westerners.

Murray, Ester Johansson. *A History of the North Fork of the Shoshone River*. Cody: Lone Eagle MultiMedia, 1996.

Osterwald, Doris B. *Rocky Mountain Splendor: A Mile by Mile Guide for Rocky Mountain National Park*. Lakewood, CO: Western Guideways, LTD.,1989.

Pickering, James H. *This Blue Hollow: Estes Park, the Early Years, 1859-1915*. Niwot: University of Colorado Press, 1999.

Schullery, Paul. *Searching for Yellowstone*. Boston: Houghton Mifflin Company, 1997.

Ubanek, Mae. *Wyoming Place Names*. Missoula: Montana Press Publishing Company, 1988.

Wasden, David J. *From Beaver to Oil*. Cheyenne: Pioneer Printing and Stationery Comp., 1973.

Whiteley, Lee. *The Cherokee Trail: Bent's Old Fort to Fort Bridger*. Boulder: Johnson Printing, 1999.

Whittlesey, Lee H. *Yellowstone Place Names*. Helena: Montana Historical Society Press, 1988.

--------------, *A Yellowstone Album*. Boulder: Roberts Rinehart Publishers, 1997.

Writers Program of the Public Work Projects Administration. *Wyoming - A Guide to its History, Highways, and People*. Lincoln: University of Nebraska Press, 1941. Bison Book reprint, 1981.

"Two roads diverged in a wood, and I - I took the one less traveled by, and that has made all the difference."

Robert Frost

Index

On the back cover and page xiv:
Yellowstone fee-paid sticker courtesy of
the National Park Service, Yellowstone
National Park. Rocky Mountain National
Park fee-paid sticker courtesy of the
National Park Service, Rocky Mountain
National Park.